CONTEMPORARY LEF
ACTIVISM VOL 1

Within many societies across the world, new social and political movements have sprung up that either challenge formal parliamentary structures of democracy and participation, or work within them and, in the process, fundamentally alter the ideological content of democratic potentials. At the same time, some parliamentary political parties have attracted a new type of 'populist' political rhetoric and support base.

This collection, along with its accompanying Volume 2, examines the emergence of, and the connections between, these new types of left-wing democracy and participation. Through an array of examples from different countries, it explains why left-wing activism arises in new and innovative spaces in society, and how this joins up with conventional left-wing politics, including parliamentary politics. It demonstrates how these new forms of politics can resonate with the real-life experiences of ordinary people and thereby win support for left-wing agendas.

John Michael Roberts is a Reader in Sociology and Communications, Department of Social and Political Sciences, Brunel University, UK.

Joseph Ibrahim is Senior Lecturer in Sociology, School of Social Sciences, Leeds Beckett University, UK.

Routledge Studies in Radical History and Politics

Series editors: Thomas Linehan, *Brunel University*, and
John Michael Roberts, *Brunel University*

The series *Routledge Studies in Radical History and Politics* has two areas of interest. First, this series aims to publish books that focus on the history of movements of the radical Left. 'Movement of the radical Left' is here interpreted in its broadest sense as encompassing those past movements for radical change that operated in the mainstream political arena, as with political parties, and past movements for change that operated more outside the mainstream, as with millenarian movements, anarchist groups, utopian socialist communities, and trade unions. Second, this series aims to publish books that focus on more contemporary expressions of radical left-wing politics. Recent years have been witness to the emergence of a multitude of new radical movements adept at getting their voices heard in the public sphere. From those participating in the Arab Spring, the Occupy movement, community unionism, social media forums, independent media outlets, local voluntary organizations campaigning for progressive change, and so on, it seems to be the case that innovative networks of radicalism are being constructed in civil society that operate in different public forms.

The series very much welcomes titles with a British focus, but is not limited to any particular national context or region. The series will encourage scholars who contribute to this series to draw on perspectives and insights from other disciplines.

Titles include:

The Far Left in Australia since 1945
Jon Piccini, Evan Smith and Matthew Worley (eds.)

Hybrid media activism
ecologies, imaginaries, algorithms
Emiliano Treré

Contemporary Left-Wing Activism Vol 1
Democracy, Participation and Dissent in a Global Context
Edited by John Michael Roberts and Joseph Ibrahim

Contemporary Left-Wing Activism Vol 2
Democracy, Participation and Dissent in a Global Context
Edited by Joseph Ibrahim and John Michael Roberts

For more about this series, please visit: www.routledge.com/Routledge-Studies-in-Radical-History-and-Politics/book-series/RSRHP.

CONTEMPORARY LEFT-WING ACTIVISM VOL 1

Democracy, Participation and Dissent in a Global Context

Edited by John Michael Roberts and Joseph Ibrahim

Routledge
Taylor & Francis Group

LONDON AND NEW YORK

First published 2019
by Routledge
2 Park Square, Milton Park, Abingdon, Oxon OX14 4RN

and by Routledge
52 Vanderbilt Avenue, New York, NY 10017

Routledge is an imprint of the Taylor & Francis Group, an informa business

British Library Cataloguing-in-Publication Data
A catalogue record for this book is available from the British Library

Library of Congress Cataloging-in-Publication Data
A catalog record has been requested for this book

ISBN: 978-0-815-36350-7 (hbk)
ISBN: 978-0-815-36394-1 (pbk)
ISBN: 978-1-351-04736-4 (ebk)

Typeset in Times New Roman
by Swales & Willis Ltd

Printed and bound in Great Britain by
TJ International Ltd, Padstow, Cornwall

CONTENTS

FIGURES

CONTRIBUTORS

Emanuele Achino received a PhD in Methodology of Social Research (Unimib) by focusing on social movements and gender studies, and he has worked with cultural and structural theoretical backgrounds over time. At present, Emanuele is a Senior Lecturer at the C.T.D.O. (Polito) in the field of European studies and cultural/urban anthropology, as well as in project management, fund-raising and networking by focusing on social engagement and by crossing borders between academic fields.

David Bates is a lecturer in Media and Cultural Studies at Newcastle University, UK, specialising in race, class, migration and cultural studies. He has previously worked as a campaign organiser for the Labour Party and as a youth worker for North of England Refugee Service.

Marco Damiani is Assistant Professor of Political Science in the Department of Political Science of the University of Perugia. He is currently studying the European political parties through a comparative approach. In particular, his research deals with the Left and radical left parties in Western Europe and the European populist parties. He has also studied the European political class and network analysis applied to the study of political power.

Marcello Gisondi is a researcher in the history of political thought at the University of Italian Switzerland (USI). He studied philosophy at Ludwig Maximilian University in Munich and graduated from the University of Naples Federico II, where he also earned his PhD. His current research focuses on both the history of populism and its current manifestation in European democracies.

Joseph Ibrahim is a Senior Lecturer in Sociology at Leeds Beckett University, UK. His research interests are social movements, political protests and social and political theory. He has recently completed projects on the application of social theory for understanding social movement dynamics, the politics of the alternative globalization movement, student politics and protests, and social movement emergence after the global financial crash. He is author of *Bourdieu and Social Movements: Ideological Struggles in the British Anti-capitalist Movement* (Palgrave, 2015).

Tennyson S. D. Joseph is a Senior Lecturer in Political Science at the Cave Hill Campus of the University of the West Indies (UWI). He attained his PhD at the University of Cambridge, UK. His publications include *General Elections and Voting in the English-Speaking Caribbean 1992–2005* (co-authored with Cynthia Barrow-Giles) and *Decolonization in St. Lucia: Politics and Global Neoliberalism, 1945–2010*. He is also a weekly contributor to the *Daily Nation* newspaper (Barbados). He served briefly as the Administrative Attaché to the Prime Minister of Saint Lucia (Kenny Anthony) between 2000 and 2003, and was an Opposition Senator in the Parliament of Saint Lucia for a brief period in 2007.

Gülden Özcan is an assistant professor in the Department of Sociology at the University of Lethbridge. She co-edited *A General Police System: Political Economy and Security in the Age of Enlightenment* (2009) and *Capitalism and Confrontation: Critical Readings* (2012). She contributed to *Alternate Routes: A Journal of Critical Social Research, Moment: Journal of Cultural Studies, Kampfplatz*, and *The Wiley-Blackwell Encyclopedia of Globalization*. Her commentaries have appeared in *The Bullet* (Socialist Project e-bulletin).

André Pusey is a Course Director in the Planning, Housing and Human Geography group within the School of the Built Environment, Leeds Beckett University. He previously worked within the School of Geography at the University of Leeds, where he was involved with the MA in Activism and Social Change. His research focuses on social movements, urban commons and social justice. He has previously published on student movements' experiments with critical pedagogical alternatives to the marketised university, urban activists' attempts to establish autonomous spaces, and militant forms of research.

Enrico Reuter is Lecturer in Public and Social Policy at the Department of Social Policy and Social Work, University of York. His research interests are the crisis of contemporary democracy, public service reform and labour market policies, notably regarding vulnerable or precarious forms of work and self-employment. He tweets about these topics as @ReuterEnrico.

John Michael Roberts is currently a Reader in Sociology and Communications at Brunel University. He has researched and published on free speech and the public sphere, digital culture, work and globalisation, voluntary activity, and political activism in public spaces. His publications include *The Aesthetics of Free Speech* (2003), *The Competent Public Sphere* (2009), *New Media and Public Activism* (2014), and *Digital Publics* (2015). He is currently completing a book on digital work.

Gregory White is a Research Associate in the Centre for Health Services Studies at the University of Kent. He is currently working on adult social care policy and, specifically, the Care Act (2014). He recently completed his ESRC-funded PhD in the Department of Social Policy and Social Work at the University of York, UK.

ACKNOWLEDGEMENTS

We would like to thank Craig Fowlie, Rebecca McPhee and Thomas Linehan for their encouragement, help and guidance. We would also like to thank the anonymous referees.

1

DEMOCRACY AND PARTICIPATION

Liberal and left-wing perspectives

John Michael Roberts[1]

Introduction

These days, as Theocharis and van Deth (2018) note, an array of avenues are open to ordinary citizens for them to become active in mechanisms, processes and structures of democracy and participation. Voting in elections is the most obvious, but of course the emergence of the Internet and social media has broadened the outlets for people to get their voices heard in society, and more and more of us are encouraged by politicians to become involved in civic participation through the likes of volunteering. Consumers are also persuaded to take an active stance on certain social issues, such as environmental issues, by buying products aligned with a social cause, and institutionalised participation, such as becoming involved in a community pressure group, is yet another outlet for democracy and participation. And, lest we forget, people can likewise get involved in protest campaigns and/or direct action groups, or attend a demonstration of some sort or another.

But this is not the whole story. Although the mechanisms of democracy and participation have changed, there has also been another significant development. Within many societies across the world, new social and political movements have sprung up that either challenge formal parliamentary structures of democracy and participation, or work with them and, in the process, fundamentally alter the ideological content of democratic potentials. Think momentarily about the Arab Spring. Starting in Tunisia in December 2010, and then spreading across a number of Arab states, the Arab Spring brought together a diverse range of protestors who used conventional democratic practices, such as protesting in well-known public spaces, squares and parks, as well as employing newer democratic media, such as Twitter, to mobilise discontent, demand greater democratic rights, call for an end to political corruption, and campaign against different types of social inequality (Hussain and Howard 2013).

At the same time, some parliamentary political parties have attracted a new type of 'populist' political rhetoric and support base. At its simplest, 'populism' signals a move away from formal, established political debates and practices towards one embedded in everyday language forms and emotions that channel popular and recognisable 'feelings' of anger, fear and hope in society, in and around specific and often national social and political issues. Popular culture is thereby an important ingredient of what is associated with 'populist' politics (Kellam 2017: 228–9). As Kellam goes on to note, populism is not strictly 'left' or 'right', but can be appropriated by groups in either of these political spectrums. So, although right-wing forces have drawn on populist rhetoric to win power – one need only think of Donald Trump – left-wing forces have also been successful at mobilising populist forces for their own electoral achievements. One notable illustration can be seen in the UK, where Jeremy Corbyn's left-wing leadership of the Labour Party has been bolstered and supported through left-wing grassroots activism that has been in place for many years, but only now finds an active welcome in the Labour Party (Perryman 2017).

This collection, along with its accompanying volume (Ibrahim and Roberts 2019), attempts to make sense of the emergence of, and the connections between, these new types of left-wing democracy and participation. Through an array of examples from different countries, it will show why and how left-wing activism arises in new and novel spaces in society, how such activism joins up with conventional left-wing politics, including parliamentary politics, and how this can resonate with the real-life experiences of ordinary people and thereby win support for left-wing agendas.

But before the chapters in the current volume are outlined in more detail, it is important, first, to gain a greater understanding of some of the debates that surround the very terms and ideals of democracy and participation. This is important for a number of reasons. First, although more abstract and theoretical ideas about democracy will be discussed throughout this volume and the second one, it is vital to remember that, for left-wing protagonists, politics should be thought of as an entry point to encourage and get ordinary people to participate in their own democratic mechanisms and institutions. More to the point, the Left should be campaigning for a widening of democratic participation in society for the many, and not the few. So, for example, the Left needs to argue that ordinary people must have a democratic voice in how economic decisions are made that affect their lives. In other words, left-wing activists need to campaign for political *and* economic democracy and participation. Therefore, although it is indeed vital for left-wing activists to enter into debates about the nature of democracy, leftists must also connect these debates to issues around participation in decision-making mechanisms across society as well. Second, an emphasis on democracy and participation immediately draws attention to empirical examples of left-wing versions of democracy and participation in action. The term 'democracy and participation' thereby encompasses a range of left-wing activism, from social movement activism, to leftist single issue campaigns, to left-wing parliamentary and local politics, to the left-wing appropriation of public spaces in cities, and so on. 'Democracy and participation' likewise provides a way of exploring the various participatory connections between and across these different left-wing currents and forms. Taking these points on board, this chapter will explore various ideas about democracy and participation, and how democracy and participation might be enhanced in society. It will do so by discussing different frameworks that have been devised to understand democracy and participation, principally by examining liberal and left-wing perspectives on democracy and participation.

The chapter therefore starts by first examining critically the classic study by Gabriel Almond and Sidney Verba on 'civic culture' and democracy (1963). Their liberal approach to democracy and participation was criticised by several scholars, and, in the 1990s, Verba and colleagues (1995) introduced a new framework to study democracy and participation. Again, however, criticisms were made of this new framework, some of which are outlined below.

Following this discussion, the chapter moves on to examine the term, 'social capital'. Arising during the 1990s as a way to explain why people might not engage in the processes of democracy and participation, and what might be done to reverse this problem, social capital is associated strongly with the work of the American political scientist Robert Putnam. For Putnam, social capital is a means to focus on issues and problems about how to build networks of trustworthiness between people in communities, which might then make them feel inclined to participate more in civic institutions. Unfortunately for critics, theorists such as Putnam tend in their respective accounts to accept the main ideological ingredients of liberal democracies, rather than acknowledging that in many respects liberal democracies might have been responsible, in part, for perpetuating particular social inequalities in the first place, which then have led to a decline in social capital. As noted by Pierre Bourdieu, whose ideas are elaborated on further below, social capital has been a means for those with wealth and prestige to reproduce their own privileges through the creation and maintenance of specific social networks.

If there is some truth to the claim that social capital reproduces at least some types of inequality, then perhaps one way forward is to create a form of democracy that explicitly forbids social inequalities from entering the demo-cratic process in the first place. By so doing, a space opens up for people to deliberate and reach a consensus among themselves about possible solutions to everyday issues and problems that affect them. Deliberative democracy, as it has become known, has therefore proved popular among some academic scholars and policymakers exactly because it aims to overcome a number of inequalities in societies so that a diverse array of individuals and social groups can get their voices heard about matters that concern them. Although laudable, deliberative democracy has nevertheless attracted criticism, not least about its wish to foster a consensus in society. The problem here for critics is that 'consensus' is often seen by them as a way to smuggle in liberal ideals about respecting equality that, in practice, gloss over real inequalities and power relations in society. The latter then serve to silence voices in society, particularly those from less privileged backgrounds. Thus, rather than create what is seen to be a somewhat fictitious 'consensus', critics are more prone to encourage dissensus between groups in society that more readily highlights social differences between them, including differences of opinions, different social backgrounds and different material resources people have access to that promote and sustain interests above other interests.

Social movements, and in particular rising global social movements such as the anti-capitalist movement, alongside various leftist global populist movements, celebrate the idea that dissensus can in fact lead to the formation of a wide-reaching progressive politics. Exactly by recognising that a 'consensus' with many mainstream political groups has in recent years failed to challenge the dominance of neo-liberalism, a host of global social movements seek to break with consensus politics in order to push political and social thinking towards a leftist and socialist direction. The chapter therefore ends by outlining some key features of global social movements, but also highlights some of their limitations in order to argue that a fully-fledged socialist politics is the only realistic way to avoid the problems inherent in liberal versions of democracy and participation. The chapter then briefly outlines the rest of the contributions.

But to begin, then, we first outline a liberal approach to democracy and participation. Gabriel Almond and Sidney Verba's path-breaking study, *The Civic Culture*, marked a watershed moment in approaches to the study of democracy and participation. Published in 1963 and comprising a comparative survey of values across five nations (United States, Great Britain, Germany, Italy and Mexico), Almond and Verba's exploration of the concept civic culture quickly established itself as a classic. The concept of 'culture' had fallen out of favour with political scientists more interested in Marxist and structural-functionalist explanations (Street 1997). Almond and Verba reclaimed this important concept for political science and sought to assess the extent to which culture could be seen as a useful conceptual device with which to explain political action. The next section outlines their arguments in more detail, as well as their limitations.

Civic culture and civic voluntarism models of participation

Almond and Verba begin their exploration by first considering the concept 'political culture'. 'When we speak of the political culture of society, we refer to the political system as internalized in the cognitions, feelings, and evaluations of its population' (Almond and Verba 1963: 13). From this initial starting point, Almond and Verba seek to make connections between the 'micropolitics' of everyday attitudes and the 'macropolitics' of systems, such as a formal political system. Simply stated, Almond and Verba take the view that a relationship can be found between a country's political system and its political culture to help form a civic culture. What is interesting to note here is that the concept of civic culture is wide enough to include implicit political attitudes within what is thought to be the realm of micropolitics located in non-political institutions, such as voluntary organisations. These non-political, everyday realms are important because they provide valuable arenas in which to experience and discuss democracy and participation, and this can then flow into more conventional political institutions (Almond and Verba 1963: 299).

For Almond and Verba, civic culture is that element in society most conducive to a stable democracy. This is because a civic culture is characterised by 'citizen' or 'political' competence and 'administrative' competence. Whereas the former refers to a person's level of political knowledge and confidence to influence politics, the latter refers to a person's expectation of fair treatment by political authorities. Almond and Verba claim that an ideal civic culture is one in which citizens are competent in being both active – participating in trying to influence politics – *and* passive, or deferential, when engaged in administrative competence. Almond and Verba found that the level of and relationship between these two categories varied across nations owing to the historical nature of each country explored. Britain, they believed, was the only country that enjoyed a civic culture where deference to authority was combined with a positive attitude towards active participation (Almond and Verba 1963: 6).

Almond and Verba's development of the concept of civic culture generated a substantial amount of critical commentary and debate around both their own work and the concept of political culture generally. One problem noted concerned Almond and Verba's conflation of different levels of analysis in their account. For example, Welch (1993) notes a tension between their wish to make *generalisations* about civic culture across nations so that comparative analysis is possible, while recognising the fact that each country requires a detailed analysis of its specific culture within its unique borders. As Welch suggests:

> The comparative project ... amounts to an attempted explanation of the presence of stable democracy in some countries and its absence in others in terms of pre-existing political conditions. It is a comparative explanation with political culture as the independent variable. The sociological project consists in an investigation of the social conditions under which democracy functions. It is a contribution to the 'empirical theory of democracy' in which a range of sociological variables is taken to be explanatory.
>
> *(Welch 1993: 14–15)*

This tension is noticeable in some of the variables used by Almond and Verba. For example, Almond and Verba work from a highly generalised attitudinal variable of what they consider should be the norm of participation. This revolves around the claim, 'One ought at least to take an interest in what goes on in the community' (Almond and Verba 1963: 128). However, this variable is so comprehensive as to be almost meaningless. McLennan (1989) makes a useful remark in this regard when he says: 'Whilst 72 per cent of Britons did endorse this requirement, one feels that more can be learned about democratic responsiveness from the 68 per cent of Italians who seemed unable even to go along with this bland formulation' (McLennan 1989: 29). Correspondingly, the 'positive' findings that Almond and Verba cite as evidence of healthy pluralist democracies in Britain and the USA can in fact show the opposite. On their own estimations, only 39 per cent of respondent in Britain believed that individuals should play an active role in politics, and only 21 per cent of American respondents believed that each individual should try and understand issues and be kept informed about them (Almond and Verba 1963: 127–9). Hardly a ringing endorsement of civic activity (see also Kavanagh 1989; Topf 1989).

This has prompted some to argue that Almond and Verba are implicitly less concerned with democratic pluralism than they are with the stability of the liberal democratic apparatus. Civic culture provides such stability by enabling individuals to be involved in civic affairs, thereby making the political system responsive to their involvement. Yet, on Almond and Verba's reckoning, citizens should also be 'deferential' to the political system and, in effect, leave political decision-making to the politicians. For Pateman (1989), Almond and Verba thereby reinstate a liberal theory defence of democratic participation. This rests upon the idea that participation within the democratic process must be constrained within the limits of conventional and parliamentary political practices. As a result, other types of democratic activism, such as extra-parliamentary politics associated with the likes of civil rights movements, gender politics, environmentalism, workplace and trade union democracy, and so on, are neglected. Pateman goes as far as to suggest that political competence on the part of individuals equalling a 'general acceptance' on their part of the political system does not adequately consider the socialisation of liberal norms and ideology within the population at large.

> The question that needs to be asked is whether or not the replies to questions designed to measure feelings of competence might also be reflecting an acceptance of the 'norms of democratic ideology', or the evaluative dimension of political culture.
>
> *(Pateman 1989: 81; see also Jessop 1974)*

The specific problem with this liberal model can be appreciated in greater detail if we momentarily explore some of Verba's later work. In particular, more than two decades later, Verba, along with two colleagues, Schlozman and Brady, addressed once again the twin themes of democracy and participation, but this time paid closer attention to the issue of inequality in democratic decision-making. *Voice and Equality* (Verba et al. 1995) was an enquiry into citizen participation based on a two-stage study that began with a representative sample of more than 15,000 individuals in the USA and was followed by more in-depth interviews with 2,517 people from the original sample; it explicitly sought to understand the neglected issue of inequality in participation and its meaning for contemporary democracy. The study looked in more depth at the micropolitics of political culture by focusing exclusively upon civic voluntarism in the United States. But, as with *The Civic Culture*, Verba et al. also rely upon an attitudinal notion of civic voluntarism. Specifically, the model they develop explores the process of participatory activism as this relates to two main variables: the *motivation* and the *capacity* to take part in political life. Both variables are analysed in relation to a third variable – the *networks of recruitment* through which requests for political activity are mediated.

According to Verba et al., the United States fosters many forms of voluntary activity. Voting is probably the best-known voluntary activity, but it is also true to say that the diverse range of voluntarism is itself bound up with unequal resources. Equality in political rights does not, of course, translate into an equality of their use. And disparities in political activity parallel the fault lines of social and political division in the United States. Taking this on board, Verba et al. suggest that participatory inequalities depend on asking why people do *not* take part in politics. Three answers present themselves: because they cannot; because they do not want to; because nobody asked. 'They cannot' suggests a lack of resources necessary to be involved. 'They do not want to' explores the absence of political engagement. 'Nobody asked' implies isolation from the networks of recruitment through which citizens become mobilised (Verba et al. 1995: 16).

Verba et al. further claim that three factors are important to take into account when looking at how and why some people get involved in their political and civic culture. These three factors are resources, engagement and recruitment, and together they constitute the *civic voluntarism model*. Out of the three factors, Verba et al. argue that resources are the most important. Three reasons are put forward to support this claim: 'First, we can measure resources with greater reliability and validity than we can measure the other factors. Second, the causal priority of resources is easier to establish. Third, a theoretical model based on resources is more interpretable' (Verba et al. 1995: 270). For Verba et al., three resources in particular are important: time, money and civic skills. These resources impact on whether people can be involved in democracy and participation. For example, some people will not, for various reasons, be able to devote much of their time to being involved in their civic culture.[2]

Even though Verba et al. tackle the issue of inequalities within the democratic process, nevertheless there are still problems with their model. In the first instance, Verba et al. do not embed their model as fully as might be the case in the historical specificity of different social inequalities. And so, for example, in the discussion of resources of time and money, there is little treatment of recent *qualitative* changes in work patterns, especially the intensification of work, which may then impact upon the time that individuals devote to voluntary activity. Instead, Verba et al. analyse specific variables such as how much free time is available through factors such as 'having a job', 'a spouse who works' and 'having children'. Yet these variables do not capture, for instance, the neo-liberal basis of social inequalities that has exacerbated social inequalities since the 1980s in countries such as the US and UK (see, for example, Moody 2018). Correspondingly, there is also little discussion in their analysis of the regulatory impact of the state and its move away from an inclusionary welfarism to an exclusionary workfare state (Sum and Jessop 2013). This is a strange neglect on the part of Verba et al. Their significant discovery, for example, that the advantaged are more active in the policy and political arena than the disadvantaged is never fully analysed in terms of the strategic neo-liberal terrain that obviously affects democratic participation in specific ways that empower the wealthy. Why are some channels of communication open to one social group and not another *at this particular point in time*? Verba et al. admit that their approach does not license them to pose such questions. As they say: 'It is not our enterprise to investigate where issue engagements come from – how government actions create attentive constituencies of those affected by policies or why certain issues generate deep passions while others do not' (Verba et al. 1995: 415). But it is exactly this missing historical and social dimension, a dimension that is concerned with passion, symbols, the state and the complexity of experiences, that needs to be explored in order to understand in more precise detail some of the characteristics of democracy and participation. One concept that emerged during the 1990s that sought to provide a more robust account of these factors in terms of democracy and participation was that of 'social capital'. It is this concept that we will therefore now discuss.

Social capital

Even though many theorists, researchers and practitioners have contributed towards establishing the analytical validity of social capital, perhaps one person stands out as the main protagonist in this increasingly researched area. Robert Putnam first used the concept in his study of regional government in Italy in the 1970s. He found that regional government proved a success in the north and a failure in the south because of historically deep-rooted traditions of civic engagement. The north had strong social and political networks that were organised horizontally rather than hierarchically, but these were absent in the south. They facilitated higher levels of trust and reciprocity that produced good government (Putnam 1993). Putnam's thesis about disconnectedness was then developed more fully in his book *Bowling Alone*, which was also greeted with huge publicity. Putnam defined social capital in the following way:

> [S]ocial capital refers to connections among individuals – social networks and the norms of reciprocity and trustworthiness that arise from them. In that sense social capital is closely related to what some have called 'civic virtue'. The difference is that 'social capital' calls attention to the fact that

civic virtue is most powerful when embedded in a dense network of reciprocal social relations. A society of many virtuous but isolated individuals is not necessarily rich in social capital.

(Putnam 2000: 19)

One of the most important aspects of this definition is the idea that social capital creates networks of generalised reciprocity between individuals. This is the idea that networks of mutual obligations are constructed through the belief that 'someone else will do something for me down the road' (Putnam 2000: 21). In other words, social capital should aim not only to bond individuals together but also to create bridges of reciprocity between individuals.

For Putnam, however, there has been an increasing trend in the US for social capital to decline across different spheres of life, including civic participation, informal social connections and so on. There has also been a decline in political knowledge and interest, a drop in partisanship, less involvement in campaign activities and less community involvement (Putnam 2000: Chapter 2). That is to say, there are fewer people active across a broad spectrum than there were in the 1960s. Putnam (2000: 47) places these trends against the backdrop of a decline in political trust and political efficacy. With political confidence low, motivation and involvement in politics are correspondingly down. Putnam then considers a variety of explanations for the decline in social capital. He identifies pressures of time and money (including changes in family structure), mobility and sprawl (especially suburbanisation and its effects on community), and technology and the mass media (most notably television viewing). All of these social changes have negatively affected social capital by reducing the social connectedness sustained by networks of engagement. Putnam laments the decline in social capital for it has many desirable individual and collective outcomes. It allows citizens, for example, to express their interest and have a louder voice, and, for wider society, among other things, it facilitates a more just and stable democracy and overall political legitimacy.

Putnam's arguments about the positive attributes of social capital have, however, been extensively criticised. Fine (2000) suggests that social capital represents, theoretically, the colonisation of mainstream economic ideology within the social sciences. Briefly stated, Fine argues that social capital adds a societal element to the normal human capital theory employed by economists. The latter theory is based on the assumption that the economy is reproduced through rational *individuals* optimising their choices and outcomes in making economic decisions. Social capital supplements this individualist thinking by suggesting that people also operate in social networks, and yet, at the same time, the focus is still on rational individuals, albeit within social networks. For Fine, human capital theory is thereby smuggled in through the backdoor cloaked under social capital theory. But a failure to appreciate the underlying social and historical structural problems of capitalism means that social capital reproduces the same theoretical limitations as human capital theory. For example, social capital provides ideological justification at a 'collective' level for certain negative effects of capitalism. Indeed, as Fine notes, social capital:

> signifies, in a sense, a matter of blaming the collective as opposed to the individual victim. When companies decamp, they leave individuals behind, apparently the work-shy unemployed; they also abandon communities, supposedly in decline for being deficient in social capital!
>
> *(Fine 2000: 92; see also Portes 1998)*

The work of Bourdieu is instructive in this respect. This is because, with Bourdieu, we discover a more critical use of the term social capital. According to Bourdieu (1986), there are a number of 'capitals' evident in society – economic, social, cultural and symbolic capitals – and each type of capital endows people with particular resources that can be used in social fields to gain advantages or disadvantages in particular ways. For example, those with high levels of economic capital obtain high economic resources in terms of income, wealth and so on. These then give these people certain advantages in social fields such as the workplace, health insurance and so on. At the same time, their high levels of economic resources reproduce specific social inequalities and power relations. For instance, they might ensure that many retain low levels of economic capital and thereby have less or no access to the economic benefits and social fields enjoyed by those with high economic capital. For Bourdieu, social capital refers mainly to the social networks constructed between different individuals and groups that might, or might not, bring them certain advantages. More precisely, social capital refers to:

> the aggregate of the actual or potential resources which are linked to possession of a durable network of more or less institutionalized relationships of mutual acquaintance and recognition – or in other words, to membership in a group – which provides each of its members with the backing of the collectivity – owned capital, a 'credential' which entitles them to credit, in the various senses of the word.
>
> *(Bourdieu 1986: 248–9)*

As Bourdieu goes on to argue, one's accumulation of social capital is dependent to a large degree on the size of social networks that one can mobilise, which then also enables one to reproduce and accumulate other types of capital – economic, cultural and symbolic – through these networks. For example, one might belong to an exclusive golf club, and through this golf club develop social networks, or social capital, which are also predicated on having economic, cultural and symbolic capital, but which also led to accumulating higher levels of these different types of capital.

In other words, the network of relationships is the product of investment
strategies, individual or collective, consciously or unconsciously aimed at
establishing or reproducing social relationships that are directly usable in
the short or long term, i.e., at transforming contingent relations, such as
those of neighbourhood, the workplace, or even kinship, into relationships
that are at once necessary and elective, implying durable obligations
subjectively felt (feelings of gratitude, respect, friendship, etc.) or institutionally guaranteed (rights).

(Bourdieu 1986: 249–50)

One of Bourdieu's main points here is that, by connecting with others through
social capital, an individual or group 'recognises' another as belonging to the
same network and, by so doing, 'reproduces the group' and 'reaffirms the limits
of the group' (Bourdieu 1986: 250).

In this respect, the social capital approach associated with the likes of
Putnam is seen as being one-sided. This is so in the sense that, in Bourdieu's
estimation, social capital is associated with both deeply encoded resources and
consciously constructed resources that express and reinforce power relations and
social stratification between groups. Bourdieu's approach to social capital is
therefore useful because it directs attention to the social processes that place
individuals in particular positions of subordination. More to the point, Bourdieu's emphasis on relations of the encoding and deeply layered nature of power
means that he is able to explore the regulation and articulation of social capital
through other mechanisms of power, such as state power. Bourdieu therefore
enriches our understanding of social capital and places it within a critical
context that takes on board the realities and strategic nature of power, stratification and so on, in society. Saying this, other theoretical perspectives on
democracy and participation have also emerged in recent years to take account
of problems with liberal theories, especially relating to issues such as inequalities in participation. One of the more familiar left-liberal theoretical approaches
that have gained popularity is that of deliberative democracy. We therefore
briefly turn our attention to this theory.

Deliberative democracy

Some of the key ideas of deliberative democracy can be summed up through the
following two quotes from two sets of eminent deliberative theorists. According
to Chambers:

[W]e can say that deliberation is debate and discussion aimed at producing reasonable, well-informed opinions in which participants are willing
to revise preferences in light of discussion, new information, and claims
made by fellow participants. Although consensus need not be the ultimate
aim of deliberation, and participants are expected to pursue their interests,

an overarching interest in the legitimacy of outcomes (understood as justification to all affected) ideally characterizes deliberation.

(Chambers 2003: 309)

For Gutmann and Thompson (2004), deliberative democracy is:

[A] form of government in which free and equal citizens (and their representatives) justify decisions in a process in which they give one another reasons that are mutually acceptable and generally accessible, with the aim of reaching conclusions that are binding in the present on all citizens but open to challenge in the future.

(Gutmann and Thompson 2004: 7)

As each definition indicates, a key characteristic of deliberative democracy in this respect is the idea that, through discursive interactions with one another, citizens can be transformed into politically and socially competent members of society. The more information one is prepared to listen to about a specific issue from a range of speakers, then the more one is willing to be open to a number of perspectives about the issue in question. In the process, one gains a more 'reasonable' standpoint towards an opposing point of view (Polleta et al. 2009). For deliberative democrats, then, it is important to ensure the necessary devices are in place that enable and encourage people to justify their reasons why a particular opinion or policy should be adopted. People should therefore 'give an account' of their viewpoint to others; 'that is, publicly articulating, explaining, and most importantly justifying public policy' (Chambers 2003: 308). Through such deliberative devices, there is a greater ability to reach a consensus between people with initially different points of view.

According to deliberative theorists, the advantage of this type of democracy is clear when we think about international relations. Dryzek (2006) argues that, in a post-9/11 world, deliberative democracy stands as the best opportunity to enrich the prospect of transnational democracy. Significantly, transnational discursive democracy seeks to put in place a decentralised system of control 'over the content and relative weight of globally consequential discourses' that stresses the power of communicative action in discussing issues in the public sphere (Dryzek 2006: 102–3). This is a more attractive type of inclusive democracy than other approaches to international democracy. For example, one current understanding of global public debate is associated with a 'war of ideas' approach in which governments clash over their respective ideologies. However, in this approach, governments invariably resort to stereotypes and agenda-setting politics when engaged in a 'clash of discourses' with opponents, and they treat debate as a public relations opportunity to dismiss adversaries (Dryzek 2006: 109). According to Dryzek, discursive democracy is more suited to our current age of interlinked transnational politics because it takes account of the reality of serious democratic engagement at different social levels. Since 9/11, the appearance of local anti-war movements across the world indicates that people have become more reflexive of the global world and are less willing to be dictated to by centralised systems of deliberation (Dryzek 2006: 115). Only decentralised networks of public deliberation can realistically get to grips with this dispersal of reflexive subjects in the world today. Global anti-war movements serve as an illustration of global deliberative networks that remain decentralised, open and equal and maintain a healthy level of reciprocity and respect between participants (cf. Dryzek 2001: 664).

Naturally, the theory of deliberative democracy is far more complex than the simple description given above. Within the limits of space in this chapter, however, it is sufficient in order to highlight some critical questions about the deliberative framework. The first point to make in this respect is that deliberative democracy is normally analysed within the remit of deliberative mechanisms. As Pateman (2012: 10) notes, specific deliberative settings and meetings are generally concerned only with issues of accountability, consensus and access to the forums, within the tightly defined purview of the deliberative forums themselves. As a result, wider structural issues about the nature of democracy and how it operates are rarely questioned in the deliberative approach.

Take the issue of mini-publics. These are often seen to be the practical embodiment of deliberative democracy. According to Goodin and Dryzek, mini-publics 'are designed to be small groups small enough to be genuinely deliberative, and representative enough to be genuinely democratic (though rarely will they meet the standards of statistical representativeness, and they are never representative in the electoral sense)' (Goodin and Dryzek 2006: 220). In this sense, mini-publics comprise 'lay-citizens' and 'non-partisans' who share a variety of viewpoints that reflect the viewpoints of wider society. Feedback from deliberative forums is collected and turned into reports that then go to elected officials to inform their policy decisions. Subsequently, mini-publics endeavour to include 'ordinary' people in deliberative decision-making on various matters. Nevertheless, Goodin and Dryzek also admit that, in reality, few mini-publics are actually included formally in the overall process of national and local state decision-making procedures (Goodin and Dryzek 2006: 225). For Pateman, this problem is not merely fortuitous. Instead, it highlights how deliberative mechanisms do not challenge the very foundations of liberal democracies. Certainly, liberal institutions do listen to some of the opinions and outcomes generated by mini-publics, but they also follow their already prescribed strategic and selective policy agendas. In other words, mini-publics:

> are specially established bodies, to which participants are invited, that meet for a limited period ... and they then disappear. That is to say, they are not integrated into the overall system of representative government or democratic institutions, nor do they become part of the regular political cycle in the life of a community.

> *(Pateman 2012: 9–10)*

As other critics have pointed out, if deliberative democracy does not take on board wider strategic policy mechanisms and political mediations of democracy and participation, and how these play out through factors such as social divisions and inequalities, then there will always be an issue about how 'even in our efforts to conceive … an ideal (deliberative) speech situation we will always be influenced by our own class, gender and culture' (Hooghe 1999: 292). And these sociological factors are themselves mediated through an array of state projects that aim to secure order and hegemony in society. Think, for example, about how, in our present-day neo-liberal environment, local authorities increasingly have to work in public–private partnerships in order to get projects off the ground. But, whereas state actors have to operate at least in principle within formal rules of accountability and transparency, private operators in these partnership networks work also through their own semi-autonomous procedures, some of which 'can subscribe to opaque governing norms and all too often these norms reinforce broader patterns of discrimination and power' (Kreiss et al. 2011: 252).

In order to confront these issues, there is a need in society for *community organising* and to build 'organisations controlled by people normally shut out from decision-making power, who then go on to fight for changes in the distribution of power' (Stoecker 2003: 493–4). Community organising thus attempts to enlist people in the organisation so that they then select the issues they want to be discussed and campaigned on. Moreover, community organising is predicated on the idea that society is based on conflicts between haves and have-nots. In contrast to community organising, community development is often managed through a development corporation that will claim to create jobs, educational opportunities and so on in deprived areas. At the same time, it must ensure profits are made for the corporation and other interested 'partners'. Community development therefore works within and accepts existing strategic and structural constraints and, in most cases, seeks to create a deliberative consensus between relevant parties through the likes of public–private partnerships (Stoecker 2003: 494–5). One way of summarising the difference between community organising and community development is to suggest that the former does not necessarily look to build a consensus between different parties, but is content to maintain a dissensus between itself and certain policymakers and groups that are preventing it from realising its own interests and goals (cf. Mouffe 2005). Community development, on the other hand, does try to build a consensus between such groups. But this division is also connected to another important issue.

Democracy and participation, especially social and political activism mediated through community organising and their cultures and practices, are more often than not an emotional type of engagement directed towards specified targets. Yet, many deliberative theorists are critical of overly emotional politics, arguing that it sometimes lacks reasoned justification for its ideals, 'as these violate the requirement for reason-giving' (Chappell 2010: 304). Nevertheless, there is another type of democracy and participation that in many respects prides itself on creating a dissensus around what it considers to be matters of social importance, and it also structures its activism in and around emotional images, rhetoric and action, as well as 'reason-giving' deliberation. This revolves around a more expressive, evaluative, constructed, interpretative, judgemental and symbolic approach to democracy and participation. It agrees with Grossberg (1992) when he says that political culture is not so much bound up with describing a set of interests as it is with articulating a set of emotions and passionate concerns about everyday life. Individuals adopt an 'affective' attitude towards life whereby they invest an emotional volition towards parti-cular experiences, practices, identities, meanings and pleasures. 'Affect is ... defined qualitatively by the nature of the concern (caring, passion) in the investment, by the way in which the specific event is made to matter ... But it too is articulated and disarticulated – there are affective lines of articulation and affective lines of flight – through social struggles over its structure' (Grossberg 1992: 82). Essentially, this means that culture is more than 'political culture' and can be accurately described as a more general cultural theory of political action (Street 1997: 104). The rise of these so-called new and global social movements has been at the forefront of organising a novel type of democracy and participation and constructing a politics of dissensus within and across societies. We therefore now turn our attention to new and global social movements.

New social movements and socialist democracy and participation

For Della Porta and Diani, social movements are characterised by three main attributes. First, social movements are involved in political and/or cultural conflict with the aim to promote or oppose social change in society:

> Accordingly, addressing collective problems, producing public goods, or expressing support for some moral values or principles does not auto-matically correspond to social movement action; the latter requires the identification of targets for collective efforts, specifically articulated in social or political terms.
>
> *(Della Porta and Diani 2006: 21)*

Second, social movements create dense, informal networks through which they operate to realise their social, cultural and political aims and goals. Different movement originations therefore coordinate their activities, and exchange information and resources between one another, through these dense networks, while maintaining their autonomy and independence. Third, social movements are defined to a large degree by their collective identities, which grow and mature over time beyond any single event. Collective identity, brings with it a sense of common purpose and shared commitment to a cause, which enables single activists and/or organizations to regard themselves as inextricably linked to other actors, not necessarily identical but surely compatible, in a broader collective mobilization.

(Della Porta and Diani 2006: 21)

Globalisation has given these movements an added impetus. In *The Power of Identity*, Castells (2010) notes that the move towards digital global network societies means that people now have a more 'reflexive' awareness of the world around them. We can be constantly connected to one another through the likes of social media, and this brings about a continual awareness of the world. Castells also argues that globalisation has created new modes of identity formation that he calls 'project identity', which is the construction of meaning on the basis of a cultural attribute, or related set of cultural attributes, that is/are given priority over other sources of meaning. New forms of belonging and meaning emerge that redefine the position of particular social groups in terms of the overall social structure. Gender and ethnic identities, for example, have developed to change institutions, 'discourses', roles and understandings of women, and ethnic communities (Castells 2010: xxvi). Global social movements therefore work within what they perceive to be global values, such as those found in global anti-war movements or global anti-poverty groups, and believe that solutions to social ills found in particular countries can be remedied through global solutions (Cohen and Rai 2000: 8–10).

In all of these instances, social movements engage in expressive and emotional politics, but, at the same time, infuse these traits into formal political and social activism. In particular, aesthetic representations of political and social issues are employed by movement activists to develop a passionate politics in and around democracy and participation. Doug McAdam's (1988) wonderful study of the civil rights movement in the 1950s and 1960s is a case in point. His research was based on an in-depth case study of the 1964 Mississippi Freedom Summer Campaign, organised by the Student Non-Violent Co-ordinating Committee (SNCC), which mobilised more than a thousand white, northern college students to register black voters and teach in the freedom schools in the South. In an extraordinary way, McAdam captures the emotions of the summer months spent in Mississippi. Interestingly, McAdam manages to convey the ability of social movements to construct spatial aesthetic representations of their own identities and politics against a prevailing power bloc associated with racial violence in the South. This occurred, first, by constructing an image of what Mississippi represented. For many freedom volunteers, this image was based on fears of and anxieties about an unknown place of racism (McAdam 1988: 73). However, this negative image was often countered by the more positive representation that volunteers had of the Freedom Summer project itself. Indeed, the 'ecstatic state' felt by many volunteers was transfigured into their general perception of the surrounding environment. As one volunteer said of

Mississippi's countryside, 'The panorama ... looks rounded and makes the environs feel like a stage set for a fantasy' (McAdam 1988: 74).

Such an aesthetic reinterpretation enabled volunteers to open up a gap that exposed racist attitudes and structures at a number of levels and in a number of places. For example, the Summer Project organised mock voter registrations in particular places so as to highlight the limited input that the black population had in the political process. A space was thereby constructed in freedom schools in which both blacks and whites mixed and learned from one another. Moreover, prevailing social mores about sexual encounters between different races were exposed. Such encounters were structured through notions of 'sexual desire'. Momentarily, therefore, a space was constructed through which were filtered different, heterogeneous social identities. The community atmosphere led many to believe that they were present at a history-making event that would change lives and society. It was a moment of liberation. Yet this form of democracy and participation was encapsulated within a more abstract aesthetic wherein volunteers started to question the foundations of the American Dream. Exposure to black lifestyles meant that many whites saw and experienced for the first time the social conditions of a disenfranchised group.

In their fascinating study of environmental protest around opencast mining in the UK, Beynon et al. (2000) found that aesthetic representations played a crucial role in the programme of action against opencast mining initiated by activists. Simply stated, opencast mining involves the removal of the earth that covers the coal seams and is, as a result, much more invasive of the countryside. Moreover, opencast mining is afflicted with various forms of pollution such as noise pollution and air pollution and is believed by some to cause medical conditions such as asthma. Beynon et al. note that the prospect of an opencast site is viewed by local residents as nothing short of disastrous. When news of the site is announced, rumours spread, and environmental activists talk with people about 'what it will be like'. These everyday accounts all turn on the ways in which the new site will affect everyday life. People turn to friends and neighbours who have experienced opencast mining in the past. At protest meetings, 'survivors' of previous opencast sites also recount in detail the disruptions caused by their development and working. The perceived threat is a powerful force, coordinating opposition. These factors not only indicate distinctively qualitative ideas around the mobilisation of alternative types of democracy and participation, they also demonstrate how communities establish moral networks and information flows between themselves that are pitted against those networks constructed by operators and so on. What we see, therefore, are different forms of activism being formed across social groups.

In respect to the discursive conflicts around opencast mining, Beynon et al. discovered that people living near a field or an area of woodland or even a derelict area construct their own aesthetic image of that area if it is purchased for opencast mining. For example, it becomes viewed as a major civil engineering site and a place of work. The purpose and use of land change in a way that people find disturbing. Large ('monstrous') earth-moving equipment is moved on to the site. Within days, the appearance of the landscape is completely changed as the countryside is torn apart. Particular discursive words are important for people to express their horror at what is going on. These words include 'dust', 'noise', 'blasting' and 'general nuisance'. Each word conjures up images and narratives of the experience of opencast mining that will be used by these people when they form groups opposing opencast mining (Beynon et al. 2000: 94–9). Therefore, these discursive terms are crucial enrolling mechanisms in bringing people together in a network of opposition. Such aesthetic narratives of the surrounding environment are often the starting point for the construction of protest networks and the formation of distinct spaces of democracy and participation.

However, there are also noticeable problems with social movements. First, it is not always clear how social movements engage with political electorates, formal representative groups such as trade unions, or democratic mechanisms associated with the nation-state. Sometimes, social movements seem to bypass these 'normal' representative structures. Yet, in so doing, social movements, particularly global social movements, engage in networking with one another instead of gaining hegemony among ordinary political electorates (Colás 2003: 116). Correspondingly, a lack of political leadership within some global protest movements means that there is sometimes confusion among members about the policy direction of the movement in question. In the Occupy Movement, for example, some US activists were hesitant about, almost suspicious of, building alliances with local trade unions, whereas other Occupy activists willingly did so (Roberts 2012; Shepard 2012).

The issue of the relationship between trade unions and social movements is important for another reason. There are a number of examples of how trade unions have attempted to forge links with community activists in local places. Women's organisations, civil rights groups, gay rights groups, human rights groups, worker centres, immigrant groups, churches and a range of other community-based groups have all, in various ways, campaigned on employment issues. Such campaigns make them natural bedfellows with trade unions, and, in different countries, examples exist where these community organisations have linked up with trade unions to campaign on common issues of concern (Fine 2005; Wills and Simms 2003). At the same time, however, it also needs to be remembered that trade unions are more adept at campaigning nationally, and sometimes globally, for workers' rights and do so *at the point of production*. In this respect, trade unions can push forward claims for workers through the rights to collective bargaining in the workplace itself and thereby try to bring together both political and economic democracy (Taylor and Mathers 2008: 29). For a leftist, specifically socialist, account of democracy and participation, this is a crucial step to take in promoting rights of individuals in society. To put the same point in plainer language, a leftist, and socialist, form of democracy and participation must aim to promote economic democracy, and not just political and social democracy.

There are, of course, different variants of socialism. One particular school of thought argues that socialism entails not the separation of labour from the means of production but its connection. Under capitalism, the vast majority of ordinary people have no control over or ownership of how they work and produce goods. Instead, most people are ruled by the profit motive and the incessant drive of capitalism to accumulate more and more capital for the sake of accumulation, irrespective of whether there is a marketplace or outlet for this accumulation. Socialism is thus a system that attempts to overcome these problems. At the most basic level, socialism should seek to eliminate the self-valorisation of capital, ensuring that the equality and freedom promised by capitalism can at last be realised (cf. Levine 1988: 6–7).

One way to ensure that labour is finally connected to the means of production is to dissolve the gap between economic and politics. To make the same point in a different way, it is vital for socialists to democratise the workplace so that the ownership and control of the workplace are no longer exclusively in private hands. Only then can socio-economic relations be regulated in a rational direction (McNally 1993: 199). In other words, a socialist society is dependent on a robust form of *economic democracy*. None of this is to say that market relations will be completely swept away. But it is to say that, under socialism, labour will have a real democratic input into economic decision-making.

Pateman (1970) argues that economic democracy must as a minimum requirement enable workers to elect their management and have a democratic voice in what is produced and/or how work relations are structured. The main point in implementing such a system is to ensure that workers are not employed as wage labourers by capital but rather join an enterprise as a fellow worker with full democratic rights (Smith 2006: 303). Worker self-management, where workers democratically control each productive enterprise, will be evident in such a system. Moreover, worker enterprises will operate in tandem with the wider community. For example, enterprises could pay a leasing fee for factors such as land, buildings and equipment – factors that are the common property of a community, which is why enterprises lease these. Money accumulated by this tax will be returned to the economy through public investment banks, otherwise known as 'community banks' (Schweickart 2002: 47). The assets of an enterprise (e.g. land, buildings and machinery) are thereby the common property of a community. An enterprise therefore has an obligation to ensure that these assets are properly looked after and repaired and replaced when necessary (Schweickart 2002: 47–8). Under council democracy and participation, then, the usual division that exists in capitalism between 'experts' (intellect) and 'non-experts' (manual) needs to be dissolved in favour of workers being given time and space within an enterprise to learn some of the rudiments of bookkeeping, accounting, marketing and so on (Lebowitz 2006: 77).

Conclusion: the structure of the book

Like its accompanying volume, the aim of this book, then, is to contribute towards, expand on and critically develop left-wing perspectives on democracy and participation through a number of its forms and by focusing on a number of different countries. The book is divided into three main parts. The first part deals with the political cultures and public spheres of the Left. Emanuele Achino starts this part by exploring further the relationship between left-wing activism and political culture. Emanuele's focus is Attac-Italy, which is a national branch of an international network of related associations known as the Association for the Taxation of Financial Transactions and Citizen's Action, or Attac. Groups formed links with one another in the late 1990s, and supporters from Italian NGOs, militants from the SINCONBAS and CGIL trade unions, advocates from the Fourth International and individuals from the Bandiera Rossa and Punto Rosso organisations (representatives of the Italian left wing) all joined together to form Attac-Italy in January 2002. However, the formation of Attac-Italy also attracted activists who had previously associated with the Italian Communist Party (PCI), as well as the radical left-wing party Rifondazione Comunista after 1991, itself a splinter group from the PCI. Therefore, the political culture and organisation background of those involved in Attac-Italy have been moved from one organisational context to one another. By drawing on interviews with members of Attac-Italy, Emanuele shows how the biographies and political culture of these activists have meant that the Italian branch of Attac has managed to avoid implementing a vertical decision-making structure and instead is willing to experiment with new and more inclusive types of democratic decision-making.

Chapter 3 moves on to consider the formation of proletarian public spheres. In this respect, Gulden Ozcan looks at how the 78-day-long resistance of the TEKEL workers in downtown Ankara, Turkey, in the winter of 2010 became a beacon of hope for many people in the country at a time when dissent of any kind was being ruthlessly suppressed by the government. The support for and solidarity with the TEKEL workers from different parts of the country, as well as from the international community, indicated the need to recover from the despair created by the persistent oppression of the working classes under the fast-paced neo-liberalisation of the 2000s. The aim of the chapter is to rethink the possibility of labour power-based politicisation for the working classes on the axis of history, theory and the TEKEL resistance. This case study enables Gulden to ask broader questions about the feasibility of identity politics as a way for workers to mobilise against neo-liberal politics, or whether a movement of resistance against neo-liberalism also requires the formation of a public sphere that explicitly incorporates labour power and the labour process as the moment that unites left-wing activists.

Chapter 4 continues the themes of political culture and the public sphere by focusing on social movements and struggles coalescing around the neo-liberal restructuring of higher education. Andre Pusey suggests that these struggles reflect the widening of exploitation in society. In a post-Fordist society, exploitation has moved beyond the confines of specific bounded workplaces such as the industrial factory and can now be situated in many areas of life. One need only think about how the rise of social media, smart machines and cloud computing has blurred the boundaries between physical workplaces and the rest of society. Many now work 'on the move' between actual workplaces, and others increasingly work at home. For Pusey, then, it is no surprise that, in our digital times, capitalism gains profits through 'immaterial labour' such as through people working via platforms or by creating new 'ideas', rather than by physically constructing commodities. Under these circumstances, universities have become direct sites of exploitation for capital as the intellectual output of academics and researchers is commodified in a variety of innovative ways. Pusey therefore argues that struggles around higher education and universities across many parts of the world are symptomatic of a transformation of the role of knowledge and intellectual production within society and the economy, and subsequently the role of intellectuals and knowledge production within social struggles.

The second part of the collection looks at the relationship between the state and leftist social movements. Chapter 5, by Tennyson Joseph, starts to analyse this relationship through a fascinating study of how peasant (agricultural worker) revolts have contributed to political development in the small, independent, semi-agrarian Caribbean state of Saint Lucia. It isolates key moments of electoral and constitutional change and demonstrates how such changes emerged out of protracted periods of agrarian revolt in the country. Part of a larger ongoing study that examines several such moments between 1945 and 2000, the chapter specifically focuses on two such periods for comparative purposes – 1952–1957 and 1992–1997. Despite occurring several decades apart, both periods witnessed significant island-wide revolts among the Saint Lucian peasantry, resulting in far-reaching political change. The 'sugar strikes' of 1952–1957 facilitated significant adjustment to the Crown colony system, advanced the process of self-government and shaped the contours of party politics and political economy well into the 1990s. Relatedly, the period 1992–1997 witnessed protests by a group calling itself the Banana Salvation Committee, during the period of the liberalisation of the banana market in Europe, and effectively brought to a close the features of domestic electoral politics and the broader political economy that had taken shape in the 1950s. Tennyson therefore shows how history informs the activism and struggles of left-wing movements, but also how they are entwined with different state forms and politics.

In Chapter 6, Gregory White reflects on austerity in the UK, the post-2008 economic crisis environment, and social movements and social policy. As

Gregory notes, contemporary social policy in the UK is at a critical impasse. Government austerity has presented an unprecedented challenge to civil society organisations, trade unions and social movements as to (1) tackling entrenched neo-liberal narratives surrounding the welfare state and (2) organising and coordinating direct action and non-institutional responses. In the midst of the crisis, the political Left in the UK has been split on decisions regarding how to act and how to organise against policies enacted by the Conservative-led coalition government of 2010–2015. Post-crisis social movements (such as Occupy London and UK Uncut) have focused on non-institutional methods – often manifesting in the form of direct action – to address social and economic injustices. The efficacy of such decisions to act has been widely researched. However, although the interest in researching links between activism and policy outcomes is strong, the lasting impact of such interventions on government policy – and in particular social policy – is less well known. Gregory therefore reflects on his recently completed fieldwork that aims to understand the relationship between post-crisis social movements and social policy. His chapter, in particular, critically engages with interview data collected from activists who have been organising locally and nationally in the UK. The chapter discusses institutional and non-institutional forms of activism – deployed in the post-crisis context – and begins to analyse the efficacy of such interventions. Further, it asks how social movements can challenge certain policy prescriptions and be effective in both institutional and non-institutional spheres. The study of social policy and that of social movements are, of course, two very distinct areas of enquiry. It is a primary motive of his chapter to bridge the two disciplines, using the economic crisis of 2008 as a backdrop.

Chapter 7 by Marcello Gisondi discusses the birth, in January 2014, of Podemos in Spain. Marcello shows how Podemos has radically changed the face of Spanish politics. It has gained important municipalities (e.g. Madrid and Barcelona); it has obtained extraordinary results, in both the European and Spanish general elections; and, finally, it has forced the main parties (PP and PSOE) to unite against it. One might simply link the birth of Podemos with the 2011 *Indignados* movement. But the roots of the party are in the anti-globalisation movements of the early 2000s. As Marcello shows, Podemos's founders were mostly young activists and academics who have gained great experience with the media since 2010 when they created the digital TV channel La Tuerka. The familiarity with traditional and digital media allowed Pablo Iglesias to become famous nationwide. In so doing, he and the other main leaders of the movement were able to share their political messages with a great audience, which later on constituted the electoral base of the party. The ideals and goals of Podemos clearly recall the tradition of the European Left. Nonetheless, its discourses are rooted in Ernesto Laclau's populist theory and involve themes that are traditionally far from leftist ideology, such as patriotism. Moreover, the electoral constituency of Podemos is greater than that of any other current radical left party in Europe (except Syriza). This is probably owing to the initial strategy of accumulation of political power adopted by Podemos: a top–down approach that is quite unusual for left-wing forces. The charismatic leaders of Podemos used the media to stimulate and reinforce grassroots movements. Currently, however, there is a conflict of ideas inside the party: some want to strengthen the democratic base, whereas others prefer to keep a more hierarchical structure. The aim of Marcello's chapter is to reconstruct the history of Podemos up until this pivotal moment through the publications of Podemos's founders and activists, their political discourses, as well as campaign materials and electoral data.

In Chapter 8, Joseph Ibrahim charts the emergence of the British anti-capitalist movement from the turn of the century to the present day. It begins with an analysis of the new wave of anti-capitalism that emerged in the 1990s with the anarchist anti-road-building networks, Earth First and Reclaim the Streets, and the protests against the supranational summit meetings of the IMF, World Bank and the G8 in the early 2000s. The second part of Joseph's chapter considers how anti-capitalism as an ideology attracted a wider social base to create anti-austerity networks such as the UK Occupy movement through to the new political group Momentum, which represents a connection between social movements and a political party form of mobilisation. Drawing on qualitative interviews and observation data, Joseph argues that, over the last 20 years, British anti-capitalist ideology has involved different strains, from anarchism to socialism and now to a renewal of social democracy.

The final part examines the relationship between the state and leftist parliamentary politics. David Bates starts this discussion by focusing on the British Labour Party. Specifically, David explores how the Labour Party's tortured relationship with public opinion on immigration has become as salient as ever following the vote in favour of Brexit in June 2016. The issue has often troubled the party throughout its history, and the current debate over how it should respond to widespread antipathy towards immigration in twenty-first century Britain looks set to divide the party still further: although Labour leader Jeremy Corbyn has praised the contribution of migrants to British society and defended the principle of free movement, other senior figures have called for a 'red line' on migration as the UK negotiates its exit from the European Union. David draws on qualitative interviews with a dozen Labour activists and councillors from the north-east of England who describe their own encounters with the immigration issue while campaigning in constituencies that voted by a majority for Brexit. Furthermore, David employs critical discourse analysis to explore how those involved in grassroots campaigning position themselves in relation to public opinion, the national media and debates in the Parliamentary Labour Party when discussing immigration. It is seen how 'public opinion' is constructed in different ways, including the strategic silencing of certain voices, in order to justify a range of suggested policy approaches to immigration.

In Chapter 10, Enrico Reuter examines how the radical Left in France relates to national sovereignty and statism. Enrico addresses these issues through three main points. First, he briefly discusses the historical specificity of France, to outline how left-wing radicalism is seen, by some, as being deeply intertwined with the ideal of the sovereign nation-state and the construction of national identity. Second, and by focusing on the current political landscape, Enrico maps how different forces of the radical left (notably decentralised non-parliamentary grass roots movements of the radical left such as 'Nuit Debout' and the more state-centred movement 'La France Insoumise' in support of Jean-Luc Mélenchon) position themselves with regards to national sovereignty and the EU, in order to analyse the key divisions within the radical left arising out of this question. Finally, Enrico situates these debates in the wider context of how left-wing movements and parties attempt to determine their strategic and programmatic orientations in light of the competitive pressures of a global capitalist order.

In Chapter 11, Marco Damiani seeks to explore and map out the common features that characterise radical left parties today and does so by noting differences between them and communist parties of the twentieth century. In particular, and drawing on an array of primary sources such as party documents and interviews with key players, three key areas are highlighted that bring out the differences between these two political groups. First, radical left political parties today are not necessarily 'anti-system' to the degree that their communist counterparts were in the last century. Second, the political culture and values of radical left parties today have severed ties with the classical left-wing and Marxist ideals of the early twentieth century. Third, radical left parties are more often than not built on a political pluralism at odds with the 'democratic centralism' practised by communist parties in the twentieth century. Around these three dimensions, then, there is the emergence of a new political family, the radical Left, which represents a clean break with the political experiences of the twentieth-century political matrix.

Note

1 John Michael Roberts is grateful to Palgrave MacMillan for permission to reproduce some material in Chapter 1 from John Michael Roberts (2009) *The Competent Public Sphere*, London: Palgrave.
2 A similar model of voluntarism is provided by Parry, Moyser and Day in *Political Participation and Democracy in Britain* (1992). Similar to Verba et al., Parry et al. adopt a broad definition of political participation. They define this as 'taking part in the processes of formulation, passage and implementation of public policies' (Parry et al. 1992: 16). This definition is broad enough, according to Parry et al., to account for a diverse range of participatory activity. However, it is narrow enough to exclude mere interest in politics. Thus the definition is designed to account for a 'form of action'. As part of this definition, Parry et al. utilise a resource-based model. Yet, with this model, they are not only interested in the individual resources held, they are also interested in the economic, social, cultural and ideological factors lying behind these resources that partly enhance or diminish these resources. Such resources can be either individual or group-based. These resources feed into a person's background, which then influences the perceived nature of the interests and issues at hand. From

these factors come modes of participation. The impact of participation is measured by the benefits perceived by active citizens and the extent to which elites respond to the participatory input of individuals and groups.

References

Almond, G. and Verba, S. (1963) *The Civic Culture: Political Attitudes and Democracy in Five Nations*, Princeton, NJ: Princeton University Press.

Beynon, H., Cox, A. and Hudson, R. (2000) *Digging Up Trouble: The Environment Protest and Opencast Mining*, London: Rivers Oram Press.

Bourdieu, P. (1986) 'Forms of Capital', in J. G. Richardson (ed.), *Handbook for Theory and Research for the Sociology of Education*, pp. 241–58, New York: Greenwood Press.

Castells, M. (2010) *The Power of Identity*, 2nd edn, Oxford: Wiley-Blackwell.

Chambers, S. (2003) 'Deliberative Democratic Theory', *Annual Review of Political Science* 6(1): 307–26.

Chappell, Z. (2010) 'A Tension between Ideal and Practice: Re-evaluation of Micro and Macro Models of Deliberation', *Representation* 46(3): 295–308.

Cohen, R. and Rai, S. (2000) *Global Social Movements*, London: Continuum.

Colás, A. (2003) 'The Power of Representation: Democratic Politics and Global Governance', *Review of International Studies* 29(S1): 97–118.

Della Porta, D. and Diani, M. (2006) *Social Movements*, Oxford: Blackwell.

Dryzek, J. S. (2001) 'Legitimacy and Economy in Deliberative Democracy', *Political Theory* 29(5): 651–69.

Dryzek, J. S. (2006) 'Transnational Democracy in an Insecure World', *International Political Science Review* 27(2): 101–19.

Fine, B. (2000) *Social Capital versus Social Theory*, London: Routledge.

Fine, J. (2005) 'Community Unions and the Revival of the American Labor Movement', *Politics & Society* 33(1): 153–99.

Goodin, R. E. and Dryzek, J. S. (2006) 'Deliberative Impacts: The Macro-Political Uptake of Mini-Publics', *Politics & Society* 34(2): 219–44.

Grossberg, L. (1992) *We Gotta Get Out of this Place*, London: Routledge.

Gutmann, A. and Thompson, D. (2004) *Why Deliberative Democracy?* Princeton, NJ: Princeton University Press.

Hooghe, M. (1999) 'The Rebuke of Thersites: Deliberative Democracy under Conditions of Inequality', *Acta Politica* 34(4): 287–301.

Hussain, M. M. and Howard, P. N. (2013) 'What Best Explains Successful Protest Cascades? ICTs and the Fuzzy causes of the Arab Spring', *International Studies Review* 15(1): 48–66.

Ibrahim, J. and Roberts, J. M. (eds) (2019) *Contemporary Left-wing Activism Vol 1: Democracy, Participation and Dissent in a Global Context*, London: Routledge.

Jessop, B. (1974) *Traditionalism, Conservatism and British Political Culture*, London: Routledge.

Kavanagh, D. (1989) 'Political Culture in Great Britain: The Decline of Civic Culture', in G. A. Almond and S. Verba (eds), *The Civic Culture Revisited*, London: Sage.

Kellam, J. (2017) 'The Perils of Being Popular', in M. Perryman (ed.), *The Corbyn Effect*, London: Lawrence & Wishart.

Kreiss, D., Finn, M. and Turner, F. (2011) 'The Limits of Peer Production: Some Reminders from Max Weber for the Network Society', *New Media & Society* 13(2): 243–59.

Lebowitz, M. A. (2006) *Build It Now: Socialism for the Twenty-first Century*, New York: Monthly Review Press.

Levine, A. (1988) *Arguing for Socialism*, revised edn, London: Verso.

McAdam, D. (1988) *Freedom Summer*, Oxford: Oxford University Press.

McLennan, G. (1989) *Marxism, Pluralism and Beyond*, Cambridge: Polity.

McNally, D. (1993) *Against the Market*, London: Verso.

Moody, K. (2018) *On New Terrain*, Chicago, IL: Haymarket Books.

Mouffe, C. (2005) *On the Political*, London: Routledge.

Parry, G., Moyser, G. and Day, N. (1992) *Political Participation and Democracy in Britain*, Cambridge: Cambridge University Press.

Pateman, C. (1970) *Participation and Democratic Theory*, Cambridge: Cambridge University Press.

Pateman, C. (1989) 'The Civic Culture: A Philosophic Critique', in G. A. Almond and S. Verba (eds), *The Civic Culture Revisited*, London: Sage.

Pateman, C. (2012) 'Participatory Democracy Revisited', *Perspectives on Politics* 10(1): 7–19.

Perryman, M. (2017) 'The Great Moving Left Show', in M. Perryman (ed.), *The Corbyn Effect*, London: Lawrence & Wishart.

Polleta, F., Chen, P. C. B. and Anderson, C. (2009) 'Is Information Good for Deliberation? Link-posting in an Online Forum', *Public Deliberation* 5(1): 1–20.

Portes, A. (1998) 'Social Capital: Its Origins and Applications in Modern Sociology', *Annual Review of Sociology* 24: 1–24.

Putnam, R. D. (1993) *Making Democracy Work*, Princeton, NJ: Princeton University Press.

Putnam, R. D. (2000) *Bowling Alone: The Collapse and Revival of American Community*, NewYork: Simon Schuster.

Roberts, A. (2012) 'Why the Occupy Movement Failed', *Public Administration Review* 72(5): 754–62.

Schweickart, D. (2002) *After Capitalism*, Oxford: Rowan & Littlefield.

Shepard, B. H. (2012) 'Labor and Occupy Wall Street: Common Causes and Uneasy Alliances', *WorkingUSA* 15(March): 121–34.

Smith, T. (2006) *Globalisation: A Systematic Marxian Account*, Leiden: Brill.

Stoecker, R. (2003) 'Understanding the Development-Organizing Dialectic', *Journal of Urban Affairs* 25(4): 493–512.

Street, J. (1997) *Politics and Popular Culture*, Cambridge: Polity Press.

Sum, N.-L. and Jessop, B. (2013) *Towards a Cultural Political Economy*, Cheltenham: Edward Elgar.

Taylor, G. and Mathers, A. (2008) 'Organising Unions, Organising Communities? Trades Union Councils and Community Union Politics in England and Wales', *Centre for Employment Studies Research, Working Paper 10*, Bristol Business School, University of West England.

Theocharis, Y. and van Deth, J. (2018) 'The Continuous Expansion of Citizen Participation: A New Taxonomy', *European Political Science Review* 10(1): 139–63.

Topf, R. (1989) 'Political Change and Political Culture in Britain, 1959–87', in J. R. Gibbins (ed.), *Contemporary Political Culture*, London: Sage.

Verba, S., Schlozman, K. L. and Brady, H. E. (1995) *Voice and Equality: Civic Voluntarism in American Politics*, Cambridge, MA: Harvard University Press.

Welch, S. (1993) *Concept of Political Culture*, London: Palgrave.

Wills, J. and Simms, M. (2003) 'Building Reciprocal Community Unionism in the UK', *Capital and Class* 82(Spring): 59–84.

PART I

Political culture and public spheres of the left

2

ORGANIZING ATTAC!

Organization and political culture of Attac in Italy

Emanuele Achino

Introduction

Attac is the acronym for the Association for the Taxation of Financial Transactions and Citizens' Action (Attac). The Italian branch of Attac is a political alliance that has grown over the last ten years and is tightly linked to other associations worldwide. Indeed, I have noted that Attac-Italy was formed in the late 1990s, when supporters from Italian NGOs, militants from the SiCobas and CGIL trade-unions,[1] advocates from the Fourth-International and individuals from Bandiera Rossa (Red Flag) and Punto Rosso (Red Point) organizations (representatives of the Italian left wing) joined together to found the national association, which was then formally inaugurated in January 2002 (Achino 2005). Furthermore, I have argued that many of those involved were already associated with the Italian Communist Party (PCI), as well as Rifondazione Comunista (RC) after 1991, when the PCI shifted into two separate parties, a more moderate party – Partito Democratico di Sinistra (DS) and one radical left-wing party, namely Rifondazione Comunista. After that, a part of RC shifted into a separate sub-party, namely the Comunisti Italiani political party (CI) (Achino 2005).

From this brief description, it is clear that the political culture of those involved in Attac-Italy has changed the sociopolitical context (Achino 2016). As a result, simply stated, left-wing political culture has also knowingly influenced the structure of the Italian branch of Attac. Accordingly, this chapter focuses on how members of Attac perceive issues of internal organization and decision-making and it considers these in relation to the associative charter formally adopted by the Italian organization. To do so, I developed a qualitative research design and I gained enough information to frame the Italian branch of Attac in terms of political culture, organization and decision-making. In fact, by analysing the past and present political biographies of militant activists, and by assuming that the political culture is able to inform organizational structure and decision-making, I suggest that these militants' political biographies have influenced Attac by providing the Italian organization with a homogeneous political and organizational background for the foreseeable future.

This chapter begins by discussing why a collective identity within organizations is important. It then moves on to argue that the political culture of militants had a role in providing the soon-to-be-born Italian organization with opportunities for collective action and constraints. By drawing on my own qualitative research based on political biographical interviews and focus groups with Italian left-wing activists, and through Boolean analysis, I gained sufficient information to frame the Italian organization in terms of political and cultural backgrounds. In fact, its history and present circumstances characterize Attac as belonging to the list of contemporary anti-globalization social movements, and the implications of this characterization for decision-making and internal organization have been investigated in the fieldwork.

Why do organization and collective identities matter?

For the purpose of investigating Attac's organizational structure, I focused on the cycle of protests that has emerged in the present globalized culture. In this age of complex social systems, recent mobilizations have had the effect of extending the debate about the relations between social movements' organizations and the political system. For example, some have suggested that, in terms of gaining and developing political opportunities and democratic transformations in society, organizations themselves – rather than individuals – are better equipped to gain access to the political opportunities on offer. Under these circumstances, organizations utilize militants to maximize their political success in and around certain sociopolitical issues (Goodwin and Jasper 2003).

However, an organization alone is not sufficient to influence the political system without connections to institutions, and collective identities related to such organizations are important in terms of political options and to fill the gap between individuals and institutional recognition. Indeed, collective identities are often said to be produced by several interacting individuals who are concerned with the orientation of their action (e.g. political action) and with the field of political opportunities/constraints in which their action takes place (see also DiMaggio and Powell 1991). In addition, individuals mutually recognize that they share certain orientations and, on this basis, they decide to act together. Yet, collective identity is a process negotiated over time and comprises a cognitive definition, active relationships and emotional investments (Melucci 1996). These aspects are used to contribute to the identification of those opportunities/constraints, and collective identities are able to emerge by interacting with institutional (formal) and associative (informal) actors (Polletta and Jasper 2001). In this context, collective identity is not in opposition to either strategy and politics or to interests and incentives, and collective identity is not a means of filling gaps left by the state-centred approach. By contrast, political interests are crucial in explaining social/political dynamics and structural organization, and analysis of the interconnections between those pre-existing political and organizational backgrounds is necessary.

It is also important to remember that collective identity is an interactive process used to act based on the field of opportunities/constraints and placed halfway between structural restrictions and cultural dynamics. Dynamics between the structural and cultural effects of participation are, in turn, able to transform the social perception of the reality and the political and organizational settings, where individuals, collective actors and institutions are recognized by each other. On this basis, social movements are also concerned with the cultural representation of institutions and decision-making, and therefore transformations affect the social imaginary and political action regardless of the institutional and associative participation for the near future.

Why do organization and the structure of political opportunity matter?

Collective identity is placed halfway between structural constrictions and cultural dynamics and is able to recognize opportunities/constraints informed by the political biographies of those involved. I also argue that political biographies are able to inform a social movement's organization and decision-making, although a social movement's organization cannot fully succeed alone without sponsorship from political parties or institutions (Kriesi et al. 1995). Moreover, the existence of a social movement's organization is often intertwined with the political system, and the complementary forms of political action suggest that the effectiveness of certain political organizations may have been wrongly conceptualized (Goldstone 2004). In fact, Goldstone (2004) noted that the ability of groups' organizations to combine different forms of contentions aiming at influencing political structures and reinforcing collective identity is the option that best allows the survival of an organization over time. Moreover, in focusing on social movements during the 1980s, Melucci (1996) noticed that organizations associated with new social movements pursue a variety of protests aimed at making institutional policies conform to their goals and the positive effects that political recognition may have in that process. However, the existence of the conventional political system and a stable structured organization has been taken for granted. In fact, the implicit model is that, once those groups leading certain protest cycles have succeeded and are incorporated into the polity through employing conventional politics, then social movements' organizations are consequentially integrated within the system.

Although scholars have sometimes been used to considering implicitly that the institutional polity and the political opportunity structure are the counterpart of those organizations placed outside the political system, much clarity on what constituted bright opportunity structures is required. To date, in fact, the political opportunity structure has been taken for granted when the emergence and success of a movement have been promoted, and it has been implicitly assumed that, once the political access is open, movements' activity also naturally develops institutional political action, and therefore the political opportunity structure will be able to offer a degree of formal participation. However, the opening of the political structure alone is not sufficient to explain the existence of social movement organizations. In fact, the relationships between social movement organizations and formal political institutions, as well as the relationships between social movement organizations and institutions, are intertwined in the political setting, and political outcomes also depend on these implicit and explicit interconnections (Achino 2005).

Although the political system has sometimes been taken for granted, the political opportunity structure approach has been useful in emphasizing certain strategic elements in the external environment of social movement organizations. By exploring the political issue, it emphasizes conditions relating to formal institutions, tending to neglect the role of critical economics and historical conditions. By focusing on opportunities, it emphasizes that opportunities are outside the organization, and rarely within the organization and from within individuals' political biographies. But, by focusing on structures, it suggests that large-scale premises are necessary conditions for certain outcomes (Goodwin and Jasper 1999).[2] Moreover, the political opportunity structure has not paid attention to those political biographies placed outside the political system and able to influence a social movement organization. To fill in the gap, I therefore propose to widen the perspective, aiming at introducing these political biographies into the investigation by considering that these political biographies are an opportunity for a social movement organization, on condition that these political biographies are recognized as being competent for individuals' and collectives' actions. So, whereas the political opportunity structure describes the macro conditions relevant for protest, an analysis of the specific context of the daily experiences of individuals within social movements' organizations is required to understand internal dynamics (action), and analysis of the external cultural/political setting is also required.

Theoretical and research questions

I propose that the political culture (Almond and Verba 1965) of militants involved in Attac-Italy has moved along a timeline, coming through the political formal/informal groups and organizations individuals experienced over time. I also propose that political culture is able to influence the cognitive maps of militants and the organizational structure available for the Italian association. On this basis, I have researched the militants who have previously had activist experiences within the more structured left-wing political parties and left-wing trade unions, as well as the militants who have previously had experiences in more informal left-wing Italian political organizations. Accordingly, I have argued that the decision-making system and the organizational structure could have been moved into Attac from elsewhere, although revised by those militants who have later moved into the Italian association. The mixture of political and organizational backgrounds is able to reinforce the internal associative decision-making and the still-existing political network available for this Italian organization.

I have also hypothesized that social movement activity and institutional political activity are different but symmetric approaches that are able to influence political outcomes, and I questioned which form of organization they have provided the association with, and which form of internal decision-making they have adopted in order to guarantee effective participation for everybody. On this basis, I broadened my perspective by including individuals' political biographical dynamics within the analysis. In doing so, I hypothesized that there is no clear set of necessary conditions for the emergence and actions of social movements' organization. Instead, it would appear that a specific social movement organization faces its own group-specific fields of external relations. Accordingly, I want to consider that the formal organization of Attac-Italy and the perception of internal decision-making provided by militants are able to inform the actual organizational structure. In fact, it is the relations between internal and external dynamics that appear to shape social movements' organizations. Although labelling such factors as 'political opportunity structure' may have shed light in the direction of looking beyond social movements' resources, we still nevertheless need to understand how the contextual and internal political culture of their specific organizations affect and impact their internally adopted decision-making.

The methodology

I have empirically investigated Attac-Italy using qualitative research methods. Specifically, I have looked at how militants have perceived the internal decision-making process within Attac-Italy by exploring the temporal perception of decision-making and leadership formation in relation to previous participation in political parties, trade unions and social movements.

To investigate these research questions, I undertook fieldwork between March 2004 and December 2005. Non-probability quota sampling was used to select various activists involved in both formal and informal participation.[3] For each group I met,[4] two interviews were conducted (one with a man, another with a woman), followed by at least one focus group per collective. Of the twenty-five local Italian organizations, six (24 per cent) were willing to participate in the research. In the end, I had eight focus groups, twelve narrative interviews, two brainstorming interviews (one in Milan and one in Trento), with some follow-up interviews in 2015–2016. The associative charter has also been uploaded to NVivo, with the aim of integrating data. The associative charter is, in fact, the formal regulation provided by the Italian organization; in addition, the charter disciplines concrete forms of participation and decision-making. Yet, by analysing the formal charter on the one hand and the social perception of the internal decision-making on the other hand, I obtained enough information to balance the effectiveness of internal decision-making, when compared with the model of decision-making adopted by the formal charter only.

After transcription of the interviews and focus groups, the data were uploaded to NVivo. NVivo employs Boolean analysis, which is an explorative method to detect deterministic dependencies between items, and logic operators are employed to do so (AND, OR, NOT, as well as fuzzy and near commands). Boolean analysis does not assume that the detected dependencies describe the data completely and assumes that there may be other probabilistic dependencies as well. Thus, a Boolean analysis tries to detect interesting deterministic structures in the data, but does not set out to uncover all structural aspects in the data set.

Organization, participation and political parties

During qualitative interviews and focus groups, individuals and groups discussed a broad range of topics. In consequence, I collected more information than expected, and, with the aim of reducing complexity, a text query search was employed to screen data (text search queries are helpful for searching words or phrases in a data set). In desk-based research, I asked, 'what do the data tell me about the organization of Attac-Italy?' and I identified certain descriptive relations. In fact, by codifying significant information (textual information) into meaningful groups (categorization), and by adopting a 'within ten words framework' (the AND command provided the combination of all those occurrences in the whole data set within ten words from a contextualized piece of text), I created a pyramidal tree model and developed a node matrix on this basis.

I therefore investigated descriptive relations by employing a query search. Specifically, I explored where 'organization AND participation AND political parties' have been discussed, and these 'organization, participation and political parties' discussions have been contextualized using a 'within ten words query search'. Moreover, textual data have been enlarged over the whole text of each interview and focus group, with the aim of contextualizing the discussion, and implicit/explicit meanings of communication have been analysed accordingly. Outputs provided a large amount of discursively constructed empirical material about the political biographies of those involved. Content analysis of these biographies allowed me to break down the data according to the main dimensions theoretically outlined, and the rationale adopted was about the precise use of words employed by respondents (see also Krippendorff 2004). In fact, I adopted the following combination of 'organization, participation and political parties (first query)'; 'organization, participation, and social movements (second query)'; 'organization, decision-making and leadership (third query)'. Each of these was compared with the associative charter by making links between fundamental (what is formally prescribed by the charter) and substantial (what is substantially perceived by militants) dimensions of associative life.

In the first instance, previous participation in political parties and trade unions was discussed, with the aim of analysing the political cultures of respondents. Certainly, the Milan group agreed on this point:

> Local groups attack [here the group is also punning on the name of the association] at the edge of the institutional left-wing … Attac has filled up with a large amount of people belonging to RC … almost all of them think that RC is probably the only viable party in the country.
>
> *(Milan 2004)*[5]

In Turin, however, the group noticed that:

> Local groups practise collective action … however, the prevailing factor was the risk of these groups being excessively politicized … the risk perceived was that coalitions were being formed between groups, something which principally occurs amongst institutionalized political parties.
>
> *(Turin 2004)*

Broadly speaking, during interviews and focus groups, participants agreed that a large number of militants who have previously been involved with the RC and CI political parties are at present involved with Attac, although previous quantitative research described a certain degree of heterogeneity on the matter (Achino 2005). However, the perceived risk of excessive politicization in terms of political parties has been also debated by the militants interviewed. In fact, in Bergamo, the discussion included a repositioning between formal political parties and informal social movements, as such:

> I experienced social movements and political parties, and it is easier to take a role in Attac. I was metaphorically born in a political party, although I actually reject political parties at all … I have worked with political parties, but never formally been a member, however, I have been involved in politics at municipality scale.
>
> *(Bergamo 2003)*

Although the question was about previous personal/biographical experiences in political parties, militants in Rome enlarged the discussion in this way:

> By paying attention to the relationships between Attac-Italy and the political system, we noticed that the conflict was not conflict against

the political parties. However, RC was the only political party able to stay in touch with us ... I mean, political parties can only help us to the extent that sometimes they accept certain instances that Attac proposes to them, honestly, in most cases RC is the only political party able to do so.

(Rome 2002)

In Rome, RC has also been identified as a potential partner for political alliance, whereas, in Cuneo, it was noticed by one respondent that:

I have been involved in the Argentine Communist-Leninist Party, and the Communist-Leninist party and the PCI when I moved to Italy, the question is where are we going? It seems, sometimes, that we are just moving toward the party system! The perceived risk is being co-opted by the political parties ... we have to consider that many members of Attac-Italy are also members of RC and of Green political parties, and we have to turn away from the political party system.

(Cuneo 2002)

On the one hand, the risk of co-option has been debated during focus groups, whereas, on the other hand, in Caltagirone it was stated that:

Political parties are on the decline, and Attac proposes political issues, and political parties should try to rethink these issues.

(Caltagirone 2004)

As is noticeable, the political background of militants has been connected to the wider political system in a vital way, and, because of time limitations, the discussion was over. A second focus group was arranged for the following day:

When we constituted the local group of Attac, there were no structured organizations able to gather people ... in this group no one was member of a political party, I mean, excluding those members of RC.

(Caltagirone 2004)

After data analysis, qualitative information therefore suggests that a leftist 'red line' from within the political biographies of militants, as well as a left-wing political culture, can be traced and demarcated and is also available for Attac-Italy. In the process, a specific political party (RC) has been identified, and certain heterogeneity has been quantitatively underlined.[6] However, the risk of being co-opted and the intrusion of political parties (into social movements' political activities) were urgently discussed during interviews and focus groups.

Organization, participation and social movements

In the previous section, I noted that a large number of militants in Attac-Italy also had experience within the RC political party. However, there was a need to establish where previous involvement in social movements had occurred over time.[7] To do this, a second query was run by combining 'organization AND participation AND social movements', and data were analysed with the aim of underlining interconnections between participation in social movements and the actual decision-making system. In the process, interconnections between the presence of militants from the RC political party and social movements were discussed as a paradigmatic issue. In fact, in Milan, the group stated that:

> Among many others, there were youth social movements, youth trade unions, anarchists' movements, environmental social movements and in this context Attac was considered such as the strongest organization. Attac has been interpreted as a structured transnational umbrella organization. Basically, Attac has been perceived in such a way ... Attac was comprised of members of RC, and the risk was about a political partnership with the FIOM trade union and the ARCI organization ... from the political party side, these political parties have always perceived such as Attac as an electoral black hole only.
>
> *(Milan 2003)*

The risk of being co-opted was discussed from different perspectives, as well as previous participation in social movements. In Turin, the group discussed these issues in the following way:

> All members of my family moved into socialism and communism, I felt better in social movements than in political parties. I mean, the PCI in the late 1960s. I have been involved in the students' movement and in the FUCI [Catholic organizations]. Honestly, in my political biography, I felt anger when I was involved in the Catholic social movements' students' organization ... Comunione Liberazione [controversially] ... I am feeling better with Attac, you know? Political parties do not consider those social movements' issues [common agreement]. However, certain political parties' dynamics ... these dynamics risk to be reproduced into social movements, also into Attac at the National Council.
>
> *(Turin 2005)*

In Cuneo, a similar discussion took place. One respondent observed:

> Attac-Cuneo and social movements will be able to revitalize the political system. I mean, by participating in such a way, we can increase awareness and political participation. However, RC has understood how to deal with

social movements [agreement]. I remember that it was clear during the Environmental Congress in Rio 1992. Moreover, we also must cope with the organizational issue. The paradox is about the dichotomy between 'active-participation' and 'passive-participation'. Do you know? Incentives for participation are also concerned with not just economic incentives, but also emotional incentives.

(Cuneo 2014)

In Cuneo, the group agreed that the connections between environmental social movements active in Rio 1992 and the RC political party (or at least the left-wing political parties at that time) were already established, and the group also noticed that the organizational issue is a key point for a successfully social movement's organization. Yet, the paradox of 'active participation' and 'passive participation' was also concerned with the ability of a political organization to provide militants with positive incentives (Oliver 1980). That is to say, the positive incentives (especially emotional and relational incentives) are able to provide an organization with the chance to survive and provide actions for the time to come.

In Caltagirone (Sicily), the discussion was concerned with the dynamics of political participation at the local level. One respondent, for example, said:

I experienced RC and I also come from Sicily, where I am still living. In this region there were huge pacifist social movements, anti-mafia social movements and a huge feminist social movement ... however, nothing has really changed ... these social movements have partially failed because those left-wig political parties had not been able to really change the political, economic and broadly the social context [the whole group agreed on that].

(Caltagirone 2015)

Sicilian social movements partially failed because the left-wing political parties were not able to concretely provide them with a positive political, economic and social background for action. The group stated that the connection between informal social movements and formal political parties is vital for the emergence of a successful civil society organization. In my research, I was also interested in where individuals had previously experienced social movement organizations, principally because I felt it was important to provide a sense of political and biographical continuity over time. In this respect, one respondent at Bergamo said they had 'been involved in the left-wing youth organizations over time', and, in Rome, another respondent noted that, 'most of us have experienced social movements since the 1970s. In fact, many of us have returned to participate in Attac after a while' (Rome 2002). In Torino, however, it was noticed that:

Self-education is the core point of this organization ... not one of us belongs to a specific political group, not one of us has a distinct political affiliation. All of us are self-motivated to participate, and Attac provided us with the political frame to do so.

(Turin 2005)

In Caltagirone, however, one man observed:

> I experienced the new-left organization from late 1960s to the late 1970s, and I have been also a member of RC, I have been also elected as a member of local government at the Municipality of Caltagirone. At a certain point, I decided not to take part any more. When I was involved in RC, I agreed on a document with which the Communist youth groups were always able to support those social movements' activities, and I was not yet involved in Attac. Now, I can confirm that the connections between Communist youth groups and the local group of Attac will work well together ... unfortunately, to date, Communist youth groups no longer exist in Caltagirone.

(Caltagirone 2015)

During focus groups, militants discussed a huge list of topics, and some key points have been identified accordingly. Among many others, the large presence of militants from the RC political party, members of previous student and youth social movements, as well as members from the New Left organization, peace groups and environmental organizations, have been able to inform and influence the development of the Attac-Italy organizational model. Moreover, even when political parties are perceived as declining organizations no longer able to transform demands coming from outside the political system, Attac-Italy has been described as an instrumental organization able to provide militants with a specific framework for action (and, in fact, this was not possible without Attac), by also affording a self-motivated approach to learning.

Finally, the discussion focused on the link between different social movement organizations rather than on individuals' political biographies, and certain dynamics were discussed accordingly. In doing so, militants compared Attac-Italy with Attac-France, as well as with the Lilliput-Network. On the one hand, in Milan, the following quote from a respondent was typical of the general discussion on this topic:

> Do you know, the 'centralized attitude' of [. . .],[8] in Attac-France? People could not stand [. . .] anymore, pain in the ass. I mean [. . .] the [. . .] was used to advancing the association for political strategy mainly. Just a few years ago, we perceived that a fracture was occurring within Attac-France, a fracture between two groups, one more institutionalized group – a centralized group – and one more informal group – grassroots group. In fact, Attac-Italy was fully of members of RC, and we frequently discussed political strategies, the risk of a political partnership with the FIOM trade

> union and the ARCI organization ... from the political party side, these
> political parties have always intended social movements and Attac such as
> an electoral black hole.
>
> *(Milan 2004)*

On the other hand, in Cuneo it was noticed that:

> In Attac-France, you know, Attac-France is quite an anti-globalization
> political party [...]... one viewpoint ... is about the pure political party
> that is a mixture of the French communist and socialist political parties.
>
> *(Cuneo 2004)*

In the conclusion, I will follow up on the observation above by briefly
commenting on different branches of Attac at an international level. For now,
however, I wish to move on to issues around organization and decision-making
matters. This is especially important because issues about, for example, the
decision-making role of leadership often arose in unexpected ways. One
respondent in Milan, for instance, stated:

> Founding members[9] faced the problem of how to determine the charter of
> Attac-Italy, and internal roles and decision-making. However, most of the
> founding members abandoned Attac-Italy later on, and they have not been
> a problem anymore! The first version of the charter provided founding
> members with a great deal of power in the decision-making process
> during the National Assembly. In fact, the first version of the charter was
> adopted as required by [...] from Attac-France, and this was the real
> problem. The charter of Attac-Italy has been amended by recognizing that
> the real power of founding members was [interruption, long silence]. The
> problem was self-solved because Attac-Italy become a new association in
> which the founding members' political power and individuals' back-
> grounds do not matter at all, and the positioning of those belonging to
> the IV International ... taking a role [metaphorical silence].
>
> *(Milan 2014)*

We therefore now move on to consider some organizational and decision-
making issues.

Organization and decision-making

Queries 1 and 2 focused on militants' participation in political parties and social
movements, and query 3 paid attention to 'organization AND decision-making
AND leadership' using a within-ten-words framework. Content analysis had a
role in reducing complexity and provided sub-dimensions for investigation, and
I constructed a tree nodes model on this basis. Yet, a node matrix has been

developed (intersections between organization AND decision-making AND leadership have been underlined), and the social perception of decision-making and the leadership formation in Attac-Italy is provided accordingly in Figure 2.1.

Decision-making and governance: local groups and national council

During the focus groups, left-wing militant activists described the organizational dynamic characterized by connections with internal decision-making. It was also noticeable that founding members' key roles had been transposed from one context (Attac-France) to another (Attac-Italy). In fact, Attac-Italy revised, at a national level, how the group organized its governance mechanisms. At the same time, its voting system (mainly majority voting) was described as being a critical issue by the activists interviewed. One respondent in Turin, for example, observed:

> We borrowed the proposal of founding members by Attac-France. In Attac-France founding members have enormous power, this was a contradiction [a group of persons – for instance, founding members – with a great deal of power], and not all Italian founding members experienced this transformation in the same way [the fact of borrowing the role of founding members from Attac-France]. When I noticed that the decision-making was a majority voting decision-making, the game was over [he means that a real difference between decision-making in a political party and in a social movement organization no longer exists. In fact, he

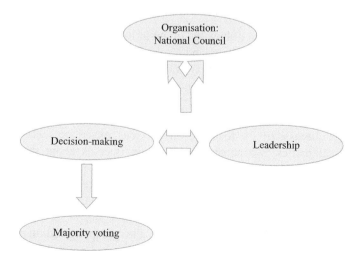

FIGURE 2.1 Tree node model: organization, decision-making and voting system

assumed that, by adopting a majority voting system, a social movement organization become more like a vertical political party than a horizontal social movement organization]. However, someone in Attac-Italy stated that I was wrong ... I experienced decision-making in different political organizations over time, and honestly, I felt bad because founding members had to know how many votes they counted on if they were to realistically make any decisions. In this context, political alliances matter, and these political alliances are the same political alliances of those political parties. Instead, we aimed at valorizing local groups of Attac. To do so, we proposed to adopt a bottom–up approach for decision-making, just a few assumptions required for discussion with local groups, and a consensus decision-making was also desirable, I have also proposed to have certain points of agreement even without having to decide.

(Turin 2015)

But, whereas the discussion in Turin centred on how the Attac-France model might be reproduced in Attac-Italy, along with a discussion about how certain problems from Attac-France could be avoided, in Rome the discussion was a slightly different one. The following quote from a respondent in Rome starts to give a sense of these slight differences:

Where have we drawn boundaries around founding members of Attac-Italy and the strength behind their vote? It was decided that those elected in political parties could not be member of the National Council. We aimed at drawing boundaries around those more structured organizations [political parties] able to influence Attac through multiple memberships [agreement].

(Rome 2002)

This quote is representative of how the group in Rome discussed how they draw 'boundaries' around membership and decision-making. They also discussed how 'multiple formal political party memberships' have also been seen as problematic for participation. Furthermore, in Caltagirone, it was stated by one respondent that:

[Huge discussion] by focusing on previous experiences elsewhere [in political parties] we agree that the main issue is about the decision-making, consensus decision-making, participating-democracy and social movements, in Attac-Caltagirone, in fact, we decide in a consensus way.

(Caltagirone 2004)

In Caltagirone, located in the south, then, the group agreed that previous participation individuals had experienced elsewhere had not influenced present activism in Attac. Moreover, the group agreed that the intersection between

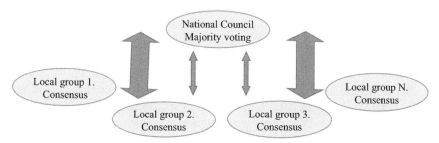

FIGURE 2.2   National Council and local groups' decision-making: majority voting and consensus approach

decision-making, participation and 'consensus system' are intertwined, and they agreed that the local groups decide in such a way. In the far north, however, in Cuneo, the group compared the local branch of Attac with the national board, as such:

> We improved the decision-making process in this group. We assumed that Attac is based on local groups, I mean, the decision-making? The decision-making shall be a consensus decision-making, although at the national board the decisions must be the expression of consent, the national council [agreement] ... it is probably true that the consensus does not work at the national council ... the majority voting and consensus decision-making are, in fact, in contraposition with each other! In doing so, the risk is to create alliances, political alliances.
>
> *(Cuneo 2004)*

Subsequently, the group underlined a dichotomy between the base (local groups) and the management group (national board), and a mismatch has been identified accordingly (see Figure 2.2). On this basis, an examination was carried out, and certain dynamics were discussed by focusing on how to improve the still existing decision-making system. The discursive approach employed in this study has been useful for this, and the affordance of a dialogical analysis of the social perceptions provided by militants.

Conclusion

In this chapter, I have combined the political biographical approach and the social perception paradigm, combining neo-institutionalism theory and the opening of the political opportunity structure perspective with the aim of informing the investigation. On the one hand, by moving from past to present political biographies, these political biographies have been able to bring the organizational heredity militants experienced elsewhere from one context to one another by informing the actual organization, and, on the other hand, the analysis of the political biographies of militants provided a structural political continuity over time. Furthermore, the neo-institutional approach was helpful in enlarging the perspective by also including a shift from an institutional political/ organizational setting to an informal political/organizational setting.

The organizational heredity militants experienced elsewhere has moved into the associative charter of Attac and, because of space limitations, I compare this associative charter and the social perception of decision-making in the conclusion only. In fact, the associative life has been intended such as fundamentally prescribed by the associative charter, whereas the substantial associative life has been intended based on the social perceptions militants provided in the field-work on decision-making and participation in political parties, trade unions and social movements over time. With the aim of analysing data, three query searches have been developed by also including the formal charter as shown in synoptic table one. Accordingly, the social perception of the decision-making and previous participation in formal/informal groups and organizations described certain dynamics when compared with the associative charter.

Although a well-defined background rooted in Italian left-wing political culture (institutional and non-institutional political backgrounds) has been already underlined, qualitative research suggests that a large number of militants previously involved in the RC political party are members of Attac-Italy, and the perceived risks of transposing models learned elsewhere (and the risk of co-option) have been largely debated. It was also stated that RC is the only political party able to form links between structural politics and social movements, and RC was also able to open doors to those radical political issues from outside the political system, for instance at the edge of the institutional left wing.

However, the charter has rigorously broken down barriers around formal members of political parties and trade unions with the aim of limiting their political influence in the Italian associative decision-making. In the process, the charter has been amended, and the role of the founding members has been reconsidered through Attac-Italy being provided with a renewed organization able to afford a radical critique of present capitalism, and social and political innovation activities. In fact, the 'large power' of founding members has been equilibrated 'in respect of … the collective discussion as proposed by … Local Group … [and by promoting] … the consensus approach for decision-making' (Art. 22). In fact, the associative charter and decision-making have been restructured through provision of an option for political participation by recognizing the key role of local groups across the country.

On the one hand, data suggest that the perceived risk of being co-opted by some left-wing political party and trade union is an issue for the militants interviewed, as well as the perception that forming some political alliances is a risky option for the time to come. On the other hand, data suggest that militants underlined a mismatch between what is formally stated in the charter (consensus approach) and the concrete decision-making at the National Council (counting votes). However, the relative power of founding members has been reconsidered, and the perception of intrusions from the outside (mainly from political parties) has been seen as compromising the genuine consensus approach characterizing the Italian social movement's organization. This is to say that data trace a line of continuity from within the institutional left-wing political culture, and the perceived risk of reproducing models has been recognized as a risky option for internal decision-making. In the process, the neo-institutionalism approach has provided an insight in terms of reproducing models learned elsewhere, by crossing borders from a well-defined institutional organization (internal to the system) to a more informal social movement organization (external to the system) placed at the edge of the institutional left wing. On this basis, the associative charter defines duties and responsibilities for local groups and for the national board, although data suggest that vertical decision-making (at least, at the national scale) is perceived by militants. However, the circular decision-making seems to work well for groups at local level. In fact, local groups from the far north to the far south of Italy agreed that they make decisions in an assembly way, which means that mutual recognition is assured, and a circular system is available for decision-making.

On the one hand, data indicate that militants perceive vertical decision-making, whereas, on the other hand, the main topic discussed by the group met in the fieldwork is the radical critique of the so-called financial economy. The radical critique of the financial economy represents, in fact, a significant political option characterizing Attac worldwide, although the repertoire of action employed by Attac-Italy seems more similar to experts' groups within social movement organizations than similar to riot groups (Achino 2005). In other words, Attac-Italy provides a radical critique and analysis of present capitalism rather than radical rioters' actions. Indeed, militants have also discussed a dichotomy between the governance at the national level (National Council) and the functioning of local groups. In fact, the main difference in the decision-making system depends on the scale of the governance. Besides, the institutional political setting and the political culture available to Attac-Italy have a role in providing the Italian organizations with political opportunities, and the RC political party opens doors for mutual understanding and for supporting the political claims Attac-Italy is used to affording.

In fact, data suggest that the Italian branch of Attac seems to be a structural organization able to survive over time (strength) rather than an expressive organization, and the shift from the left-wing political parties represents continuity with the political backgrounds of those involved in the Italian organization. Moreover, Attac-Italy is able to provide militants with a specific framework for action, but not enough information about emotional and relational incentives is available, and these emotional and relational incentives remain an issue for the future.

Finally, although these left-wing political backgrounds are able to reinforce individuals' and collective identities and political actions, a comparison between different branches of Attac worldwide would be useful to hint at a line across countries able to shape forms of participation nationally and internally.

Notes

1 SiCobas (Confederation of Workers' Committees) is an Italian left-wing trade unions network founded at the beginning of the 1980s. Sicobas is locally based and organized from below, and no vertical structure is implied in the decision-making system. CGIL (the Italian General Confederation of Workers) is the oldest Italian left-wing con-federated trade union, founded in 1944, and is hierarchically organized. The main difference between the two is the organizational form, one horizontal (SiCobas), the other vertical (CGIL).
2 The recognition process between institutional actors and actors from within the civil society comes before the opening of the political opportunities structure and is a constituency element of political participation (Laclau 2000). Although it is not a mechanical relationship between institutional and non-institutional actors, I assumed that the recognition process is a purpose of the opening of the political structure opportunities. However, it was previously noticed that 'political recognition' is not an issue for those involved in Attac-Italy (Achino 2005). I also assumed that the political biographical process is a process moving from individuals' past to present biographies and moving to the future and informing actions for the time to come. However, owing to space limitations, I wrote about past and present only.
3 Militants may be formally enrolled; others may participate informally to avoid stereotyping.
4 Local groups of Attac were visited in Torino, Milan, Bergamo, Rome, Cuneo and Caltagirone in Sicily.
5 With the aim of anonymizing the data, I quote where I attended qualitative interviews/focus groups and the year of the interview/focus groups only. The quotations have been directly extracted from NVivo.
6 In the fieldwork, a structured questionnaire was presented to participants (Achino 2005). Among many others, one question was: 'have you participated at least once in the following political parties and/or trade unions? (N = 263). Results are as follows (N = 263): Previous enrollment: yes (frequency 152, 57.8%). If you have previously answered 'yes', could you please specify which of the following you have been formally enrolled in at least once? PCI: frequency 37, 14.1%; PDS: frequency 19, 72%; Ppus, LC: frequency 13, 4.9%; DP: frequency 13, 4.9%; RC: frequency 67, 25.5%; Verdi: frequency 21, 8%; CGIL: frequency 57, 21.7%.
7 In the fieldwork, a structured questionnaire was presented to participants (Achino 2005). Among many others, one question was: 'have you participated at least once in the following social movements organizations, divided up into decades (1980s, 1990s, 2000s)'? (N = 263).
   M. Studentesco 1980: frequency 20, 7.6%; M. Ambientalista 1980: frequency 50, 19%; M. Animalista 1980: frequency 11, 4.2%; M. 1980: frequency 62, 23.6%; M. Pacifista 1980: frequency 49, 18.6%; M. Femminista 1980: frequency 13, 4.9%; M. omosex 1980: frequency 3, 1.1%; M. sindacale 1980: frequency 39, 14.8%; M. terzo mondo 1980: frequency 24, 9.1%; M. No Global 1980: frequency 2, 0.2%; M. D. Umani 1980: frequency 2, 0.8%; M. Immigrati 1980: frequency 2, 0.8%.
   M. Studentesco 1990: frequency 58, 22.1%; M. Ambientalista 1990: frequency 67, 25.5%; M. Animalista 1990: frequency 16, 6.1%; M. Antinucleare 1990: frequency 26, 9.9%; M. Pacifista 1990: frequency 90, 34.2%; M. Femminista 1990: frequency 6, 2.3%; M. omosex 1990: frequency 7, 2.7%; M. sindacale 1990: frequency 38, 14.4%; M. terzo mondo 1990: frequency 55, 20.9%; M. No Global 1990: frequency 29, 11%; M. D. Umani 1990: frequency 48, 18.3%; M. Immigrati 1990: frequency 33, 12.5%.

M. Studentesco 00: frequency 17, 6.5%; M. Ambientalista 00: frequency 41, 15.6%; M. Animalista 00: frequency 20, 7.6%; M. Antinucleare 00: frequency 18, 6.8%; M. Pacifista 00: frequency 169, 64.3%; M. Femminista 00: frequency 12, 4.6%; M. omosex 00: frequency 18, 6.8%; M. sindacale 00: frequency 58, 22.1%; M. terzo mondo 00: frequency 75, 28.5%; M. No Global 00: frequency 225, 85.6%; M. D. Umani 00: frequency 73, 27.8%; M. Immigrati 00: frequency 74, 28.1%.

8 This quotation and the following quotations have been anonymized.

9 Founding as in original members, those who created the group.

References

Achino, E. (2005) *Identities on Movements*. PhD dissertation, Milan: University of Milano-Bicocca.

Achino, E. (2016) 'What Is Your Gender? Gender and Participation in Attac-Italy', *Journal of Gender Studies* 25(2): 155–168.

Almond, G.A. and Verba, S. (1965) *The Civic Culture*, Boston: Little, Brown.

DiMaggio, P.J. and Powell, W.W. (1991) *The New Institutionalism*, Chicago: University of Chicago Press.

Goldstone, J.A. (2004) 'More Social-Movements or Fewer? Beyond Political Opportunity Structures to Relational Fields', *Theory & Society* 33(3): 333–365.

Goodwin, J. and Jasper, J.M. (1999) 'Caught in a Winding, Snarling Vine: The Structural Bias of Political Process Theory', *Sociological Forum* 14(1): 27–54.

Goodwin, J. and Jasper, J.M. (2003) *The Social Movements Reader: Cases and Concepts*, Hoboken: Blackwell.

Kriesi, H., Koopmans, R., Duyvendak, J.W. and Giugni, M. (1995) *New Social Movements in Western Europe: A Comparative Analysis*, Minneapolis: University of Minnesota Press.

Krippendorff, K. (2004) *Content Analysis: An Introduction to Its Methodology*, Thousand Oaks: Sage.

Laclau, E. (2000) *Contingency, Hegemony, Universality*, London: Verso.

Melucci, A. (1996) *Challenging Codes*, Cambridge: Cambridge University Press.

Oliver, P. (1980) 'Rewards and Punishments as Selective Incentives for Collective Action: Theoretical Investigations', *American Journal of Sociology* 85(6): 1356–1375.

Polletta, F. and Jasper, M. (2001) 'Collective-Identity and Social-Movements', *Annual Review of Sociology* 27(1): 283–305.

3

TEKEL RESISTANCE IN TURKEY

The making of the proletarian public sphere

Gülden Özcan

The TEKEL (Tobacco and Alcohol Monopoly of Turkey) workers' resistance took place in a period when the repression of social opposition was paving the way to despair. Although the austerity policies that put the burden of the 2007 economic crisis on the working poor had fueled opposition through broad social movements throughout the world, in Turkey such mass-based action was yet to come (Karaağaç and Kaya 2010). The TEKEL workers' action first emerged in December 2009 as a protest against a law regulating the precarization of public employees—that is, Section C of Article 4 of the Public Employees' Law, commonly known as 4/C.[1] Then, as part of a more fundamental stand against privatization, it sparked a more comprehensive opposition to neoliberalism.[2] More than 6,000 TEKEL workers occupied downtown Ankara (the capital city) in their self-made nylon tents for 78 days in the winter of 2009–2010, opening a space for hope for certain social groups in Turkey. The national and international support from different grassroots organizations and social opposition groups, extended to the resistance by TEKEL workers, pointed at the will and necessity to shake off despair. The distinctive features of the TEKEL workers' resistance have been much debated, yet subsequent, seemingly bigger, events in the recent political history of Turkey (such as the Gezi Resistance in the summer of 2013; the powerful emergence of the left-wing Peoples' Democratic Party (HDP) in late 2013; bloody sabotages against HDP and other organized left-wing organizations, starting in July 2015 following HDP's electoral success in June 2015; and the plotted coup d'état of July 2016, following state of emergency and decree laws) paused the discussions on the significance of the TEKEL resistance. In this chapter, with the intent to revise and reinitiate these discussions, I look at the TEKEL resistance from a long-neglected angle of the theory of the public sphere: the proletarian public sphere.

In the second half of the 1990s and early 2000s, the concept of the public sphere has been much discussed in both academic circles and in the parliament in Turkey. The bourgeois public sphere, analyzed by Jürgen Habermas, has been the center of debate with a view to various neighboring issues such as laicism, liberal democracy, legitimacy crisis, women's visibility in the public sphere, the colonization of lifeworld by the market. However, these discussions have hardly related to Oskar Negt and Alexander Kluge's *Public Sphere and Experience* ([1972]1993) and the term 'proletarian public sphere.' One should, of course, note the exceptions of a few attempts to include the book's central themes in the literature.[3] The rather low-level popularity of the book in English-speaking academia and the facts that it was translated to English two decades after its publication in German in 1972 and that it has not been translated into Turkish yet can be considered to have had an effect on this lack of interest. Nevertheless, without doubt, the book is important in that it offers a stance countering Habermas's arguments for the bourgeois public sphere. It relies on the potential of the term proletariat as the dialectical opposite of the term bourgeoisie. Thus, it has the potential to contribute much to the discussions on the public sphere in general.

This chapter, then, aims to reconsider the politicization of the working class based on labor power through the axes of history, theory and TEKEL resistance. My main question is the following: What are the political implications of the rise of labor as a unifying force and the meeting of experiences that originate from labor processes with action in the neoliberal order of things? I believe it is important to start the analysis of the definitions and means of politics from the public sphere, despite the fetishization of the concept in liberal theory and the commodification of the actual public sphere by the bourgeoisie. Knowledge of the actors, means and mentalities that have a role in the structuration of the public sphere as the sphere of social reproduction sheds light on a number of issues regarding the different processes and historical roots of socialization. In his tenth thesis on Feuerbach, Marx says: 'The viewpoint of the old materialism was *civil* society; that of the new one is *human society* or *socialized* humanity' (Marx 1968: 667; original emphasis). Hence, the socialization process shall be reconsidered in depth within the scope of historical materialism and dialectical materialism. This is not just a procedural issue; it is rather important because it is an infrastructural issue. The means and technologies effective in the socialization of the workers who constitute the greater part of the social need to be analyzed in more detail, and the organizations that claim to be mass movements of workers should be able to discuss and put into effect alternative forms of socialization.

In the first part of the chapter, I focus on the concept of the public sphere, which was defined by the early philosophers of the Enlightenment as the only sphere of politics, and by Hannah Arendt as the only condition for political action; which Habermas tries to improve so as to ensure that its procedures benefit the whole society; and which is considered as the 'conventional bourgeois public sphere' by Negt and Kluge. I also discuss the place that the TEKEL resistance occupies in this sphere in which the workers matured their resistance. In the second part, I take issue with the management of and control over the sphere that offer a place for workers' activities outside the workplace. Negt and Kluge name this sphere as 'the new sphere of industrial production' created by the media cartels. I would rather call this sphere 'the market public sphere,' claiming that it is not 'new' and that its origins can be traced back to the nineteenth century. Here, I also underline the market public sphere, which has regulated and thus controlled the leisure activities of the working class in Turkey in the post-1980 period, pointing at the methods and tactics that were used through TEKEL resistance against this gigantic public sphere of the market. In the third part, I focus on the concept of the 'proletarian public sphere' and the theoretical and practical advantages of considering TEKEL resistance within the scope of the proletarian public. I argue that the TEKEL resistance hosts both the aspiration for and an actual example of the proletarian public sphere. In the concluding part, I try to point at the possible sites of and for struggle for future resistance.

The private sphere of public interests versus the public sphere of private interests

Reflecting on the questions of the relationship between collective interests and experiences in modern capitalist societies, and the mechanisms through which these experiences are constituted on which basis and by whom—that is, what are the actors, sphere and context of modern politics—brings in the concept of public sphere and the related debate. According to the early philosophers of the Enlightenment, the public sphere is related to the specific definition of democracy, meaning the institutionalization of the use of reason by autonomous citizens for public interest, determined collectively. The main element of the condition for acting together is the institutions that are specified on constitutional grounds. These might include political parties, professional organizations, trade unions, charity organizations, educational institutions and local administrations. These spaces for social integration, defined by modernity, are those spheres of political action where the members of society voice their demands and interests. According to Negt and Kluge, the revolutionary bourgeoisie offered this concept in order to fix society as a totality through the empathy raised by the concept of public opinion. This has been preserved as a political goal in bourgeois societies, built on commodity production. It is for this reason that there were not that many instances of questions about the extent of the representativeness of the public sphere for the society as a whole. For there emerged a possibility to define society with a view to a formation different than commodity exchange, private property and free market—a possibility to base it on a different foundation (Negt and Kluge ([1972]1993). In this sense, the bourgeois public sphere could develop an awareness with the masses that created that very sphere. Reforms and alternatives are possible—just as the advertising sector makes one consider it a possibility to buy something that one knows it would be impossible to buy through one's lifetime.

For Arendt (1998), the public sphere has world-creating potential, and living together in the world means that 'a world of things is between those who have it in common, as a *table* is located between those who sit around it; the world, like every in-between, relates and separates men at the same time' (Arendt 1998: 52). In modern industrial societies, however, the 'table,' located in-between people so as to provide a space for shared interests, disappears owing to the rise of labor or, as famously worded, 'the rise of the social.' Arendt (1998) finds the reason behind the demise of political activity in the rise of labor, as she argues at the outset that labor activity excludes shared interests. A parallel view appears in Habermas's conception of the public sphere as he depicts the public sphere as 'a sphere between civil society and the state, in which critical public discussion of matters of general interest was institutionally guaranteed' (Habermas 1991: xi). He separates the political, economic and civil spheres and locates the public sphere in the civil societal space. In other words, Habermas follows Arendt in distinguishing the public from the state and free-market relations and immediate family relations.

According to Habermas, the growth of a market economy led to the degeneration of the bourgeois public sphere. Like Arendt, he defines the problem as the rise of the social—without naming it that. The public sphere in the world of letters, Habermas claims, 'had the kind of "political" character by virtue of which it was removed from the sphere of social reproduction' (Habermas 1991: 160). Since the middle of the nineteenth century, it has become more and more difficult to apply the distinction between public and private to the emerging social sphere, and the rational-critical discussion of the public sphere, Habermas insists, has been replaced by a private world of consumption culture. By idealizing a public sphere that is separate from the sphere of social reproduction, Habermas construes the citizen 'as a mere "consumer" of the public sphere' (Verstraeten 1996: 350). Habermas's conceptualization estranges the production process of the public sphere from the end product of the bourgeois public sphere and, hence, reproduces the contradictions embedded in the bourgeois ideology. The bourgeois public sphere takes on a commodity-like character by virtue of which it became detached from the process of social production. That is, as a concept—and as a significant part of liberal discourse—it is alienated from the social forces that produced it, and in turn is fetishized as the sole realm to be involved in politics.

Negt and Kluge, on the other hand, start from the limitations of the bourgeois public sphere and point at the dialectical co-existence of different public spheres and the existence of 'counter' publics. Basically, they distinguish three public spheres: (1) the classical bourgeois public sphere (an invention of the revolutionary bourgeoisie proposed by benefiting from the social empathy of the concept of public opinion with the aim of unifying society); (2) new public

spheres of industrial production (a public made up by the profit-driven sophis-
ticated world of media corporations, marketing and human relations); and (3)
the proletarian public sphere (composed of the proletarian context of life).
However, these public spheres are not separated by demarcated borders. They
share the same space as elements of a dialectical relationality. This mutuality is
more than the relation between the outlines of different public spheres. They
relate to each other by each creating its own counter sphere and thus the space
for the other sphere. The classical bourgeois public sphere might at first sight
seem to be the sphere of domination. However, it also embodies the new public
spheres of industrial production and the proletarian public sphere. At the same
time, it forms a mechanism for exclusion that reflects the contradictions arising
from this embodiment. This sphere does not have use value for the experiences
and interests of the greater part of society (for the producers). The use
values of the new public spheres of production are significant for the advertising
and marketing sectors. But, in these spheres, one can observe the elements of
everyday life. These spheres embrace and process everyday life as raw materials. They emerge with the claim to reach and affect the private spheres of the
individuals, discarding the intermediary sphere as defined within the scope of
the conventional liberal public sphere. Thus, they largely use the public–private
distinction of the conventional bourgeois public sphere; they concentrate on the
private sphere and redefine it both as the object in which communication
originates and as the center of profit (Negt and Kluge [1972]1993). Commodities participate in this sphere as subjects themselves.

Negt and Kluge are concerned with the public sphere in terms of the
organization of collective experiences rather than institutions and procedures.
Their main problematic relates to the mechanisms and means that create the
social plane of experiences, and for whose benefit this social plane works and
for which effects. Experience (*Erfahrung*) here means mediated experience in
Hegelian terms, and it is conceived with a view to the dialectical process. They
argue that immediate experiences will acquire mediated and transformative
character in the majority that is socialized in the proletarian public sphere.

Following Knödler-Bunte et al. (1975), one can note three main factors that
distinguish Negt and Kluge's approach from that of Habermas. First, Habermas
puts the bourgeois public sphere at the center of his analysis. For him, the
proletarian public sphere forms a repressed part of the bourgeois public sphere
from the very beginning. But Negt and Kluge point at the mutual co-existence
of the bourgeois and proletarian public spheres. Thus, their approach offers
the grounds to observe the different forms of publicness that emerge from the
structural transformations in the production system. Second, Habermas's
approach tends to bypass the contradictions between the ideal of the public
sphere envisaged through the bourgeoisie in the Enlightenment process and the
form that its historical reality took. Negt and Kluge, on the other hand, reveal
these contradictions through considerations of different public spheres together
with the structural transformations of the mode of production. Thus, they inevitably

exclude ahistorical discourses and they inevitably prescribe a historical analysis. Third, Habermas overestimates the normative value of the bourgeois public sphere: for example, he trusts its openness to supposedly rational-critical deliberations, democratic procedures and predictable institutions. Thus, in terms of the political extensions of his analysis, he opts to search for ways to ameliorate the procedures of the bourgeois public sphere. Negt and Kluge, on the other hand, start from the relations between the different forms of the public sphere and human experience and interests connected to the social practices of everyday life. In this respect, in terms of the political extensions of their analysis, they opt to reveal the revolutionary potential of the proletariat through redefinitions of the proletarian public sphere on the basis of unpredictable experiences and interests. Therefore, they do not allow the reduction of the concept of the public sphere and the opposition that would arise from thereon to the institutions and procedures of the bourgeois public sphere (Knödler-Bunte et al. 1975).

Bourgeois society was built on the basis of some interests that are not social—that is, that do not concern the society as a whole. Everything is for society (as in the discourse on human rights), and yet the real society cannot be observed. Here, the interests at hand are those of the bourgeoisie; what is at issue is the publicization of the private interests of the bourgeoisie. On the other hand, the public interests of the working class are privatized in bourgeois society. For example, elections, movie premieres, parades, parliamentary discussions are considered public facts, whereas working in a factory or watching TV is read as a private fact (Negt and Kluge [1972]1993). In other words, social experiences that human beings produce in their everyday lives are interrupted via public–private distinction. They are talking about a public sphere where the experiences of a considerable part of society bring in complete indifference of the working class to the social relations that are alienated and reified owing to the characteristic of the relations of production. This makes it harder for workers to recognize their importance in a societal setting that does not belong to them. Workers are faced with a dilemma when they happen to enter into the bourgeois public sphere, assuming a position therein: the public sphere can only be subjected to private use, for it can only function through this rule of private use. It does not rely on the rules, which serve for the organized state of the specific experiences and interests of the workers. The public sphere as such is the sum total of the individual spheres and it depends essentially on the rejection of the proletarian context of life. This is because it is a definition totally independent of the objective conditions. The form through which the public sphere exposes itself conforms and works in tandem with the social structure of production and the history of its institutions. Thus, capital is private property and it has to belong to the private sphere. However, capital is under public control; raw material, means, money and workers are in fact parts of the public sphere (Negt and Kluge [1972]1993).

The bourgeois public sphere, too, separates the real makers of experiences from the means of production. In this respect, the way the public sphere has been created is masked and pushed into oblivion. 'All reification is forgetting,' say Max Horkheimer and Theodor Adorno ([1944]2002: 191). Now workers are left with a reified and alienated public sphere. How they shall act in that sphere is defined by the laws. Workers communicating through the language of the laws cannot act freely in this sphere to which they are strangers. The bourgeois public sphere prescribes a special education; it requires a new spoken and body language. Workers who cannot comprehend this language develop an uncondi-tional attachment to this sphere, which is composed of spaces and objects that manipulate their feelings and thoughts at every turn. Otherwise, they are doomed to stay in their private spheres. Moreover, if workers do not have a language of their own, they will be destined to lose their own life experiences in the stereotypical life form offered by the bourgeois public. In this respect, the representation and legitimacy crisis of liberal democracy is not accidental.

In this instance, the public sphere of the working class, which can be observed empirically, emerges as a variation of the bourgeois public sphere. To understand the working-class public sphere, it would be apt to focus on the concept of 'class as a relation and process.' As E.P. Thompson (1957: 131) explains, '[p]roduction, distribution and consumption are not only digging, carrying, and eating, but are also planning, organising and enjoying.' These experiences bring workers together or separate them from each other, in and outside the production process. Then it is the experiences of the proletariat that determine the content of Arendt's 'table' more realistically. In other words, the workers come together (and are separated) through the experiences that arise out of the shared use of the labor force. Their organization on the basis of real experiences and interests will produce class consciousness. But how would this happen in the alienated labor process and reified relations in the sphere that falls out of the labor sphere, circumscribed by commodities?

The commodity character of the bourgeois public sphere results from a dual structure. First, this is to do with the fact that it is constructed in distinction from its constituents/producers to be presented to them as if a foreign space. Second, it is related to the prerequisite that one has to buy certain valorized talents that will serve to follow the necessary procedures to represent and/or be represented in the bourgeois public sphere. The decommodification of the public sphere can be achieved by the claim of those who produce social relations and through their own methods to re-embrace it. Therefore, every mass movement does not necessarily lead to this claim. This requires a certain process and a physical space for the workers to share their experiences with each other. The TEKEL resistance, in its 78-day-long 'Sakarya Street' experience, was perhaps most successful in this respect: it showed to a large part of society the possibility that the bourgeois public sphere could be reclaimed. The TEKEL resistance could appeal to a considerable part of society as the experiences shared in the resistance space and the aggregated interests were not just those of the workers at the resistance site, but also corresponded to the experiences and demands of other workers (and certainly the unemployed) who could share the atmosphere on Sakarya Street *via* their televisions, computers and newspapers. For the same reason, the TEKEL resistance, which grew out of a bourgeois public sphere style of organization, namely the trade union TekGıda-İş, could go beyond the limits of this organization and thus could push the boundaries of the bourgeois public sphere.

Here, it should not be ignored that the structure—against which the TEKEL workers had struggled—had well-organized, systematically running means and mechanisms with its intellectuals, politicians, legislators, media bosses, public relations specialists and multinational corporations. Each and every one of these instruments played its function when needed. Hence, questions regarding the privatization of TEKEL (e.g., to which capital owners it would be sold; how this process would be hidden from the public; how the workers would be controlled by the union; how the effect of this process on the election of the union chair would be minimized; the legal status of the workers in the factories that were sold; the share of public workers from the desecuritization) and similar issues were considered and calculated in great detail, and the most effective answers were put into practice by the ruling classes. The pressures exerted by the multinational corporations for the privatization of TEKEL, the strategies they pursued to have a share of TEKEL's profit and/or to cut off its effect in Turkey's and the world's tobacco market (Lawrence 2009; Aysu 2010),[4] the promise Recep Tayyip Erdoğan—then prime minister—gave to the Türk-İş (Confederation of Turkish Trade Unions, with which the TEKEL workers' union TekGıda-İş is affiliated) chair Mustafa Kumlu that the tobacco processing factories that were sold in 2007 would be kept operating with their workers until the end of 2009 ('Başbakan Hangi Sendikacıları Dolmabahçe'ye Çağırdı' 2010), all these were projected outcomes of these mechanisms.

Nevertheless, the issues, which were of vital importance for bourgeois politics—as there was an ongoing fight between the old ruling elite and the new ruling elite over power—and thus were pushed into the political agenda in Turkey during the TEKEL resistance, could not undermine the agents of the resistance and the importance of their action itself in the eyes of society. All these issues directed toward the society are indeed 'movements of minorities, or in the interest of minorities.' As Marx and Engels ([1848]1977) state: 'in all these battles [the bourgeoisie] sees itself compelled to appeal to the proletariat, to ask for its help, and thus, to drag it into the political arena' (p. 47). It is only the movement of the proletariat that 'is the self-conscious, independent movement of the immense majority, in the interest of the immense majority' (Marx and Engels, [1848]1977: 47). The TEKEL resistance could raise such awareness— despite the counter effort by the mass media—by preserving its significance in the sociopolitical agenda. Hence the importance of the creation of the counter public sphere. The public sphere can have a use value for the proletariat only when it contains a space for the organization of the workers' experiences. Otherwise, the existence and/or consideration of a public sphere that allows only for the organization of bourgeois interests and the bourgeoisie's private life experiences creates a political environment where the experiences, interests and concrete existence of the working class are excluded—or marginalized—in the reified bourgeois public. In the consideration of the proletarian public sphere, on the other hand, the practical political experiences of the proletarian public sphere constitute the vital point. This is to do with the close relation between the concept of the proletarian public sphere and the practices of social production and reproduction, which form the basis of politics in capitalist societies.

In-between the mysterious charm of the bourgeoisie and its repulsiveness

The history of capitalism reveals that the ways workers make use of non-working time and place have been rigorously considered by political economists, ruling authorities and capital owners. For example, in the eighteenth century, weavers who could easily live by working three days a week were targeted based on the claim that they should not have time to idle and should be made to work every day of the week, with lower wages providing more profit (Thompson [1963]1991). On the other hand, one of the main issues in nineteenth-century England, where capitalism developed and started to expand in the real sense of the term, was finding a way to unite workers with different cultural backgrounds on the same cultural plane. The aim was to define a standard, more productive popular culture that would supersede popular cultures, which differ among groups of workers (Storch 1977). This was owing to two factors. First, it was difficult to get to know workers with different cultures, to foresee their actions under different circumstances. Second, workers' different cultures and the way they practiced these cultures generally resulted in rebellion. Control over workers' street festivities, preemption of heated debates in the bars, regulating the consumption of alcoholic beverages, determining workers' 'leisure time' activities beforehand, and teaching workers the new form of property through moral codification were required to make them more productive and docile. In time, a series of measures, such as the system of licensing that regulated bars, the limitation of sports on the streets with specified spaces and with the prerequisite to obtain permission, the publication of newspapers that would make news to invoke property rights, were taken to regulate the social life and thus lived experiences of the working class (Thompson 1967; Storch 1982; Hunt 1999). These measures also enabled the commodification of cultural activities. In other words, the foundations of the 'culture industry' were laid in this period.[5] The aim was to minimize the sharing of the experiences gained by the proletariat on the basis of labor exploitation.[6]

As Miriam Hansen points out, in bourgeois society, the normative function of culture was carried to the center of the market public sphere, under the name of 'arts and literature' (Hansen, in Negt and Kluge [1972]1993). Certainly, culture is not a static notion, but most of the time it is normative. Thus, the shaping of culture in commodities and its congealment in objects through its normative function suppress its transformative, rebellious features. What is at stake is to activate the critical aspects of the culture, its parts that are production driven by experiences. But the culture industry is a sector that was developed to preempt the popularization of the rebellious nature of working-class culture.[7] In Turkey, it is possible to observe the mass culture practices in the aftermath of the 1980 military coup d'état, in the process of the consolidation of the free market and thenceforth. One such example is the preemption of the potential of the Nawruz celebrations to transform into rebellion by the Kurdish peoples by means of encapsulating the celebrations into an official ceremony by the institutions of the bourgeois public sphere. Besides, the movie theaters that had served the working class in the 1970s were locked into the shopping malls—that is, the most functional part of the market public sphere. In these theaters, there is no problem with screening the movie *Devrimden Sonra* (*After the Revolution*). This is because, as the audience members take a couple of steps forward under the glamorous lights, they would be attracted to the commodities presented.[8] It would be apt to note that similar practices in the post-1980 period destroyed those social reproduction spheres that fall outside the working time and place of the working class.

As Marx noted, if material reality would change thought, and if the workers are required to find the thought pattern necessary to mediate immediate experiences themselves, such a mediation process can only take place in an environment where workers can share and discuss their immediate experiences. In Turkey, such an environment could be found until the late 1980s. Trade unions, political parties, professional organizations, coffee houses, neighborhood relations all offered such discussion platforms. However, the 1980 military coup d'état and the accompanying legal regulations prepared the grounds for neoliberal economic policies and the culture of neoliberal capitalism. The efforts toward de-unionization and flexible and insecure working conditions led to a sharp turn in working-class culture. The effect of television on popular culture was significant at this point. The establishment of private channels in the early 1990s and the extension of the products of the culture industry through this commodity that reaches into each and every house have been instrumental in explaining the basics of the world of commodities to the working class. Capitalism gains its real power when it brings in its own culture and materializes in the life experiences of the working class. This culture carries with it the loss of history. People who are deprived of a personal account of history are circumscribed by a number of out-of-context values that are presented in the public sphere of the television and other mass media, in other words, in the public sphere of the market. They are forced to accept and integrate these values into their lives. As a consequence they acquire '[t]he capacity to let go of one's past, the confidence to accept fragmentation' (Sennett 1998: 63).

The success of the market public spheres lies in their accomplishing the instillation of bourgeois values into people at an incredible speed. The architecture and internal design of shopping malls, for example, enable the rapid adjustment of people from diverse backgrounds to the codes of conduct required by these malls that mushroom in cities. In the school system, as part of the conventional bourgeois public sphere, a considerable amount of time and effort is reserved for teaching 'civil' codes of conduct. The speed of the teaching process that is put into force in today's shopping malls is incomparable in this respect. There are two sources of the success of the public spheres of the market: they appeal to the fantasy worlds of the people and they individualize the daily issues that relate to private life. Neither the conventional bourgeois public sphere nor the unions and labor parties as proletarian public spheres can respond to the daily needs of the proletariat. The public spheres of the market meet workers' everyday needs, offer solutions to the problems that concern workers' most intimate spheres. Thus, compared with the conventional bourgeois public sphere, they pose a greater threat to the proletarian public sphere. The public spheres of the market tend to respond to a series of intimate problems and needs that are exposed to the manipulations of the advertising and marketing sector. While meeting the workers' needs by means of commodities, they open the way to the reification of social relations and offer ideological subtexts that are congealed in the commodities.

Negt and Kluge's account of media cartels is exemplary. According to Negt and Kluge, the mass media themselves form a 'macro commodity.' The things 'put on sale' here are the predetermined contexts of life and learning. It is an industrial complex that can gather the commodities of education, entertainment and information in a single body (Negt and Kluge [1972]1993). Thus, when following the mass media, people are forced to buy all these commodities at once—as if buying the whole aisle in order to buy a single product; it is necessary that one buys a certain definition of entertainment if one wants to buy education. Hence, the market public spheres, focused on exploitation, reproduce all the contexts of life as objects of opportunities (Negt and Kluge [1972]1993).

The proletarian public sphere mediates existence and consciousness to the extent that it represents a form of interaction that is defined in terms relating the vital interests of the working class to the whole society (Knödler-Bunte et al. 1975). Here it would be apt to look at the conceptualization of reification by George Lukács (1971), who defines the world, circumscribed by commodities, as the 'second nature.' He notes that, in the second nature, relations are totally reified, and, hence, it is rather difficult for class consciousness to develop— actually, the opportunity for the first nature seems dim under capitalism (Lukács 1971). He thus emits pessimism about resistance. In this respect, Lukács orients us to the following question: Where will the revolution be organized if the time and space outside the work life suffer from reification? Will it be organized within the boundaries of the working time and space, with the discipline and surveillance mechanisms making it ever harder for workers even to smile, let alone to organize. This can take us at most to unionization and its limits that I noted in the previous section. But the alternative revealed by the TEKEL resistance is that the world outside the work life is not as deadlocked as noted by Lukács, and that both the commodification and reification in capitalism are uneven, and this can be manipulated to create a proletarian public sphere (Paulson 2005). TEKEL workers, through their resistance, undermined the commodity character of the public sphere, while at the same time reproducing the non-reified or less reified forms of the relations by using them. What they achieved could not be done through union organization alone.

The weakness of the unions stems from the fact that they follow the procedures of the bourgeois public sphere in organizing as they are embedded in the bourgeois public sphere. This often separates them from the context of production, which reinforces their power. They create a plane where the voice of the producers' experiences is hardly heard. When media initiatives emerge through a product or a program (for example, matchmaking shows) that offer a remedy to the everyday problems of the workers, the union tries to face it with opinions and policies. But the one-sidedness of media products (and commodities) can only be overcome by creating counter products (Negt and Kluge [1972]1993). One can note live broadcasts by the Workers Films Festival Society during the TEKEL resistance as an instance of such counter-product formation. These live broadcasts were realized not by the union's efforts but in response to the need that emerged through the urge of the experiences, shared in the proletarian public sphere: first, workers' need to communicate with their families, then national and international interest in the resistance, and afterwards, the indifference of the mass media to the resistance necessitated these broadcasts. Later, these broadcasts went beyond the initial intention and offered evidence of the power of the TEKEL resistance, which cannot be expressed in words. They promised to function as exemplary products for the use of the centralization of numerous local struggles. The means of communication with ever-expanding limits in today's capitalism do not necessarily offer a communication venue for workers to share their experiences. Although they offer alternatives to the private ownership of the means of communication, the use of these spheres for ensuring the unity of workers requires another sphere of struggle. This struggle was waged during the resistance of the TEKEL workers with the fight between the bourgeois means of communication and the proletarian means of communication.

Negt and Kluge view the proletariat not as a totality but as a plurality based on the mediated experiences of those who constitute the working class, whose needs vary. They find the fault for the defeat of working-class movements in the organizations that are formed with reference to a totality. For Negt and Kluge, such specific needs as childcare, sexuality, work and leisure-time activities cannot find a place and most of the time are ignored in these movements and organizations. The new public spheres of production and bourgeois public sphere, on the other hand, meet these needs by top–down regulation. Negt and Kluge define these spheres as the 'real life bloc.' Capitalism cannot demolish this life bloc as it feeds off it. The workers, on the other hand, cannot organize a countermovement against this bloc that also nurtures them—that is, also against themselves. Even if they organize such a countermovement, it is doomed to failure, or they can at most enable better working of this bloc (Negt and Kluge [1972]1993). Here it is necessary to transform this bloc by the real experiences of the working class and to create an opposition from within. This, in turn, can be accomplished by the politicization of basic vital interests; a long-term socialist strategy might be developed just then. The TEKEL workers' resistance gains meaning at this point. For they emerged out of this bloc and started with their union—an organization that was established in the bourgeois public sphere and according to its procedures. Then, the momentum gained by the movement forced them to create a new real-life bloc. They had already observed that they could not win through the union procedure. Ultimately, they left the arena they occupied at the call of their union, but the last two months of the 78 days were built on the transformation of this bloc.

Publicizing the TEKEL resistance: an example for the proletarian public sphere

Workers plan and organize the work in their workplaces despite the unending surveillance of the capitalist. Thus, the transformation of the organization and planning of the infrastructure can only be achieved through action in the proletarian public sphere—rather than interventions in the superstructural factors of the bourgeois public. Advertisement and marketing as the major components of the market public spheres process everyday life as raw material. They emerge directly from the demand for access to the individual's private sphere, and not through the conventional bourgeois public sphere. The conventional bourgeois public sphere is built on the manipulation of workers' interests. As these interests can only be expressed in the bourgeois public sphere, they are bound to remain as objects of the bourgeoisie's interests. Thus, it is the 'real life bloc' that should first be transformed. The interests of the workers should be experienced in a proletarian public sphere in order that they are not restricted to the realm of possibilities. For, if the masses struggle against a ruling class that relies on the public sphere without transforming this bloc, this struggle is futile, as the public sphere is formed by their participation, and thus struggling against it would mean struggling against themselves.

In the social spaces where proletarian interests merge with universal bourgeois organizations, one cannot talk about just the bourgeois public sphere. The proletarian public spheres that develop through use of bourgeois organizational forms (such as labor parties, unions, professional organizations) not only merge real proletarian interests and experiences, but also organize them so as to enable the transition to a certain stage of the proletarian public sphere (Negt and Kluge [1972]1993). In this instance, it is possible to note two proletarian public spheres that correspond to two stages in the formation of the proletarian public sphere: first, there is the proletarian public sphere that is organized in bourgeois form. Second, there is the proletarian public sphere that develops from within such a bourgeois form of organization and transcends it. The second one hosts the real revolutionary potential. Here it is possible to underline that, in the case of the TEKEL resistance, the workers created their own proletarian public sphere by negating the bourgeois form of organization. In parallel, they could adjust the support of similar bourgeois organizations to their real proletarian interests. Although the action did not result in a concrete achievement, it was successful in forming an example: it vividly displayed the possibility of the proletarian public sphere.[9]

Although the type of proletarian public sphere that was developed by using the bourgeois form of organization at the foundation stage of the proletarian public sphere, which hosts the real revolutionary potential, is needed from time to time, this does not mean that similar organizations will necessarily go through this change. Lack of this change leads to two problems. On the one hand, they are distinguished from the bourgeois public sphere in terms of their outer perimeters, but they cannot offer organizing capacities that would develop alternatives inside. Such organizations are turned into the objects of politics just like the workers who are commodity objects in the economic system. Thus, the movements they develop cannot go beyond defending existing positions, and transition from the state of object to that of real subjects turns out to be impossible. In the worldwide discussions on the Left within the context of the crisis of global capitalism, it has frequently been pointed out that the real deficit of the Left is the lack of concrete, realist proposals for solving the problems. Besides, in these discussions, unions are blamed for hindering new achievements and the development of their members' capacities (Panitch 2011). Unlike the path to the crisis in capitalism in the 1970s, in which the organized workers' movement was decisive, the path to the 2007 crisis was marked by unorganized workers and workers' inability to defend their rights. Flexible production, which has extended from the 1980s onwards, an increase in the proportion of informal workers and unemployment made it difficult to unionize, and unions were weakened. Workers were deprived of a militant union-based movement that would address the developments, leading to the crisis and to the crisis at hand. They could not go beyond being objects and constituents of bourgeois politics.

On the other hand, unions and labor parties that are organized in a bourgeois style face the risk of polarization. If the working class organizes itself as another camp in bourgeois society, it loses its potential for a proletarian public sphere that embraces the whole society. If the organization of the proletarian context of life cannot evolve into such a public sphere, this camp—regardless of the underlying intention to get rid of the bourgeois context—will reproduce the mechanisms of the bourgeois public sphere. It will continue to live with exclusion, pseudo-publicness and the dictatorship of the procedural rules. This is a familiar picture in Turkey. According to Negt and Kluge ([1972]1993), this state of affairs signifies, above all, 'how remote the camp mentality of many communist organizations is from the Leninist conception of the party' (pp. 62–63).

For, once the related procedures acquire supremacy in the labor party, the party loses its revolutionary potential to embrace the society as a whole. The role of the unions in the unfolding of the polarization and the negative effects of this polarization on the workers are revealed in the following words by a worker who had participated in the TEKEL resistance:

> Sümerbank [a state-owned bank funding the construction of textile factories and the development of the textile industry in Turkey] had already been privatized in my city, Malatya. Then Sümerbank workers chanted, 'do not stay silent, as you keep silent next will be your turn' ... And we happened to stare at them, pardon my language, as if a cow staring at the train. We used to think that we would not have our turn. But it turned out to be such. If we had supported the Sümerbank workers then, we might not have experienced our turn.
>
> *(Aşık 2010)*

The unions' problem with collective action continued during the resistance of the TEKEL workers. The unions with mass representation did not comply with the decision to go on a general strike; they did not encourage their members to support the TEKEL resistance, even on an individual basis; and they left the TEKEL workers alone with the decision-making mechanism of the union of which the latter are members, and that of the workers' federation. The failure to turn promises of a general strike into a real call, despite the workers' demands, can be read as a result of this polarization. In this respect, it seems that the TEKEL resistance evinces the impotency of the unions. The transformation of the momentum achieved by the TEKEL workers into a more comprehensive and effective movement could only be possible with a call for a general strike or for a state of agency, encompassing all the popular forces that would circulate among organized structures. But this opportunity was missed.

Negt and Kluge note that three factors should work together for the emergence of a proletarian public sphere: (1) the motor of the public sphere should be the interests of the productive class; (2) it should be possible to create a mediator to form the relation between the specific interests of the producers and the interests of the whole society; (3) the effect of disruptive and deterrent means (such as the police force) of the bourgeois public sphere should not be strong in the formation of the proletarian public sphere (Negt and Kluge [1972] 1993). In this respect, the workings of these three factors can be observed in the TEKEL workers' occupation of the bourgeois and market public spheres,[10] and their success in splitting these spheres away from the commodity form and creating their own proletarian public spheres. It would be apt to analyze the meaning of each factor in the TEKEL resistance.

First, there is the case of the tobacco-processing workers who arrived in Sakarya Street (Ankara, Turkey) and set up their tent city. The basic motor behind their act was that they had been deprived of their already-acquired rights by the privatization of their factories and by the fact that the same factories were sold without the workers. They had launched protests and activities in the cities in which they used to work, but they could not reach a wider community. The last option proposed by their unions was to go to Ankara and voice their demands there. They did not plan to stay in Ankara for 78 days, as they travelled from 21 different cities. The demands that they had started to voice against privatization were turned into a demand to be transferred to another public institution, instead of the transfer to the precarious 4/C status (Section C of Article 4 of the Public Employees' Law), which suggests that workers from privatized public institutions would be hired by other public employers (possibly in other cities) as temporary, sessional workers with lower wages and fewer benefits. A TEKEL worker explained their reason for going to Ankara and the transformation they experienced as follows: 'On my part, I am in this struggle for money. But as of now the scales fell from my eyes. Now I'm struggling for my children's future' ('Türkiye iç savaşa gidiyordu, bunu biz yıktık' 2010).

The TEKEL resistance created awareness among the workers of the 4/C status imposed by the government. The TEKEL workers met with laborers in other sectors who shared the same destiny with them. Sümerbank workers shared the conditions of 4/C, which they had already been experiencing. Teachers and health-sector workers who were within the scope of the 4/C status came to Sakarya Street to express both their support for the TEKEL resistance and their demands. A wider section of the society could realize that the problem also concerned professions such as education and health services, deemed relatively 'basic and guaranteed.' The resistance thus extended its focus to the wider context—that is, the new work order, precarious work that further impoverished the youth, women and migrant workers and deprived them of the right to a health service, education and retirement. This also offers an answer to Metin Özügurlu's (2010: 51) question: 'Might the tendency to precarious work that homogenizes the working class be the link that organizes a united class movement?' Negt and Kluge, too, note that the demands and experiences that workers use in politicization processes should be widely acceptable. For example, a single demand such as wages would limit the labor movement within the existing sector. A claim related to the fact that the definition of work and working in a capitalist system brings forth a total meaninglessness, on the other hand, has the potential to appeal to society as a whole (Negt and Kluge [1972]1993). But it seems difficult to start with such a claim in contemporary capitalism. For the culture of capitalism has already fixed work— even overwork—for an income that would just ensure the reproduction of labor as a moral necessity, as a norm. Therefore, it seems rather difficult for a resistance to start merely with demands that contain issues other than work conditions and wages. Nevertheless, once resistance starts on these grounds, the proletarian public sphere might host other basic and new demands that happen to be binding on the wider society, as well as everyday demands that have immediate effects on the workers' lives. For example, the resistance of the TEKEL workers revealed that back pain and asthma are common health problems among the workers, making this commonality a public matter.

Another similar everyday issue is related to security during the resistance. Although the police forces attacked the TEKEL workers with pepper gas and pressurized water cannons and shut them up in a sports hall in the first days of the resistance, the police forces refrained from violence after the workers took shelter in the TÜRK-İŞ headquarters in downtown Ankara and during the process when the tent city was built. Despite the continuity in the threats and verbal harassments from the ruling circles, the fact that the police force did not intervene directly in the resistance square was highly useful. Thus, the workers could spend time on developing tactics and not on protecting themselves from the police force. On the other hand, there have been complaints that the workers could not leave the tent city owing to possible police intervention, and thus they fell short of a more vivid activism—in fact, they were locked up in the tent city ('Serdar Akbudakla Röportaj' 2010). This is certainly a well-founded criticism. A more vivid activism might have had more effect on the masses, and might have made more people aware of the TEKEL workers' presence on Sakarya Street. Such activism might have further developed the formation process of the proletarian public sphere, for tactic development emerges from within activism itself.

Here, based on the TEKEL experience, a fourth condition might be added to the three proposed by Negt and Kluge: the working of the proletarian public sphere in accordance with tactics that are developed jointly based on changing conditions, and not in accordance with top–down, predetermined strategies. Hence, as the TEKEL resistance was a movement composed of multiple ingredients, it was required to be flexible enough to adopt different tactics in accordance with changeable conditions, any time, anywhere. The conventional bourgeois public sphere, which mostly operates through strategic plans, could thus be manipulated by means of varying tactics. In this respect, the struggle that would be launched in the proletarian public sphere would more likely be a *war of positions* than a *war of maneuvers* (Gramsci 1971). For, dissolution of the commodified character—as the hidden face of the bourgeois public sphere, and as the most apparent face of the market public sphere—cannot happen all of a sudden. It requires strong social support that would be gathered in time and a sufficient number of people willing to establish the public sphere—that is, willing to create the grounds to express and share their experiences and vital demands, and to search for solutions. To earn this consent asks for the war of positions.

In this sphere, created and used by the TEKEL workers throughout 78 days of resistance, one can observe the spontaneity of the working class and its turning into an agency (Hacısalihoğlu et al. 2010).[11] Agency-cum-class is a must for the development of capacities for forming tactics. They are the organizers, producers in the workplace, and they will succeed in organizing the resistance based on such experiences. It is in this respect that they could turn the 'controversies' imposed by bourgeois politics into 'reciprocities' in this process (Özuğurlu 2011), for the historicity of Turkey's working class that appeared in their agency paves the way to overcome the dominant discourse that turns them against each other. It helps them to see that discrimination based on identities is a matter of ahistorical discourse initiated by ruling circles. As more than once noted by TEKEL workers, they were the ones who created the real 'democratic opening' for the Kurdish issue in Turkey—which was the motto of the AKP government then, although nowadays the same party with the same leadership acts in the complete opposite direction when it comes to the Kurdish issue—for they could find the grounds that would carry them beyond 'pseduo patriotisms' to discuss the origins of the problem:

> We do not have any distinction among each other as workers. We have been resisting here for days. We are here, shoulder to shoulder, all workers, from Diyarbakır to Tokat, from Hatay to Bitlis. We have been eating on the same table for days. We are here, as Turks and Kurds. It is not them who realized the opening; it's us.
>
> *('Direnişteki TEKEL İşçileri ile konuştuk' 2009)*

The fact that workers are historical subjects enables their experiences to materialize from within the proletarian life contexts; they embrace the historical processes as historical subjects. Therefore, one should focus on the historicity of the working class rather than the history of the working class. The history of the working class puts forth the working class as an object without agency. The historicity of the working class signifies the approach to the working class as a living, acting subject that continually accumulates experiences. Looking at the experiences would offer the details of our historicity.

It is necessary to recognize workers' intellectual, organizing, remedial capacities, for persuasiveness and commitment are important for the proletarian public sphere. If the TEKEL workers had not counted upon their leftist supporters, if they had not believed that they would not leave them alone, they would have opted to stand at a distance from those they used to label 'nasty communists' in their own words. It was necessary to participate in the experiences, and in the problems that the workers brought in from within the center of their everyday lives, and the leftist supporters in Ankara were successful in doing so.[12] Thus, it was a reciprocal learning process: those who happened to approach the workers with an imposing mentality were quick to understand that they should rather take a share in the existing experience.

Conclusion: rethinking the working-class movement

In his analysis of the floating values created by flexible production, Richard Sennett (1998) asks: '[h]ow can a human being develop a narrative of identity and life story in a society composed of episodes and fragments?' (p. 26). In parallel, Metin Özuğurlu (2011) defines the new working class as those whose 'destinies are being united while their lives are being fragmented' (p. 181). It is the common use of the labor force that merges the destinies and makes the life story possible. In today's capitalism in crisis, one has to insist on the commonizing feature of labor. The transformation of the different, yet in many respects similar, experiences with the exploitation of labor into real experiences through an organized movement can only be possible with this insistence. The importance of the TEKEL resistance is due to the fact that the workers could act through this cooperation and attract the attention of wider society. The new working conditions—or better, precarious work—have a big share in the experiences that unite workers today. Precarious work has the potential to dissolve the old hierarchies that cause fragmentation among workers. Today, almost all wage earners, regardless of their abilities, rank and educational level, work on temporary contracts and/or a part-time basis. Public institutions with contracted personnel have increasingly resorted to subcontractors. So, resistance should be forged through campaigns, social networks and organizations based on the instability of work.

The success of the TEKEL resistance is due to the fact that the activists were laborers: the workers were successful in organizing this struggle because they were familiar with organizing production, as they were trained to do in the production process. It is significant that this experience displayed the possibility of such organization. Immediate experiences were mediated through the practices of reflection, discussion and sharing in the proletarian public sphere, and, hence, subjective experiences were turned into a dialectical contrariety, in which the working class participated. This platform should also be used and developed in the periods that do not host radical activism. It is necessary to find those life practices that connect the workers to the wider society.[13]

As a conclusion, the public sphere should be understood together with all the dynamics of the social—with all institutions, actors, practices and spaces (such as law, the press, public opinion, public employees, workplaces, streets, squares). In this respect, Negt and Kluge do not approach the public sphere as an intermediary sphere between the state and society. Instead, they build their analysis on the concrete sphere of social reproduction. For them, the public sphere is produced and reproduced by real people and their real needs (Krause 2006). It also corresponds to a production process; it is not an external object that precedes the person, nor a sphere in which one can participate after it is built. The concept concerns a continuous state of being and displaying potentials. Experience refers to a dialectical process; it is a state of a sort of attachment to others and the reality beyond lived moments and feelings. Reclaiming the public sphere necessitates creating new solidarity spheres by the acknowledgment of the interpersonal nature of identities—which are forced to divisive functions in neoliberal public spheres—and the prioritization of the unifying experiences of the working class. Last but not least, in the cases where instances of anti-systemic resistance are not organized in the form of proletarian publicness, they are doomed to act as raw material for capitalist exploitation.

Notes

1 In 1994, 4/C was created to employ temporary workers in government jobs that lasted less than 10 months. In 2004, the AKP government approved an amendment to this article that included workers who had been laid off owing to privatization. These temporary contracts have been especially prevalent in education and health care. Rather than employing people in full-time, year-round forms of employment, AKP continues to hire recent graduates and health-care providers on limited-term contracts of less than 10 months.

2 Here it would be apt to note Abdullah Aysu's (2010) warning: 'Those whom we named as TEKEL workers in Ankara were not working for TEKEL. They were indeed working in Tobacco, Salt, Tobacco Leaf processing. For, we shall remember that TEKEL had been completely privatized, including its royalty' (p. 208; translation is mine).

3 The book *Kamusal Alan* by Meral Özbek (2005) includes a Turkish translation of a chapter from Negt and Kluge's *Public Sphere and Experience*. Additionally Mustafa Kemal Coşkun (2007) offers an analysis of the conceptualization of the 'proletarian public sphere' in the conclusion of his book, especially pp. 115–123.

4 In his article, Lawrence (2009) gives a brief account of how BAT's patience in waiting for the right time for a share in Turkey's tobacco market since the 1980s caused its failure vis-à-vis Philip Morris, which gained 'success' in Turkey's tobacco industry by means of setting up a factory in partnership with Sabancı Holding; the account is presented from the perspective of capital. For the same story, told from the perspective of labor, see Aysu (2010).

5 Max Horkheimer and Theodor Adorno use the concept of 'culture industry' for the mass production of culture in an advanced capitalist period. I argue that the foundations of this period were laid in the eighteenth and nineteenth centuries— although we cannot point at mass production in that period (Horkheimer and Adorno [1944]2002).

6 When we consider the modern scientific method, it is not surprising that all these measures were implemented as meticulously as in a laboratory setting. The Royal Society, established in England in 1660 by such names as Sir William Petty and Robert Boyle, who acted as counselors to the government, hosted the emergence of a new literature that focused exclusively on 'population.' Population was important, for, in the transition to a labor-intensive production system, each and every body within the labor force it embodied had a certain value for the wealth of the nation. Thus, it is not surprising that, for Sir William Petty, known as the 'Columbus of the Statistics,' 'each dead young English means 69 sterling worth loss' (Pasquino 1991).

7 Negt and Kluge ([1972]1993) refer to the concept of 'culture industry' offered by Horkheimer and Adorno ([1944]2002), as 'conscious industry.' In doing so, they focus on the public use of reason.

8 *Devrimden Sonra (After the Revolution)*, 2011, Director: Mustafa Kenan Aybastı. The movie, composed of eight short films, gives an account of a possible post-revolutionary order in Turkey. Emphasizing a certain definition of socialism, the movie runs through didactic accounts of the appropriate practice of property relations, a health system and the use of public goods in a socialist system.

9 This does not necessitate a bourgeois type of organizing for every proletarian public sphere experience. For example, those who organized the Wall Street occupation in New York signified the opportunity for publicness that does not arise out of the union/labor party-based organizations, familiar for bourgeois publicness, and thus is amorphous and emerges spontaneously and, hence, created a sphere that had already shaped its form of organization in the movement, at the very beginning.

10 The prime minister of the time named the action at Sakarya Street as an 'occupation.' He was not that mistaken ('Başbakan Yanıltıyor, Ne İş Bırakmak Yasadışı Ne de Direniş' 2010). But the occupation by the TEKEL workers should be evaluated as

a process of occupation with a reverse move. TEKEL workers occupied a sphere whose creators had been plundered and that had been occupied by the market and bourgeois politics. They did so in order to reclaim it.

11 Elif Hacısalihoğlu et al. (2010) discuss the spontaneity of class with quotes from Luxemburg. Although they emphasize spontaneity, they do not deny the importance of union-based organizing.

12 Here it would be apt to note some of the successful work by the organizations: physicians provided a 24-hour volunteer service, within the scope of the Turkish Communist Party (TKP; Ankara branch) and the Turkish Physicians Association (Ankara branch). Besides, TKP members issued TEKEL diaries and distributed them among the workers; thus, they created a news network. The team of the International Workers' Film Festival realized live broadcasts from the resistance site on the Internet (www.sendika.tv). Halkevleri (People's Houses) members set up their own tents, with the name 'TEKEL University,' thus bringing together TEKEL workers, university students and academics (Hacısalihoğlu et al. 2010; Özcan 2010).

13 Here, for example, the protests by Halkevleri (People's Houses) against increased costs for public transport in Ankara are important. Public transport might at first sound like a minor issue in terms of public activism, but it is a vital need for the majority of the people. A movement that voices itself through this need and that advocates for related claims has the potential to reach many people and get the support of wider social sectors. Such a claim might drive a worker who has rightist political views into the movement ('Batıkent Metrosuna Binlerce Yolcu Parasız Bindi' 2010; 'Eylemci-Vatandaş Elele Ücretsiz Otobüse' 2011; Ballıktaş 2011).

References

Arendt, H. (1998) *The Human Condition*, Chicago and London: University of Chicago Press.

Aşık, M. (2010) 'Hasan Uyanıyor!' *Milliyet* (Turkish daily), February 26, at: www.milliyet.com.tr/hasan-uyaniyor-/melih-asik/guncel/yazardetayarsiv/26.02.2010/1204144/default.htm (accessed on December 1, 2017).

Aysu, A. (2010) 'TEKEL ve Tütünün Öyküsü,' in G. Bulut (ed.), *TEKEL Direnişinin Işığında Gelenekselden Yeniye İşçi Sınıfı Hareketi*, Ankara: Nota Bene.

Ballıktaş, B. (2011) 'Halkevlerinden Ulaşım Zammına Metroda Protesto.' *Bianet*, at: http://bianet.org/bianet/toplum/127011-halkevlerinden-ulasim-zammina-metroda-protesto (accessed on December 1, 2017).

'Başbakan Hangi Sendikacıları Dolmabahçe'ye Çağırdı.' (2010, February 3) At: www.odatv.com/n.php?n=basbakan-hangi-sendikacilari-dolmabahceye-cagirdi-0302101200 (accessed on December 1, 2017).

'Başbakan Yanıltıyor, Ne İş Bırakmak Yasadışı Ne de Direniş.' (2010) *Bianet*, at: http://bianet.org/bianet/insan-haklari/119847-basbakan-yaniltiyor-ne-is-birakmak-yasadisi-ne-de-direnis (accessed on December 1, 2017).

'Batıkent Metrosuna Binlerce Yolcu Parasız Bindi.' (2010) At: www.sendika.org/yazi.php?yazi_no=29080 (accessed on December 1, 2017).

Coşkun, M.K. (2007) *Demokrasi Teorileri ve Toplumsal Hareketler*, Ankara: Dipnot Yayınları.

'Direnişteki TEKEL İşçileri ile konuştuk … "Ölmek Var, Dönmek Yok."' (2009) *Kızıl Bayrak*, at: www.kizilbayrak.net/sinif-hareketi/haber/arsiv/2009/12/30/select/roeportaj/artikel/136/direnisteki-tek.html (accessed on December 1, 2017).

'Eylemci-Vatandaş Elele Ücretsiz Otobüse.' (2011) *Milliyet*, at: www.milliyet.com.tr/Gundem/SonDakika.aspx?aType=SonDakika&ArticleID=1334593&Date=04.01.2011&Kate

gori=gundem&b=Eylemci%20-%20vatandas%20el%20ele%20ucretsiz%20otobuse (accessed on December 1, 2017).

Gramsci, A. (1971) *Selections from Prison Notebooks*, ed. and trans. Q. Hoare and G.N. Smith, London: Lawrence & Wishart.

Habermas, J. (1991) *The Structural Transformation of the Public Sphere: An Inquiry into a Category of Bourgeois Society*, trans. T. Burger, Cambridge: MIT Press.

Hacısalihoğlu, E., Uğurlu, G. and Yücesan-Özdemir, G. (2010 21. Yüzyılda Sosyal Hak Mücadelesi: TEKEL Direnişi. *II. Sosyal Haklar Ulusal Sempozyumu*, at: www.sosyal haklar.net/2010/2010index.htm (accessed on December 1, 2017).

Horkheimer, M. and Adorno, T. ([1944]2002) *Dialectic of Enlightenment: Philosophical Fragments*, Stanford: Stanford University Press.

Hunt, A. (1999) *Governing Morals: A Social History of Moral Regulation*, Cambridge: Cambridge University Press.

Karaağaç, B. and Kaya, Y. (2010) 'Turkey: Capital's Crisis, Labour's Burden,' *Relay: A Socialist Project Review* (29, January–March): 32–34.

Knödler-Bunte, E., Lennox, S. and Lennox, F. (1975) 'The Proletarian Public Sphere and Political Organization: An Analysis of Oskar Negt and Alexander Kluge's *Public Sphere and Experience*,' *New German Critique* 4: 51–75.

Krause, M. (2006) 'The Production of Counter-Publics and the Counter-Publics of Production: An Interview with Oskar Negt,' *European Journal of Social Theory* 9(1): 119–128.

Lawrence, S. (2009) 'British American Tobacco's Failure in Turkey,' *Tobacco Control* 18: 22–28.

Lukács, G. (1971) *History and Class Consciousness*, trans. R. Livingstone, Cambridge, MA: MIT Press.

Marx, K. (1968) 'Thesis on Feuerbach,' in K. Marx and F. Engels (eds.), *The German Ideology*, Moscow: Progress.

Marx, K. and Engels, F. ([1848]1977) *Manifesto of the Communist Party*, Moscow: Progress.

Negt, O. and Kluge, A. ([1972]1993) *Public Sphere and Experience: Toward an Analysis of the Bourgeois and Proletarian Public Sphere*, trans. P. Labanyi, J.O. Daniel and A. Oksiloff, Minneapolis: University of Minnesota Press.

Özbek, M. (2005) *Kamusal Alan*, Adıyaman: Hil Yayınevi.

Özcan, G. (2010) 'The TEKEL Strike in Turkey: Workers are Teaching, Students are Learning,' *The Bullet: Socialist Project, E-Bulletin* (326), at: www.socialistproject.ca/ bullet/326.php (accessed on December 1, 2017).

Özuğurlu, M. (2010) 'TEKEL Direnişi: Sınıflar Mücadelesi Üzerine Anımsamalar,' in G. Bulut (ed.), *TEKEL Direnişinin Işığında Gelenekselden Yeniye İşçi Sınıfı Hareketi*, Ankara: Nota Bene.

Özuğurlu, M. (2011) 'The TEKEL Resistance Movement: Reminiscences on Class Struggle,' *Capital and Class* 35(2): 179–187.

Panitch, L. (2011) 'The Left's Crisis,' *The Bullet: Socialist Project, E-Bulletin* (536), at www.socialistproject.ca/bullet/536.php (accessed on December 1, 2017).

Pasquino, P. (1991) 'Theatrum Politicum: The Genealogy of Capital, Police and the State of Property,' in G. Burchell, C. Gordon and P. Miller (eds.), *The Foucault Effect: Studies in Governmentality*, Hemel Hempstead: Harvester Wheatsheaf.

Paulson, J. (2005) *Uneven Reification*, Santa Cruz: University of California, unpublished PhD thesis.

Sennett, R. (1998) *The Corrosion of Character*, New York: W.W. Norton.

Serdar Akbudakla Röportaj. (2010) 'Emek Piyasasında Kardeşleşildi,' in G. Bulut (ed.), *TEKEL Direnişinin Işığında Gelenekselden Yeniye İşçi Sınıfı Hareketi*, Ankara: Nota Bene.

Storch, R.D. (1977) 'The Problem of Working-Class Leisure. Some Roots of Middle-Class Moral Reform in the Industrial North: 1825–1850,' in A.P. Donajgrodzki (ed.), *Social Control in Nineteenth Century Britain*, London: Croom Helm.

Storch, R.D. (ed.) (1982) *Popular Culture and Custom in Nineteenth-Century England*, New York: St Martin's Press.

Thompson, E.P. (1957) 'Socialist Humanism,' *The New Reasoner* 1: 105–143.

Thompson, E.P. (1967) 'Time, Work-Discipline, and Industrial Capitalism' *Past & Present* 38(1): 56–97.

Thompson, E.P. ([1963]1991) *The Making of the English Working Class*, London: Penguin.

'Türkiye iç savaşa gidiyordu, bunu biz yıktık.' (2010) At: www.t24.com.tr/haberdetay/71618.aspx (accessed on December 1, 2017).

Verstraeten, H. (1996) 'The Media and the Transformation of the Public Sphere: A Contribution for a Critical Political Economy of the Public Sphere,' *European Journal of Communication* 11(3): 347–370.

4

REFUSE, RESIST, REVOLT

Cognitive capitalism and the struggle for the general intellect

André Pusey

Introduction

This chapter focuses on social movements and struggles coalescing around the neo-liberal restructuring of higher education (HE). HE has increasingly become a battleground. Protest has ranged from a series of high-profile university occupations in the US during 2008 and 2009 (After the Fall Communiqués 2010; Levenson 2011), the student protests and occupations against the removal of the Education Maintenance Allowance (EMA) and tripling of university tuition fees in the UK during the winter of 2010 (Browne 2010; Hancox 2011; Ibrahim 2011; Solomon and Palmieri 2011; Younis 2011), the Quebecian student strike of 2012 (Spiegel 2015a, 2015b, 2016), and, more recently, protests against the ongoing colonial legacies of the university (Newsinger 2016). This chapter maintains that, through the transition from Fordist to post-Fordist modes of production and the concurrent rise of 'immaterial' (Lazzarato 1996) forms of labour, the university is directly a site of capitalist production (Edu-Factory 2009). It is argued, therefore, that the struggles around HE and universities across many parts of the world are about more than simply a resurgence of cycles of student protest that have waxed and waned over the course of the mid to late twentieth century. Instead, they are symptomatic of a transformation of the role of knowledge and intellectual production within society and the economy and, subsequently, the role of intellectuals and knowledge production within social struggles. Using Marx's (1993) 'fragment on machines' from the *Grundrisse*, this chapter concludes that the struggles around education are struggles against the enclosure of the general intellect through cognitive capitalism and for mass intellectuality, the general intellect unchained from capital's capture.

Restructuring the university

There has been extensive discussion of the numerous ways in which universities and HE are being restructured according to neo-liberal logic (Radice 2013). These debates have been wide ranging. For example, many have directed their arguments against the increased precariousness of academic labour (Bousquet 2008), others the increased anxiety associated with academic working conditions and the introduction of metric systems and an audit culture that commodifies the outputs of academic work (Ball 2004; De Angelis and Harvie 2009; Hall and Stahl 2015; Harvie 2000). Other focuses have been a critique by educators of the transformation of the student into a consumer and the spiralling of student debt (Federici 2014). Critics have attacked these reforms as representing a 'great university gamble' (McGettigan 2013) and suggested the university is in 'ruins' (Readings 1996). Some have mourned the erosion of the public university in the face of corporate encroachment and marketization and attempted to defend it from attack (Newfield 2008). Other have focused their critique on the 'gendered, sexualised, raced and classed politics of motherhood' within marketized universities (Amsler and Motta 2017).

Enda Brophy (2011) has observed that the university increasingly seeks to commodify its intellectual production and market itself, developing its 'unique selling points' in order to find its niche within an increasingly global market for HE products and providers. Gigi Roggero (2011) argues this transformation of the university has been occurring concurrently with the convergence of the figures of the student and the worker, and that increasingly the divide between these two figures is porous, where it exists at all. In turn, these transformations of labour and the university are occurring within a period that has experienced an increased focus and integration of communication, culture, knowledge and affect within the valorization of capital. Or, as Brophy (2011: vii) puts it, these categories have been 'put to work with unprecedented intensity'.

Although the elements of these reforms may be context-specific, across vast parts of Europe and North America the response has been a wave of struggles that have shared certain commonalities: against increases in tuition fees, against precaratization of working conditions, against marketization of education. This 'assault on the university' (Bailey and Freedman 2011), or what Giroux (2014) has described as neo-liberalism's 'war on education', has unsurprisingly been met with an acceleration of education struggles. Ostensibly these may be viewed as defensive fights, calls to protect the public university from corporate encroachment and privatization, or to reform the existing 'neoliberal university'. However, I argue below that they are far more radical than this and that they call into question the nature of the society we live in.

As capitalism becomes increasingly reliant on the production of knowledge, codes and affects, it is also simultaneously reliant on increased levels of cooperation, collaboration and sociability. The struggles that have emerged around education and knowledge production have not only been resistive, but have also contained strong elements that have experimented with prefigurative alternatives and merged with autonomous education projects outside universities (Noterman and Pusey 2012; Roggero 2011). These have produced forms of 'minor knowledge' and are projects that contain examples of a future general intellect freed from capital's apparatus of capture, seeds of another social world. Before moving on to discuss this in greater detail, the next section briefly outlines some of these struggles.

Refuse, resist, revolt: the three Rs and pedagogic resistance

During 2008, protestors in Italy organized the first mobilization against austerity measures related to the 2007–8 financial crisis (Zamponi 2012). This movement became known as the 'anomalous wave' and developed into the largest in Italy in thirty years. Protestors galvanized around the slogan 'We won't pay for your crisis'. The slogan's double meaning refers to both the global 2007–8 economic crisis and the crisis of the university and the Bologna process. These protests were to become emblematic of the emerging cycle of education struggles that are not only protesting relatively contained issues around educational reform but are also engaged in struggles around the 'double crisis' of the university and the economy. Furthermore, there is a self-consciousness about both the increased centrality of the neo-liberalized and corporatized university within the economy and the increased importance of the knowledge economy more broadly within 'cognitive capitalism' (Vercellone 2007).

The anomalous wave in Italy was quickly followed by struggles elsewhere. In the US, during December 2008, students occupying the New School for Social Research in New York City suggested that activists needed to 'occupy everything'. This was a call for the immediate occupation of not only the New School NYC, or even universities more generally, but of 'everything' – the occupation and appropriation of the entire socio-spatial realm. This expansive call to action summons up the long history of occupation as a revolutionary tactic. But retrospectively, we can also see this slogan as heralding the new wave of occupations in the struggles during the post 2007–8 financial crisis: Tahir Square in Egypt in 2011 and the Occupy encampments around the world to name just a few (Halvorsen 2012; Lunghi and Wheeler 2012; Mason 2013; Pickerill and Krinsky 2012; Van Gelder 2011).

Between September and December 2009, occupations of university campus buildings spread across California, including at UC Berkeley and UC Santa Cruz (After the Fall Communiqués 2010). At these protests, the slogan 'Occupy Every-thing', coined by the New School occupiers, was extended to 'Occupy Everything. Demand Nothing!' This simple slogan embodied a refusal of mediation and representation. In place of the 'rational demands' and media-based activism often accompanying protest and student occupations, these activists simply proposed a refusal, negation. Encompassed within this simple slogan was a nod to the politics of communization. Indeed, a vocal element of these protests was openly invoking the rhetoric of communization. Communization can be described as a 'problematic' rather than a fully formed theory (Noys 2011). It developed out of French ultra-left currents during the 1970s and has since morphed into several tendencies, analytic and prefigurative communization (Clare and Habermehl 2016). Arguably, the Californian students were utilizing a prefigurative form of communization, with antecedents in the French journal *Tiqqun* and the Invisible Committee (see Merrifield 2010). It views communism as something to be put into practice not in the distant future, after some transitionary stage, but now, through immediate communizing measures. Therefore, the occupations by the Californian students are not simply seen as ways to attract media attention, 'speak truth to power', or even apply pressure to university administrations. Instead, they are viewed as processes of reappropriation and decommodification.

During the autumn/winter of 2010, England experienced a series of increasingly militant protests against the removal of the EMA and the proposed tripling of university tuition fees by the coalition government (Browne 2010; Ibrahim 2011). These protests were notable for refusing to be controlled by either the lecturers' union, the University College Union (UCU) or the National Union of Students (NUS). Indeed, at the first major demonstration of this movement, protestors refused to be marshalled by protest stewards, occupied and damaged the Conservative Party headquarters at Millbank and were roundly condemned by the presiding head of the NUS, Aaron Porter (BBC 2010). This effectively marked the withdrawal of the NUS from any relevance to this movement, and future national and local demonstrations largely operated without any official NUS involvement or funding (Penny 2010; Robertson 2010; Sealey-Huggins and Pusey 2013). At the second national demonstration, protestors evaded police 'kettles' and ran through the streets, making up the route as they moved through the city. At the demonstration to mark the final decision about these reforms, protestors fought with police outside Parliament and attacked prominent government buildings, corporate targets and even a car carrying members of the Royal Family. Although protests began to recede after the bill was passed, at a demonstration in Manchester in the New Year of 2011, protestors pelted the head of the NUS, Aaron Porter, with eggs, again demonstrating the disdain for him and perhaps the NUS bureaucratic apparatus more generally (Fox 2011). After the rally, protestors set off on their own unofficial march away from the out-of-the-way park where the NUS had organized the rally and into Manchester city centre.

These protests utilized a diverse repertoire of contention (Tilly 2008). One prominent feature of these protests was the 'book block', a tactic that utilized shields made to represent books. An iconic image of these protests is that of demonstrators attempting to defend themselves from police batons with copies of seminal texts, such as George Orwell's *1984* and Aldous Huxley's *Brave New World*. This provided the protests with a poignant symbolism, as knowledge struggled against its further commodification and was forcibly suppressed by the state. More than twenty university campuses were occupied as part of this struggle, some for several weeks (NCAFC 2010). These occupations formed important spaces through which the movement organized and mobilized further (Salter and Kay 2011). Many of these occupations included prefigurative and pedagogical elements (Hall 2011) that began to build critical spaces of free association and experimental self-education, contributing towards processes of (re)politicization and the transformation of student subjectivities (Pusey 2016).

Although these protests dissipated with their apparent 'defeat', new protests emerged in 2013 around cleaners' wages and cops off campus (UCLU 2013). In Sussex, protests erupted during 2013 about the university outsourcing support staff jobs. Students occupied the university conference centre for more than six weeks. Sussex developed an innovative 'pop-up union' (Nişancıoğlu and Pal 2016). The Sussex protests utilized a yellow square, which was adapted from the Quebec student protests a year earlier.

In Quebec, during 2012, approximately 75 per cent of students went on strike as part of a mass struggle over a 75 per cent increase in student tuition fees. Perhaps most prominent among the array of tactics used by the movement was the utilization of the red square as a symbol of being 'squarely in the red' or 'squarely in debt' (Spiegel 2016, 2015a). This movement not only shut down most colleges and universities in the province for six months but also mobilized thousands of supporters. At its height, nearly three-quarters of Quebec's post-secondary student population were on strike (230,000), and Spiegel (2015b) suggests that the largest demonstration was attended by up to 500,000 people.

This is far from an exhaustive list of education struggles and merely gives an indication of the kinds of contestation being organized around higher-education struggles since 2008. It misses out the highly militant student struggle in Chile during 2011 and the Rhodes Must Fall campaign, which started in Cape Town and spread to Oxford (Chaudhuri 2016). But it gives an account of some of the high points of struggle and the transnational nature of the contestation around HE. This chapter now moves on to argue that these struggles are symptomatic of the centrality of HE to the economy and encompass resistance to the enclosure and commodification of the general intellect.

Universities, cognitive capitalism and the struggle over the general intellect

The struggles discussed above are symptomatic of a transformation of the role of knowledge and intellectual production within society and the economy, and subsequently the role of intellectuals and knowledge production within social struggles. Using Marx's 'fragment on machines' from the *Grundrisse* (Marx 1993), I argue that the protests around education are struggles against the enclosure of the general intellect by cognitive capitalism and for mass intellectuality, the general intellect unchained from capital's capture.

The concept of the 'general intellect' is introduced by Marx in a passage in the *Grundrisse* commonly referred to as the 'fragment on machines' (Marx 1993). In the 'fragment on machines', Marx uses the term 'general intellect' to refer to the general 'social knowledge' of a society – what could be described as its collective intelligence, or perhaps the limits of what we know about ourselves at any given period. In the *Grundrisse*, Marx focuses on forms of 'fixed capital' such as machinery as embodying the general intellect, as well as human beings, contending that:

> Nature builds no machines, no locomotives, railways, electric telegraphs, self-acting mules etc. These are products of human industry; natural material transformed into organs of the human will over nature, or of human participation in nature. They are organs of the human brain, created by the human hand; the power of knowledge, objectified. The development of fixed capital indicates to what degree general social knowledge has become a *direct force of production*, and to what degree, hence, the conditions of the process of social life itself have come under the control of the general intellect and been transformed in accordance with it. To what degree the powers of social production have been produced, not only in the form of knowledge but also as immediate organs of social practice, of the real life process.
>
> *(Marx 1993: 706; emphasis in the original)*

From this starting point, Paulo Virno (2004) understands the general intellect to include all the 'formal and informal knowledge, imagination, ethical tendencies, mentalities and "language games" that are not the property of an individual or corporation but are rather immanent to the productive capacity of society itself'. The general intellect is, therefore, the driving force of production in society, from the immaterial, such as languages and codes, to the concrete, such as bridges and cars – the cumulative creative potential of society. The general intellect incorporates not only an immaterial capacity but also knowledge that has become materially embodied in physical objects, such as machines and the built environment. This is not, however, to say that physical objects have their own isolated productive capacity, but rather that a manifestation of the general intellect can be found in those phenomena that augment the productive capacity of the general intellect.

Dyer-Witheford (1999: 233) states that 'in [the] contest [for the general intellect] the contemporary proletariat fights to actualise the "general intellect", not according to the privatizing, appropriative logic of capital, but in ways that are deeply democratic and collective, and hence truly "general"'. This indicates a struggle against the enclosure of knowledge (Federici and Caffentzis 2007) and for a generalization or 'commonization' (Clare and Habermehl 2016) of the general intellect. A key space and place of this 'value struggle' (De Angelis 2007) over the general intellect is the university, 'for no site could be more vital to capital's harnessing of collective intelligence than academia' (Dyer-Witheford 1999: 233). One of the ways capital harnesses academic 'doing' (Holloway 2010) is through metrics systems and the struggle over the implementation of measure (De Angelis and Harvie 2009; Harvie 2000).These are key mechanisms for imposing market-like conditions upon academia and transforming the production of knowledge and teaching into commodities.

According to Dyer-Witheford, analysing an article by Negri and Lazzarato, in the 'ivory-tower' era of the university, when universities were:

> only partially integrated into capitalism, or marginal to its central func-
> tions, academics appeared (however much this actually mystified real
> interconnections) to be removed from industrial activity and its attendant
> class-conflicts. It was from this position of apparent exteriority that the
> intellectual could commit or engage himself with political movements.
>
> *(Dyer-Witheford 1999: 234)*

We can describe this era as that of formal subsumption, where capital takes command of labour processes previously organized outside or prior to the capital relation. Today, however, with the corporatization and marketization of universities, 'university teachers find themselves unequivocally involved in capital's appropriation of "general intellect"' (Dyer-Witheford 1999: 234). This is real subsumption, where the labour process of academic production is reorganized by capital for its own benefit. Negri and Lazzarato suggest these changed conditions, 'create the grounds for a new relation between dissenting academics and oppositional social movements. Rather than descending from the heights of the university to commit themselves to a cause largely external to their daily experience, possibilities emerge for academics to make more "transverse connections"' (cited in Dyer-Witheford 1999: 234). This leads Dyer-Witheford to suggest that this may mean academics 'lose some preten-sions as the bearer of great truths and grand analysis, but become the carriers of particular skills, knowledges and accesses useful to movements in which they participate on the basis of increasing commonalities with other members of post-Fordist "mass intellect"' (1999: 234–235).

Dyer-Witheford suggests that, in order to effectively harness the mass intellect to accumulation, capital must maintain a certain degree of openness within the universities. Part of what capital seeks in its subsumption of academia is the creativity and experimentation of social labour power, qualities vital to a high-technology economy based on perpetual innovation. But, if industry is to benefit from such invention power, it cannot entirely regiment the institutions of education (Dyer-Witheford 1999: 235). It is this seemingly unavoidable condition 'of an economic order based on general intellect' that, in Dyer-Witheford's view, gives a 'limited but real porosity to universities' (1999: 235). Capital, therefore, needs the creativity and cooperation of the academic commons. Dyer-Witheford optimistically suggests that:

> this porosity can be exploited by dissident academics – to research and teach on topics of value to social movements in opposition to capital; to invite activists and analysts from these movements onto campuses and into lectures and seminars; and to use the university's resources, including its easy access to the great communication networks of our age, to circulate news and analysis that are otherwise marginalised.
>
> *(Dyer-Witheford 1999: 235)*

This is certainly the case in some instances; for example, some academics have developed programmes on activism and social change, and, of course, there are numerous other examples that are perhaps less overt in their stance. We can also think of the various struggles to include/make space for marginalized and 'minor knowledges'.[1]

Dyer-Witheford concludes that:

> In academia, as elsewhere, labor power is never completely controllable. To the degree that capital uses the university to harness general intellect, insisting its workforce engage in life-long learning as the price of employability, it runs the risk that people will teach and learn something other than what it intends.
>
> *(Dyer-Witheford 1999: 236)*

I argue below that this is what we are experiencing though the rise of the movements outlined above.[2] Fundamentally, this is about struggles over measure (De Angelis and Harvie 2009) and the law of value being introduced into the university.

Within elements of the Italian workerist tradition, and especially the writings of Antonio Negri, the figure of the 'mass worker' was the embodiment of the worker in the Fordist era of capitalist production (Negri 1988). The 'socialised worker' came to replace it with the development of 'post-Fordist' and 'cognitive' forms of labour, at least within the eyes of some post-autonomist theorists. Dyer-Witheford argues that:

> corporations went 'cognitive' in the 1960s and 70s not just because computers and biotech innovations were available, but also because high technology restructuring offered a weapon against the massive unrest that beset industrial, Fordist capitalism – whether by automating unruly factories, networking outsourced global production costs or green revolutionizing the sites of peasant struggle. But making the shift from industrial to cognitive capital – or from Fordism to post-Fordism – required pacifying and restructuring academia. After the immediate discipline of police action, shootings and academic purges, the neoliberal response was radical reorganization.
>
> *(Dyer-Witheford 2005: 75)*

The 'radical restructuring' that Dyer-Witheford suggests was neo-liberalism's response to the earlier Fordist 'mass worker' and student cycles of struggle incorporates some of the demands of these earlier struggles, such as the demands for formerly marginalized knowledges within the university; we can regard this as a 'weapon of inclusion' (Roggero 2011). This restructuring also introduces a regime of liberalization that makes universities productive for cognitive capitalism.

Post-Fordism utilizes the 'general intellect' through its deployment of cooperative and collaborative forms of labor, something that has led some, notably Paulo Virno, to describe it as the 'communism of capital' (Virno 2004: 11). We can extend this analysis to 'cognitive capitalism'. Matteo Pasquinelli suggests that, 'in technical terms, the expression "communism of capital" refers to a process of colonization of any aspect of human life that can be transformed into a credit line' (Pasquinelli 2010: 5), that is the process of marketization and financialization of the world, part of the ongoing process of primitive accumulation and enclosure (Bonefeld 1988; Midnight Notes 1990). Pasquinelli analyses the 'communism of capital' as causing (or relying upon?) a 'cannibalism of the common' (Pasquinelli 2010: 5). Returning to the university then, capital relies on the openness and criticality of the university in order to cannibalize it, but this comes with the risk of refusal and labour acting in excess of this capture. Thus the student-workers of the struggles discussed in this chapter are part of a broader struggle over the cannibalization of the university common.

According to Virno, 'mass intellectuality is the prominent form in which the general intellect is manifest today' (Virno 2007: 6). Virno describes mass intellectuality as the 'entirety of post-Fordist living labor' (Virno 2007: 6). Mass intellectuality then is the 'collective intelligence and accumulated intellectual powers that extend horizontally across society' (Virno and Hardt 1996: 262). This appears to point towards the general intellect in its liberated form, breaking free from or slipping past capital's 'apparatus of capture' (Deleuze and Guattari 2004). The university relies upon the cooperation of the common. The problematic of contemporary education struggles is to find ways to exceed this capture and cannibalization, in order to throw off this apparatus of capture and enclosure entirely, liberating the general intellect.

Taking this further and relating it back to struggles around HE discussed above, the University of Utopia (2010: np) states that it does not want 'mass education or education for the masses but mass intellectuality', continuing that:

> mass education is based on the assumption that people are stupid and must be made not-stupid (i.e. Educated). Mass intellectuality recognizes that education maintains the population in a condition of stupidity (i.e. Intelligence Quotient) regulated through examinations and other forms of humiliations (i.e. Grades and Assessments).

The University of Utopia (2010: np) suggests that, 'mass intellectuality is based on our common ability to do, based on our needs and capacities and what needs to be done'. What needs to be done

> raises doing from the level of the individual to the level of society. In the society of doing, based on what needs to be done, my own needs are subsumed with the needs of others and I become invisible (i.e. Free).
>
> *(University of Utopia 2010: np)*

This invocation of mass intellectuality can be seen to be the result of a process of social struggles to free the 'general intellect' of its containment by capital and, in this case, education.

For Franco Berardi, 'the birth of the student movement in the 1960s was the sign of the mutation of the social scenario out of which emerges this new figure of mass intellectuality' (Berardi 2009: 63). Beradi continues:

> no longer are intellectuals a class independent of production, or free individualities that take upon themselves the task of a purely ethical and freely cognitive choice; instead the intellectual becomes a mass social subject that tends to become an integral part of the general productive process.
>
> *(Berardi 2009: 63)*

This argument concurs with Dyer-Witherford and harks back to the discussion outlined above regarding the centrality of the academy in the struggle over the general intellect, because 'intellectuals no longer find the realm of political action to be outside of their daily practices; it now lies in the transversal connections between knowledge and social practices' (Berardi 2009: 66).

The current struggles around HE and universities across many parts of the world are therefore about more than simply a resurgence of cycles of student protest that have waxed and waned over the course of at least the mid to late twentieth century. Instead, they are symptomatic of a transformation in and increased centrality of the role of knowledge and intellectual production within society and the economy, and subsequently the role of intellectuals and knowledge production within social struggles. At the point at which the university is being incorporated further into capital's circuits, integrating students and academics into the general productive process, it is simultaneously relying on the communicative capacity, collaboration and cooperation of their labour power. However, it needs to control this while maintaining the porosity and freedom that facilitate this continued production for capital. The university relies upon the cooperation of the common. The problematic of contemporary education struggles is the need to find ways to exceed this capture and cannibalization in order to throw off this apparatus of capture and enclosure entirely, liberating the general intellect, perhaps utilizing what Neary and Hagyard (2010) term the 'pedagogy of excess', an 'overflowing' (Holloway 2002). As Jason

Read states: 'Wealth is no longer produced by bodies put to work in the closed spaces of the factory but by knowledge, communication, and interactions through-out society' (Read 2003: 104). As part of this process, capital also becomes more dependent on social forms of knowledge, cooperation and communication. Read elaborates:

> At the heart of the capitalist mode of production there are relations of cooperation, which are not only productive for capital but productive of the material possibility of relations that exceed those reinforced by the competitive market of labour and the hierarchy of the technological division of labour.
>
> *(Read 2003: 101)*

There are several ways the recent cycles of struggle around HE do this. First, through a refusal of the conditions being imposed on the existing neo-liberal university. The struggles outlined at the beginning of this chapter represent a 'scream' of refusal of these processes (Holloway 2002). Although notionally they are organized and mobilized around the specifics of their particular context, from localized cuts and restructuring of institutions through to national campaigns against fees and cuts, they are also part of a broader rejection of the HE status quo and, by implication given the analysis above, they become struggles over the alienation of their labour within cognitive capitalism, the capturing of their doing and the commodification of the creative and cooperative capacities. As Roggero states:

> We have to recognise that in cognitive capitalism we run into a situation in which the resistance to the expropriation of knowledge is immediately the struggle against the relations of exploitation because this resistance poses the question of the collective control of the (cognitive) production of the common against capitalist capture.
>
> *(Roggero 2010: 363)*

The second way these struggles do this is through the creation of alternatives. Many of these movements have either directly experimented with forms of alternative education (Pusey and Sealey-Huggins 2013) or contained pedagogical elements (Neary and Amsler 2012). These struggles, therefore, create 'pedagogies of resistance' (Thompsett 2017) and exist within a longer history of free university experiments (Amsler 2017; Kanngieser 2008). Struggles are involved in the production of common spaces (Pusey and Chatterton 2016) where it is possible to reimagine education and the university, 'and by extension the rest of our lives'.

For Hall (2017), 'the idea of an alternative questions the legitimacy of formalised spaces'. From inside and against the hegemonic institution, alter-natives articulate the limits of formal education, including its problematic nature as a public or private good. Here, the idea of the school or university as a form of enclosure of knowledge and practice is refused through public intellectualism or educational activity that is conducted in public.

Through critiquing and resisting the neo-liberalization of academia and acting within the 'double crisis' (Edu-Factory 2009) and creating examples of how academic labour, knowledge production and learning could take place in common, these movements point to an excess that could refuse the enclosure of these practices as subsumed within capital and recreate them as mass intellectuality, the general intellect unchained from the capital relation. This is counter the subsumption and valorization of academic labour that characterizes the contemporary university. Instead, this is a process of self-valorization (Negri 1991), the self-determining, self-organized autonomous activity of scholars and 'student-scholars' (Neary 2013).

Conclusion

This chapter has argued that the mobilizations, struggles and movements coalescing around universities and HE go beyond mere iterations of previous cycles of student struggle. Instead, this chapter suggests that these are struggles against the enclosure of the general intellect through cognitive capitalism and for mass intellectuality, the general intellect unchained from capital's capture. It has argued that the subsumption of the university and the valorization of academic labour have not only been met with resistance through this wave of struggles, but have also created experiments with alternatives. These experiments have involved the production of common spaces from which to reimagine education and the university in a non-commodified form. These self-valorizing practices point towards an excess – and overflowing – that critically interrogates and undermines formalized educational space and begins to develop new practices where it might be possible to engage in knowledge production learning and teaching in common.

Notes

1 This is not, however, an unproblematic or straightforward process, as this 'porosity' cannot only be exploited by 'dissident academics' in order to 'subvert' the academy from within, but can also be used to boost the cultural capital and profile of an academic in order to enhance their own career. Even if this is not explicitly the case, the university can attempt to co-opt these subversive spaces within the institution for its own ends, recapturing them as part of a 'rebellious' liberal image.
2 There is, however, a substantial difference between exceeding capital's total capture of the university in the form of teaching as a transgressive act and a rebellious labour force actively resisting the commodification of its labour power. Although it is certainly possible to use the university to teach 'freedom and defiance' or even the uncovering/or creation of marginalized 'minor knowledges', it remains to be seen whether these can be put to use in a struggle inside and against the university, so as to go beyond it.

References

After the Fall Communiqués. (2010) *After the Fall: Communiqués from Occupied California*, at: https://libcom.org/files/afterthefall_communiques.pdf (accessed 16 October 2018).

Amsler, S. (2017) '"Insane with Courage": Free University Experiments and the Struggle for Higher Education in Historical Perspective', *Learning & Teaching* 10(1): 5–23.

Amsler, S., and Motta, S. C. (2017) 'The Marketised University and the Politics of Motherhood', *Gender & Education* 1–18, early view.

Bailey, M., and Freedman, D. (eds) (2011) *The Assault on Universities*, London: Pluto.

Ball, S. J. (2004) *Education for Sale! The Commodification of Everything*, London: Department of Education and Professional Studies Annual Lecture, Institute of Education (June 2004).

BBC. (2010) 'NUS President Condemns the Violence during Tuition Protest', at: www.bbc.co.uk/news/av/uk-11728264/nus-president-condemns-the-violence-during-tuition-protest (accessed 31 May 2017).

Berardi, F. (2009) *Soul at Work*, Los Angeles: MIT Press.

Bonefeld, W. (1988) 'Class Struggle and the Permanence of Primitive Accumulation', *Common Sense* 6: 54–65.

Bousquet, M. (2008) *How the University Works*, New York: NYU Press.

Brophy, E. (2011) 'Translator's Foreword', in G. Roggero (ed.), *The Production of Living Knowledge*, Philadelphia, PA: Temple University Press.

Browne, J. (2010) *Securing a Sustainable Future for Higher Education: An Independent Review of Higher Education Funding and Student Finance*, at: www.gov.uk/government/publications/the-browne-report-higher-education-funding-and-student-finance (accessed 31 May 2017).

Chaudhuri, A. (2016) 'The Real Meaning of Rhodes Must Fall', *The Guardian*, at: www.theguardian.com/uk-news/2016/mar/16/the-real-meaning-of-rhodes-must-fall (accessed 31 May 2017).

Clare, N., and Habermehl, V. (2016) 'Towards a Theory of "Commonization"', in M. L. De Souza, R. J. White and S. Springer (eds), *Theories of Resistance: Anarchism, Geography, and the Spirit of Revolt*, London: Rowman & Littlefield.

De Angelis, M. (2007) *The Beginning of History*, London: Pluto Press.

De Angelis, M., and Harvie, D. (2009) '"Cognitive Capitalism" and the Rat-race: How Capital Measures Immaterial Labour in British Universities', *Historical Materialism* 17(3): 3–30.

Deleuze, G., and Guattari, F. (2004) *A Thousand Plateaus*, London: Continuum.

Dyer-Witheford, N. (1999) *Cyber-Marx*, Urbana, IL: University of Illinois Press.

Dyer-Witheford, N. (2005) 'Cognitive Capitalism and the Contested Campus', in G. Cox and J. Krysa (eds), *Engineering Culture*, Brooklyn: Autonomedia.

Edu-Factory Collective. (2009) *Toward a Global Autonomous University*, Brooklyn: Autonomedia.

Federici, S. (2014) 'From Commoning to Debt: Financialization, Microcredit, and the Changing Architecture of Capital Accumulation', *South Atlantic Quarterly* 113(2): 231–244.

Federici, S., and Caffentzis, G. (2007) 'Notes on the Edu-factory and Cognitive Capitalism', *The Commoner* 12: 63–70.

Fox, T. (2011) 'Hundreds of Students Chase Aaron Porter through Manchester', at: http://manchestermule.com/article/hundreds-of-students-chase-aaron-porter-through-manchester (accessed 31 May 2017).

Giroux, H. A. (2014) *Neoliberalism's War on Higher Education*, Chicago, IL: Haymarket Books.

Hall, R. (2011) 'Occupation: A Place to Deliberate the Socio-History of Re-Production', *Roundhouse Journal: Reimagining the University* 2: 54–63.

Hall, R. (2017) 'Alternative Education', at: www.richard-hall.org/2017/06/02/notes-for-alternative-education/ (accessed 9 June 2017).

Hall, R., and Stahl, B. (2015) 'Against Commodification: The University, Cognitive Capitalism and Emergent Technologies', in C. Fuchs and V. Mosco (eds), *Marx and the Political Economy of the Media*, Leiden: Brill.

Halvorsen, S. (2012) 'Beyond the Network? Occupy London and the Global Movement', *Social Movement Studies* 11(3–4): 427–433.

Hancox, D. (2011) *Summer of Unrest*, London: Random House.

Harvie, D. (2000) 'Alienation, Class and Enclosure in UK Universities', *Capital & Class* 24(2): 103–132.

Holloway, J. (2002) *Change the World Without Taking Power*, London: Pluto Press.

Holloway, J. (2010) *Crack Capitalism*, London: Pluto Press.

Ibrahim, J. (2011) 'The New Toll on Higher Education and the UK Student Revolts of 2010–2011', *Social Movement Studies* 10(4): 415–421.

Kanngieser, A. (2008) 'It's Our Academy: Transforming Education Through Self-organized Universities', *Arena Journal* 29/30: 25–34.

Lazzarato, M. (1996) 'Immaterial Labor', in P. Virno and M. Hardt (eds), *Radical Thought in Italy*, Minneapolis, MN: Minnesota Press.

Levenson, Z. (2011) 'Occupying Education: The Student Fight Against Austerity in California', *NACLA Report on the Americas* 44(6): 25–28.

Lunghi, A., and Wheeler, S. (eds) (2012) *Occupy Everything!: Reflections on Why It's Kicking Off Everywhere*, New York: Minor Compositions.

McGettigan, A. (2013) *The Great University Gamble: Money, Markets and the Future of Higher Education*, London: Pluto.

Marx, K. (1993) *Grundrisse*, London: Penguin.

Mason, P. (2013) *Why It's Still Kicking Off Everywhere*, London: Verso Books.

Merrifield, A. (2010) 'The Coming of The Coming Insurrection: Notes on a Politics of Neocommunism', *Environment & Planning D: Society &and Space* 28(2): 202–216.

Midnight Notes. (1990) 'The New Enclosures', *Midnight Notes* 10: 1–9.

NCAFC. (2010) 'List of University Occupations', at: http://anticuts.com/2010/11/27/list-of-university-occupations (accessed 9 June 2017).

Neary, M. (2013) 'Occupying the City with the Social Science Centre – An Interview with Mike Neary', at: http://undercommoning.org/occupying-the-city/ (accessed 9 June 2017).

Neary, M., and Amsler, S. (2012) 'Occupy: A New Pedagogy of Space and Time', *Journal for Critical Education Policy Studies* 10(2): 106–138.

Neary, M., and Hagyard, A. (2010) 'Pedagogy of Excess: An Alternative Political Economy of Student Life', in M. Molesworth, R. Scullion and E. Nixon (eds), *The Marketisation of Higher Education and the Student as Consumer*, London: Routledge.

Negri, A. (1988) *Revolution Retrieved: Selected Writings on Marx, Keynes, Capitalist Crisis and New Social Subjects, 1967–83*. Trans. Ed Emery and John Merrington, London: Red Notes.

Negri, A. (1991) *Marx Beyond Marx*, New York: Autonomedia.

Newfield, C. (2008) *Unmaking the Public University*, Cambridge, MA: Harvard University Press.

Newsinger, J. (2016) 'Why Rhodes Must Fall', *Race & Class* 58(2): 70–78.

Nişancıoğlu, K., and Pal, M. (2016) 'Counter-conduct in the University Factory: Locating the Occupy Sussex Campaign', *Global Society* 30(2): 279–300.

Noterman, E., and Pusey, A. (2012) 'Inside, Outside, and on the Edge of the Academy: Experiments in Radical Pedagogies', in R. Haworth (ed.), *Anarchist Pedagogies*, Oakland: PM Press.

Noys, B. (ed.) (2011). *Communization and its Discontents*, New York: Minor Compositions.

Pasquinelli, M. (2010) 'Communism of Capital and Cannibalism of the Common: Notes on the Art of Over-Identification' *Abandon Normal Devices Festival*, Manchester, 1–7 October, at: https://kruzok.files.wordpress.com/2011/05/pasquinelli_communism_of_capital1.pdf (accessed 31 May 2017).

Penny, L. (2010) 'Out with the Old Politics', at: www.theguardian.com/commentisfree/2010/dec/24/student-protests-young-politics-voices (accessed 31 May 2017).

Pickerill, J., and Krinsky, J. (2012) 'Why Does Occupy Matter?', *Social Movement Studies* 11(3–4): 279–287.

Pusey, A. (2016) 'Strike, Occupy, Transform! Students, Subjectivity and Struggle', *Journal of Marketing for Higher Education* 26(2): 214–232.

Pusey, A., and Chatterton, P. (2016) 'Commons', in M. Jayne and K. Ward (eds), *Urban Theory*, London: Routledge.

Pusey, A., and Sealey-Huggins, L. (2013) 'Transforming the University: Beyond Students and Cuts', *ACME: An International Journal for Critical Geographies* 12(3): 443–458.

Radice, H. (2013) 'How We Got Here: UK Higher Education Under Neoliberalism', *ACME: An International E-Journal for Critical Geographies* 12(2): 407–418.

Read, J. (2003) *The Micro-politics of Capital*, New York: SUNY Press.

Readings, B. (1996) *The University in Ruins*, Cambridge, MA.: Harvard University Press.

Robertson, M. (2010) 'Aaron Porter Is No Longer Fit to Lead the Student Movement', at: www.theguardian.com/commentisfree/2011/jan/11/nus-porter-failed-student-protestors (accessed 31 May 2017).

Roggero, G. (2010) 'Five Theses on the Common', *Rethinking Marxism* 22(3): 357–373.

Roggero, G. (2011) *The Production of Living Knowledge*, Philadelphia, PA: Temple University Press.

Salter, L., and Kay, J. B. (2011) 'The UWE Student Occupation', *Social Movement Studies* 10(4): 423–429.

Sealey-Huggins, L., and Pusey, A. (2013) 'Neoliberalism and Depoliticisation in the Academy: Understanding the "New Student Rebellions"', *Graduate Journal of Social Science* 10(3): 80–99.

Solomon, C., and Palmieri, T. (2011) *Springtime: The New Student Rebellions*, London: Verso.

Spiegel, J. B. (2015a) 'Rêve Général Illimité? The Role of Creative Protest in Transforming the Dynamics of Space and Time during the 2012 Quebec Student Strike', *Antipode* 47 (3): 770–791.

Spiegel, J. B. (2015b) 'Masked Protest in the Age of Austerity: State Violence, Anonymous Bodies, and Resistance "In the Red"', *Critical Inquiry* 41(4): 786–810.

Spiegel, J. B. (2016) 'Performing "In the Red": Transformations and Tensions in Repertoires of Contention during the 2012 Quebec Student Strike', *Social Movement Studies* 15(5): 531–538.

Thompsett, F. (2017) 'Pedagogies of Resistance: Free Universities and the Radical Re-imagination of Study', *Learning & Teaching* 10(1): 24–41.

Tilly, C. (2008) *Contentious Performances*, Cambridge: Cambridge University Press.

UCLU. (2013) 'Cops off Our Campus', at: http://uclu.org/policy/up1302/cops-off-our-campus (accessed 9 June 2017).

University of Utopia. (2010) 'Sharing', at: www.universityofutopia.org/sharing (accessed 13 May 2017).

Van Gelder, S. (2011) *This Changes Everything: Occupy Wall Street and the 99% Movement*, San Francisco: Berrett-Koehler.

Vercellone, C. (2007) 'From Formal Subsumption to General Intellect: Elements for a Marxist Reading of the Thesis of Cognitive Capitalism', *Historical Materialism* 15(1): 13–36.

Virno, P. (2004) *A Grammar of the Multitude*, Los Angeles: Semiotext(e).

Virno, P. (2007) 'General Intellect', *Historical Materialism* 15(3): 3–8.

Virno, P., and Hardt, M. (1996) 'Glossary', in P. Virno and M. Hardt (eds), *Radical Thought in Italy*, Minneapolis, MN: Minnesota Press.

Younis, M. (2011) 'British Tuition Fee Protest, November 9, 2010, London', *Interface: A Journal for and about Social Movements* 3(1): 172–181.

Zamponi, L. (2012) 'Why Don't Italians Occupy? Hypotheses on a Failed Mobilisation', *Social Movement Studies* 11(3–4): 416–426.

PART II

The state and social movements

5

PEASANT REVOLTS AND POLITICAL CHANGE IN SAINT LUCIA

The rise and fall of peasant movements, 1952–1957 and 1992–1997

Tennyson S. D. Joseph

Introduction

In the strict application of Marxist political theory and political economy, small peripheral states, arising out of the underdevelopment of their productive forces, suffer from a corresponding underdevelopment of their anti-systemic movements. This theme of peripheral underdevelopment and the related handicapped character of the revolutionary forces in such conditions has often resulted in the intellectual neglect of the experiences of the left and radical movements in the so-called peripheral countries. However, despite their 'peripheral' status, the experiences of anti-systemic movements outside the dominant economic centres can provide important insights into the state of global radical politics. This is so because the level of development of the 'periphery' is by and large a consequence and reflection of the state of development of the capitalist centre, to which the hinterland is linked by the structural economic relations.

The argument being presented here is that the social relations, modes of production and the general 'level of development' not only of the productive forces but also of the radical movements on the periphery cannot be understood outside their connection to the social and economic character of the capitalist centre. To understand the state of radical and left-wing movements on the periphery, therefore, is to understand the state of radical movements globally, particularly as the under-developed nature of the so-called periphery is the result of the periphery's historical remaking in the image of, and its connection to, the core. As argued by Amilcar Cabral (1969), it is this historical reconnection to the economic needs of the metropole that results in the destruction of the natural and organic development of the productive forces of the periphery and puts the colony 'out of history'. Indeed, it is his explanation of the manner in which the politics of the periphery is tied to the politics of the core, which is one of the signal contributions of Immanuel Wallerstein's world-systems theory to under-standing the politics of the so-called under-developed regions of the globe (Wallerstein 1974).

It is on this basis, therefore, that this chapter presents the experience of peasant movements in the small, semi-agrarian independent Caribbean state of Saint Lucia, as part of the global story of left-wing and radical move-ments that have emerged to respond to exploitative social and economic relations in specific localities. The experience of peasant struggles in Saint Lucia is conceptually interesting for several reasons, and knowledge of that experience can assist in the advance of knowledge on global radical movements.

First, the study of the role of anti-systemic revolts among agricultural work-ers in facilitating political change presents possibilities for comparative analysis against urban-based radical politics, in other political formations. Further, the study of peasant revolts in a predominantly agro-based economy contributes to the theoretical debates about the applicability of Marxist notions of the centrality of proletarian activity as the critical factor in social change to countries where the peasantry has had a significantly large impact on political change. Another conceptual question thrown up by the Saint Lucian and wider Caribbean experience is the extent to which such peasant-based radical politics continues to remain viable, given the shift towards tourism and services and the collapse of the sugar, banana and other agro-based economies in the mid 1990s, given the region's new mode of insertion into the global political economy.

Finally, this chapter deliberately highlights the link between peasant revolt and political change as a normative perspective countering currently dominant views that suggest the futility of anti-systemic revolt. One of the consequences of the retreat of Marxist social science that emphasises the causal linkages between socio-economic change and political activity of the underclass is the tendency among academic theoreticians (as distinct from activists) to downplay or ignore the efficacy of the politics of revolt. With the postmodern turn, the emphasis now is on individual agency and a general suspicion of any structur-alist perspective. One of the enduring features of Marxist social science is the methodology that it offers for the study of social change. By focussing on breaks in continuity and qualitative transformations of the underlying productive base, Marxist methodology best explains how a social formation moves from one distinct political economy to the next. Although other perspectives, such as structural functionalism, may be useful in studying 'normal change' or non-antagonistic contradictions, only the Marxist method allows for the study of qualitative transformation, or deep shifts in the underlying political economy. The experience of peasant revolts in Saint Lucia suggests strongly that there is clear link between significant advances in political development and specific revolts among the peasantry, thus validating the utility of Marxist theories of social change.

One of the critical features of the Saint Lucian case is that many of the strikes that occur, particularly in the early period, are fought directly over the wages of sugar workers. In the final days of the sugar industry, these wage strikes and negotiations determined the success or failure of the industry, confirming the utility of Marx's labour theory of value as a basis for understanding social change. This study of peasant revolts in Saint Lucia is, therefore, undertaken utilising Marxist theory of political change to normatively argue against notions of the irrelevance of Marxism at the theoretical level and the futility of popular struggles at a practical level.

It is within these normative and conceptual frameworks that this chapter is situated. It examines the relationship between peasant struggles and political change in Saint Lucia in two historical periods – the periods 1952–1957 and 1992–1997. These two identified periods are chosen for several reasons. First, they represent the beginning and end of the dominance of the banana industry, an industry that had the most influential effect on the political life of Saint Lucia in the twentieth century, and as such they fit into the category of moments of qualitative transformation of the political economy. Second, the identified protests come forty years apart, and, as such, an opportunity is presented for historical comparative assessment of the changing impact of the peasantry on the politics of the country. Third, the two episodes are useful as they allow for the tracing of the political changes that have taken place in the political economy of Saint Lucia over time, particularly in relation to Saint Lucia's location in the global political economy.

The chapter therefore seeks to show conclusively the role of peasant struggles in ushering in, and destroying, qualitative transformations in the dominant productive base and, by extension, the general political economy of Saint Lucia. It therefore has three main tasks. It will first clarify the specific application of the term 'peasant' to the context of Saint Lucia. Following this, the chapter will present the historical account of the two identified instances of peasant revolt, first the events of 1952–1957 and later those of 1992–1997, showing the corresponding political outcomes that emerge out of each period of protest. Finally, the chapter turns its gaze towards the present and closes with the conclusion that the revolts of 1992–1997 might have signalled the end of the politics of agrarian revolt in Saint Lucia, as a result of a new mode of participation in the global economy with the shift towards tourism and financial services.

A Caribbean peasantry?

Given the unique historical contexts in which Caribbean small agricultural producers have emerged, it is necessary to clarify the specific usage of the socio-economic group referred to as 'peasants' in this chapter. This uniqueness of the West Indian peasantry is captured in a description by Saint Lucian Nobel Prize-winning economist W. Arthur Lewis, who observes that:

The history of the peasantry in the British West Indies differs essentially from the history of the peasantry in almost every part of the world. In tracing the evolution of agricultural tenures in Europe or Asia in modern times, the student begins invariably with a peasant possessing rights, however circumvented, to the land, and follows either the process by which the peasant liquidated his lord, as in France, or the process by which the lord expropriated the peasant, as in England. But modern West Indian history begins without a peasantry, and is of particular interest because in tracing it, we trace the birth and development of an entirely new class which has profoundly affected the foundations of West Indian society.

(Lewis 1936: 1)

Given its uniqueness, one writer, Frucht (1967), has used the notion of 'neither Peasant nor Proletarian' to highlight the fluidity of the productive bases and social relations of Caribbean agrarian rural producers. He argues that:

the situation may be comprehended by making use of Marx's analytic distinction between the means of production, that is, the tools and techniques, and relations of production, that is, what we usually mean by the social division of labour as well as the articulation of the productive economy and the social organization, including property and power relations.

(Frucht 1967: 295)

According to Frucht (1967: 295–296), the fluid nature of the category arises out of the fact that feudal and capitalist means and relations of production exist and impact simultaneously on the agrarian producer.

On grounds similar to those established by Frucht, therefore, Lewis claims that, in the Caribbean context,

the term 'peasant' covers a variety of tenures ... The peasant may hold his land leasehold, rather than freehold. He may occasionally hire himself out to neighbouring plantations when work is slack on his own holding, or, similarly, may hire labour occasionally to help him with particular operations. And he may combine other activities, such as shop keeping with the cultivation of his land ... [I]t is sufficient to define a peasant as a man who devotes the major part of his time to cultivate land on his own account, with the help of little or no outside labour.

(Lewis 1936: 2–3)

These interventions by Lewis and Frucht, however, ignore the segment of the landless 'rural proletariat' who were also integrally involved in the struggles of the two periods identified in this chapter. In this regard, the insistence by Sidney

Mintz (1979: 194) that 'peasant communities ... may include in their membership some or many persons who are landless and even wage-earning; but their
proletarian status is cloaked by the many relationships they have with the
landed' completes the understanding of the category of 'peasantry' utilised in
this work.

What is significant here is the fact that Saint Lucia's insertion into the global
economy as a monocrop producer, first of sugar cane and later bananas, placed
the peasantry at the vanguard of political struggles in the late twentieth century.
Peter Adrian (1996), in his work *Metayage, Capitalism and Peasant Development*, argues that, 'the dominant form of production in any specific historical
period is the vehicle for social and structural change in any society'. On the
basis of this observation he describes the Saint Lucian social arrangement of
sharecropping, '*metayage* as a significant force in social change in general, and
in rural development in particular' (1996: 1). Similarly, Sidney Mintz asserts
that 'Caribbean peasantries represent a mode of response to the plantation
system and its connotations, and a mode of resistance to imposed styles of
life' (in Barrow 1992: 9). Like Mintz and Adrien, it is argued here that the
specific location of the Saint Lucian peasantry in the context of the country's
insertion into the global economy as a primary producer of export agricultural
goods as its main economic activity made the peasantry an objectively powerful
political force (see Louis 1982). The task now is to examine the role of the
peasantry in two identified periods, to assess their impact on political change in
Saint Lucia.

Peasant revolts and political change – 1952–1957 and 1992–1997

The protests of 1952–1957 and their political effects

Between 1952 and 1957, Saint Lucia experienced two major upheavals in the
rural agricultural sector that were to have profound effects on political developments. The first was the 'Brown Strike' of 1952, named after W.G. Brown, a
newly elected independent member of the Saint Lucia legislative council who
led a strike of sugar workers in the Roseau Valley for pay increases. The official
colonial reports on the strike reduce the cause of the strike to competition
between the two main trade unions existing at the time, the first, the Roseau
Peasants and Workers Union led by Brown and the other, the more established
Saint Lucia Cooperative Workers Union (SLCWU), the trade union arm of the
Saint Lucia Labour Party (SLP), led by key figures such as George Charles,
Oleo Jn Baptiste and Carl La Corbiniere.

A Colonial Office security report explains the origin of the 1952 strike in the
following way:

> Strike at Roseau was certainly organised by Brown, who has been telling
> workers ever since [the 1951] election that he can get them $2 a day with

corresponding increase for women. Apparently workers believed him, or decided to give him a trial, notwithstanding the fact that the Cooperative Workers Union have negotiated their wage for the past six years and concluded, in February, a very satisfactory agreement ... Cul-de-sac workers[1] appear to have followed suit on their own account without intimidation. Brown's reasons for failing to take part in the wage negotiations, of which he was aware, are obscure, and the strength and organisation of his recently registered union are unknown. He himself remains elusive, vexatious and irresponsible as ever.

(Public Records Office – Colonial Office Reports 1952a)

Despite the Colonial Office's blaming the strike exclusively on the personality and personal political ambitions of Brown, a more thorough examination suggests wider causes. The 1952 sugar strike can best be understood in the context of the decline of the Saint Lucia sugar industry occurring simultaneously with a moment of constitutional and political transition towards self-government. In short, deep economic and political changes were manifesting themselves in heightened militancy and politicisation among the peasantry.

It is instructive that the strike took place in 1952, one year after the attainment of universal adult suffrage. Prior to this, the only room for political participation by workers' representatives was in 'city council' elections and, more importantly, in the form of labour representation via the trade union movement. The Saint Lucia Cooperative Workers Union was therefore formed in 1945 as the vehicle through which both the economic and political aspirations of the working people were pursued (see Charles 1994). Once formed, the SLCWU found its principal membership among the peasantry.

When the 1952 sugar strikes occurred, Saint Lucia was in the early stages of experiencing the politics of popular participation. The early political leaders were trade unionists organising largely among agricultural workers, and the targets of their political activity were the owners of the three remaining operational sugar factories, one in Dennery owned by Denis Barnard, and the other two in the Roseau and Cul-de-Sac valleys, owned principally by Harold Devaux (Jackson Commission Report 1957: 3). In the context of the economic decline of sugar production, the maintenance of low wages became the principal concern of the sugar proprietors and the defining issue motivating their politics. They perceived every instance of labour mobilisation as a threat to their continued existence, and their survival needs placed them in natural opposition to the trade union movement.

A similarly supportive stance on the continuation of the sugar economy was shared by the British Colonial Office, and this defined its stance on the process of constitutional decolonisation. The production of sugar for export was the country's main economic activity, and, in the midst of British considerations for constitutional change, notions of 'economic viability' became the central argument dictating the pace of constitutional change. In 1951, 'sugar represented

47 per cent of the total value of exports, and had the largest single impact on the utilisation of the labour force' (Acosta and Casimir 1985: 45). There was, therefore, a clear link between the continuation of the sugar industry, the control of labour and the pace of constitutional change. Thus, deeply intermeshed with this question of 'economic viability' was the insistence of the British government on a 'demonstration of political responsibility' by the labour leaders as a criterion for further constitutional advances. The eruption of the 1952 strikes, therefore, intervened in this intellectual, political and economic climate and began the process of creating new conditions that forced the Colonial Office to introduce legislative changes and pushed the old sugar interests to reconsider their continuation in the industry.

Despite the Colonial Office's blaming of the 1952 upheavals on the opportunism of the 'maverick' W.G. Brown, 'who has set up himself as a martyr who is being persecuted by Government and has threatened strikes and commotions if he is unseated', the strike could be attributed to more than the recklessness of Brown. Of significance is the fact that the main trade union, the SLCWU, joined the strike in support of Brown, a development that the colonial office explained as the SLP's wish to 'keep the peace with the constituents of Brown's district so that if he is unseated their candidate may be persona grata'. Similarly, the report noted as 'significant' the fact that 'A.M. Lewis, President of the Labour Party is defending Brown' (Public Records Office – Colonial Office Reports 1952a).[2]

It is clear that the colonial authorities were very concerned about the potential for political mischief to be caused by W.G. Brown. An intelligence report of 26 January 1954 described Brown as a 'genuine communist and out to make all the trouble he can on the usual lines', and as being 'a grave menace to the security of Saint Lucia' (Public Records Office – Colonial Office Reports 1954). More chillingly, the report hinted at the eventual deportation of Brown to his native Bermuda on the basis of being an undeclared bankrupt 'owing Barclays Bank about £30,000 which the bank could not recover from him because the loan was outside the terms of their charter' (Public Records Office – Colonial Office Reports 1954).

The report of the Malone Commission, which was established to investigate the causes of the 1952 strike, suggests clearly that the commissioners were sympathetic to the deteriorating circumstances of the sugar interests. The report rejected the view that the sugar estates were offering the workers substandard wages or that pay increases were warranted. The commissioners held that:

> any idea that the willing and able-bodied cane-cutter or header of canes employed at Roseau and Cul-de-Sac is existing on a breadline wage, or that the work is unduly heavy or the discipline onerous is quite incorrect ... The evidence went to show that able-bodied adults working for the Roseau and Cul-de-sac companies could earn wages in the sugar industry which were not unreasonable, and that they had ample leisure time at their disposal.
>
> *(Malone Commission Report 1952: 11)*

Much of this claim was based on the semi-autonomous economic relationship of the peasantry with the plantation sector. This was taken by the Malone Commission as evidence of their estate labour as being 'additional income' to supplement their livelihoods as share croppers (*metayers*) or independent producers. The semi-autonomy of the peasants was seen as a disadvantage to the sugar companies, as the peasant farmers 'seem to make very little effort to increase the tonnage per acre' (Malone Commission Report 1952: 13). The reduced output to the sugar factories was blamed on the competing poles of employment in the commercial and urban sectors, a reflection of the shifting nature of the country's mode of insertion into the global economy. Thus, the Malone report observed that the Saint Lucian was 'becoming more and more disinclined to cultivate his own garden plot ... [F]irst coaling, then the American forces "invasion"; then the Castries reconstruction offered inducements difficult to resist' (Malone Commission Report 1952: 14).[3]

The official reports on the Brown strike clearly treated the strike as a largely industrial matter. As a result of the uncertainties over wage rates, one of the outcomes of the strike was the decision to create a wages council to determine the rates for the various tasks involved in sugar production. This was intended to undermine the trade union, as the Malone Commission ruled that it 'could not conscientiously recommend that full negotiating authority be given to a trade union whose membership does not represent a substantial proportion of the workers engaged in the industry'. The main reason for insisting on the wages council, therefore, was the Commission's belief that it was:

> almost a certainty that if the position which has obtained in the past is allowed to continue there will be other competing ambitious aspirants springing up on irresponsible bases and bringing about situations where sound trade unionism and healthy industrial relations will become impossible
>
> *(Jackson Commission Report 1957: 5)*

One of the main economic consequences of the 1952 strike was that it signalled the decline of the traditional sugar plantocracy in Saint Lucia. Thus, following the 1952 strike, according to a later report:

> the owners of two of the private companies gave notice to the Administrator of Saint Lucia of their decision to go into voluntary liquidation; this was crystallised and in October 1953 a public limited liability company was formed under the name of Sugar Manufacturers Limited [to acquire the assets of the liquidated companies].
>
> *(Jackson Commission Report 1957: 3)*

Meanwhile, the Dennery Factory Company, owned by Denis Barnard, continued under private ownership (Jackson Commission Report 1957: 4). The new company was incorporated 'with a nominal capital of $2,000,000 of which $500,000 compromised 6 per cent Cumulative Preference Shares and $1,500,000 Ordinary shares' (Jackson Commission Report 1957: 3). With the formation of Sugar Manufacturers Limited, therefore, in addition to the colonial government of Saint Lucia loaning the company $900,000, the government also acquired 250,000 of the available shares (Jackson Commission Report 1957: 4). The 1952 strike, therefore, had a clear impact on ownership and the class structure, particularly in the country's main industry, and thus signalled important shifts in the underlying political economy and class relations of the society.

An important economic consequence of the strike was that it initiated the process of the termination of sugar production in Saint Lucia. Principal among the reasons for the decision by the private sugar owners to go into voluntary liquidation was the uncertainty of profits due to the erratic nature of labour demands. Thus, in their submissions to the Malone Commission, the factory owners consistently highlighted the fact that profits could only be determined by the price of labour, and, as the growing militancy of the trade union movement introduced an unknown variable into the equation, the owners expressed their unwillingness to work under such conditions. As will be seen later, it was around this time that alternatives to sugar, namely bananas, were being explored, and this shift was to have a profound impact on the political economy of Saint Lucia.

One important political consequence of the 1952 strike was the consolidation of the left-wing SLP as the dominant political force in Saint Lucia. Despite the attempt by the Malone Commission to discredit the SLCWU and the political leaders of the SLP, the 1952 strike established the SLP as the main mass-based political organisation in the country. Having won convincingly the first elections under universal suffrage in 1951, the eventual expulsion and later deportation of W.G. Brown removed the only organised political force capable of undermining its base among the workers and peasants, from both an industrial relations and electoral perspective. Between 1952 and 1957, therefore, the SLP was the main beneficiary of the British government's concessions towards constitutional change. Thus, it was the SLP that benefitted from the 'committee system' in 1955 in which three elected members were allowed supervisory roles within specific departments in the civil service, minus executive decision-making power. Similarly, and most importantly, it was the SLP members who were the beneficiaries of the 'full ministerial system' in 1956, under which a select number of elected members were allowed to sit in the executive council as 'ministers' (see Joseph 2011a: 28).

It is against such a context of the 'settlements' associated with the 1952 strike that the five-week strike in the sugar industry was to erupt between 25 March and 29 April 1957. Whereas the 1952 strike was attributed to Brown, the 1957 strikes were deliberately and consciously organised by the SLCWU in response to the refusal of Sugar Manufacturers Ltd to recognise the union 'as the sole body for negotiating terms and conditions of employment for the sugar workers' (Jackson Commission Report 1957: 7–8). This request from the union was in keeping with its rejection of the wages council as the mechanism through which wage negotiations would be settled, preferring the collective bargaining mechanism instead. When, however, the union acceded to requests to nominate two representatives to the wages council, the hostility of the employer group to trade unionism became very evident in its obstinate claim that the union 'did not qualify for such representation' (Jackson Commission Report 1957: 9). The 1957 strike was, therefore, rooted in a trial of strength between the labour union and employers, a contest that was rooted in the employer's belief that any concessions to labour unionism would result in its economic ruin.

Thus, when on 25 March 1957 there was an abrupt stoppage of work on the Roseau Plantation, and when labour union officials appeared on the scene in full support of the strike, these developments were in keeping with the long-standing tensions between the SLCWU and the sugar owners. By 28 March, with the stoppage of work at the Dennery sugar factory, production on the island had come to a complete stop, with police reinforcements from the nearby Windward Islands being engaged to assist with keeping the peace (Jackson Commission Report 1957: 12). These developments signalled the plunging of the country into a new crisis associated with the struggles for wages in the sugar industry. During the strike:

> scores of persons were taken to court between 3 and 26 April 1957 and charged with offences ranging from the use of offensive weapons to disorderly behaviour and intimidation. Many were fined between $40 and $50 and received jail sentences of between three and six months.
>
> *(Joseph 2011a: 17; see also Public Records Office –*
> *Colonial Office Reports 1952b)*

An important political development during the strike was the emergence of John Compton[4] as a leading member of the SLP. At the time of the strike, Compton was the president of the eastern branch of the SLCWU, a member of the legislative council and the minister of trade under the ministerial system. He proved to be a key militant personality, organising several roadblocks, and was in the front lines of the strike action. He too was arrested and charged for obstructing a truck belonging to Grace Augustin, the first female legislator in Saint Lucia, who at the time had been a leading agriculturist, an appointed member of the legislative council and a conservative defender of colonialism (see Joseph 2011b).

In political terms, the 1957 strike completed the processes of social and economic change that had been set in train by the events of 1952. A report in *The Voice of St. Lucia* (Sunday 26 May 1957: 2) estimated that the government of Saint Lucia needed 'a total of $120, 950 to offset the estimated drop in revenue as a result of the recent strike'. Most significantly, the final shock of the 1957 strike brought to an end the old political economy of sugar, as, following from their earlier anxieties of 1952, it broke the resolve of the planters who had remained in sugar. Following the strike, the traditional private sugar manufacturers sold their remaining shares in Sugar Manufacturers Ltd, leaving the government as the sole owner. Despite the later attempts by George Charles, the first chief minister of Saint Lucia, to salvage the sugar industry, the period following the 1957 strike witnessed the rapid shift of Saint Lucia out of sugar into bananas.

An interesting development in this regard was the emerging conflict between George Charles and John Compton over the future direction of the economy of Saint Lucia. Whereas Charles's economic approach continued to revolve around the continuation and strengthening of the sugar industry, Compton was among the earliest SLP politicians who consciously and deliberately pursued the possibilities of the banana industry as an alternative to sugar. A Colonial Office report provides an interesting account of a secret meeting in London between John Compton and Van Geest, the future banana magnate who would dominate the economic life of the West Indies, which reveals clear intent on the part of Compton to support Geest in facilitating the establishment of the banana industry in Saint Lucia (see Public Records Office – Colonial Office Reports 1960).

This shift to banana production was undoubtedly the most important outcome of the 1952–1957 strikes. By 1960, banana production for export had become the dominant economic activity in Saint Lucia. The banana economy radically overturned the social relations of the old sugar economy. With bananas, the former plantation-dependent cane producers were now transformed into independent suppliers of an export crop directly to a global company. Acosta and Casimir (1985: 43) cite a 1970s report that indicates that, 'farms less than 10 acres were responsible for at least 56% of the banana crop'.

An important feature of the structure of the banana industry was the formation of a Banana Growers Association in which small, medium and large producers could directly elect directors who would, among other things, negotiate prices with Geest, act as the representative body liaising with government and serve as a cooperative in respect to the sourcing of subsidised inputs and other benefits. In a direct sense, therefore, the development of the banana industry had given rise to a 'new class', and, although still rooted in peasant social relations, these relations were now constructed upon new global trade arrangements and new domestic production relations, qualitatively different from those of the sugar economy.

Under the new arrangements, the political relations of banana production were mediated through the Saint Lucia Banana Growers Association (SLBGA). Although the decisions and make-up of the SLBGA were heavily skewed towards the power of the larger growers – and it would be the place through which the United Workers Party (UWP) government of John Compton, who had later broken from the SLP, would manage his support among banana producers – one of its important positive features was its empowerment of the previous cane producers as 'shareholders' of the association. Acosta and Casimir provide the following summary of its early history and structure, highlighting the manner in which it facilitated the empowerment of the banana producers:

> [I]n 1967, the House of Assembly of St. Lucia (under the St. Lucia Corporation Act) re-established the Association as a Statuary Corporation on which the powers were conferred for the marketing of bananas. This act ensured government participation in the policies formulated by the merchants to whom large growers gave a supervisory role over to the Board's finances, as well as making provision for accountability.
>
> *(Acosta and Casimir 1985: 49)*

Indicating that 'government's participation did not lessen the level of disenchantment and dissatisfaction expressed by the majority of the growers and related population', they report the membership in the Association in 1967 as 17,000, but in 1977–1978, a membership of less than 6,400 was counted, with the growers divided into four categories: 'grower', 'small grower', 'medium grower' and 'large grower' (Acosta and Casimir 1985: 49).

A new social class, 'the banana farmer', had therefore been born. In material terms, the impact of the influx of banana revenues could be visibly seen in the improvement in the living conditions of the banana producing regions and the country as a whole (Williams and Darius 1998). Although the banana industry would result in several negatives, such as environmental degradation and social factors such as the loss of educational opportunities for banana children due to their prioritisation of farming over schooling, there is little doubt that the domestic politics of Saint Lucia, by the early 1960s, had become a direct reflection of the mode of production and social relations of the banana economy.

The banana economy radically transformed the framework that had facilitated the earlier political domination of the SLP. Coincident with the rise of bananas, in 1964, a new political party, the UWP, led by John Compton, won the general election. Much of the political base of the SLP had been constructed upon its trade union activities among the peasant groups, in the context of their proletarian-type relations with sugar plantation owners. Following the shift to bananas, and with erstwhile cane farmers, headers and weighmen transformed into independent banana producers, the power base of the SLP was effectively eroded. The 1964 electoral victory of the UWP set the framework for much of the remaining pre- and post-independence (1979) period of Saint Lucia.

Between 1964 and 1997, Compton's UWP completely dominated the politics of Saint Lucia, winning every election except that of 1979, when a resurgent left-wing SLP defeated the UWP, only to collapse in 1982 owing to an internal split. Much of this political domination was constructed upon the specific local and global arrangements of the banana industry. The reality of special preferences in the UK market was the global dimension of the economic infrastructure of the banana arrangements. Within this infrastructure was carved a space for Geest industries as the sole buyer of West Indian fruit, as the price setter and as the provider of a secure market. At the local level, the SLBGA facilitated the organisation of all producers, which guaranteed Geest its supply, as well as serving as the UWP's political power base.

The link between bananas and the political hegemony of John Compton has best been captured by George Odlum, who argued that:

> The industry and politics became completely intertwined, and the government saw bananas so much as a UWP-thing that they were less than straight in highlighting the negative possibilities of the industry ... There was a happy corollary to this. John Compton himself saw the banana business as being so closely linked with his political fortunes, that over the past thirty years he fought indefatigably to preserve the industry from all the vicissitudes which threatened its survival.
>
> *(In Joseph 2011a: 7)*

These political arrangements would come to a sharp end following another round of peasant revolts in the 1990s. Whereas the 1952–1957 revolts had brought to a close the political economy of sugar and had given rise to the banana economy, the revolts of 1992–1997, culminating in the electoral defeat of the Compton-founded UWP, were to bring to a close the political economy of bananas.

The protests of 1992–1997 and their political effects

Just as the revolts of 1952–1957 had erupted in the context of the decay of the politico-economic structural framework of the sugar economy, then, similarly, were the peasant uprisings of the 1990s the result of shifts in the global trade arrangements for banana exportation. The spark for the banana uprisings of the 1990s can be traced to resistance by organised farmers to attempts by the Compton government to assert control of the SLBGA, in a moment when the movement towards the Single European Market, and the liberalisation of world trade in bananas were undermining the stability of the domestic banana industry. Compton's efforts at securing his power base in the SLBGA, therefore, represented his domestic political response to global adjustments in the banana industry.

The first signs of conflict emerged in 1988 when the Compton government sought to dissolve the entire board of the SLBGA by an Act of Parliament on 25 October (see Joseph 2011a: 103). As is usually the case in moments of conflict, the impact of larger external structural forces are manifested in specific and particular ways at the local level, and, in this instance, the issue that first sparked the revolt was a 5 per cent levy on banana profits. As noted in Joseph (2011a: 103),

[C]entral to the conflict between the SLBGA board and the UWP government was the board's criticism of the government's decision to introduce a 5% levy on banana profits for the construction of roads in the banana-producing areas. Resistance by the SLBGA board to what was perceived by the government as a necessary structural requirement in the face of growing international pressures on Caribbean bananas was seen as requiring the sharpest response by the state. The minister of agriculture argued that 'the board had emerged into a direct confrontation with the government at a critical time for the industry with the approach of the European Single Market'. This was viewed as 'a state of affairs which could not be allowed to continue in the country's main industry'.

(See Joseph 2011a: 103–104)

As a result, the government, via an Act of Parliament on 25 October 1988, effectively dissolved the SLBGA board and toppled the chairman, Rupert Gajhadar, along with the existing farmer-appointed directors (*The Voice* 1988b).

A newspaper report of the environment in which the bill was first piloted provides a clear sense of the political tension that was building when the government first attempted to push the bill through the parliament:

It was a virtual 'banana storm' when the debate started. Noise and excitement outside the parliament chamber came from a group of banana farmers and St. Lucia Labour Party (SLP) followers provided debaters inside with additional vigour. The current chairman of the SLBGA, Rupert Gajhadar, leading the protest outside, was also a big subject inside the house. It was this man, they said, that had been leading a small 'clique' of banana growers into direct confrontational politics with the government. The new bill was being piloted to deal with this threatening situation, the government repeatedly said.

(The Weekend Voice *1988: 4*)

This conflict presented a moment, for the first time since the birth of the banana industry, in which peasant banana producers perceived their interests as separate from that of Compton's UWP, and it also opened the door for the long-marginalised SLP to build an alliance with the hitherto pro-Compton banana farmers. The dominant group at the vanguard of the strikes was the Banana Salvation Committee (BSC), which included key players such as Patrick Joseph, Abel Wilson, Elizabeth Charles and others. Between 1998 and 1994, the BSC launched a series of 'no-cut strikes' intended to deny Geest and later the Windward Islands Banana Development and Exporting Company (WIBDECO)[5] of a supply of fruit, as a way to protest against the government decisions perceived as harmful to the farmers' interests.

From the first skirmish with the government in 1988, the entire period up to 1993 can be seen as a long period of struggle between the government and the banana community. A perusal of the newspaper headlines in Saint Lucia between 1988 and 1993 provides a clear catalogue of conflict between the government and the BSC in a context of the loss of preferential markets and the movement towards liberalised globalised trade. The headlines in *The Voice* newspaper, such as '1988 – Year of Intense Activity' (1988c: 9), 'Banana Protest' (1988a: 1), 'Politics Goes Bananas' (29 October 1988) 'Banana Strike Looms' (1993b: 1–14), 'Growers Threaten New Strikes' (1993c: 1–14) and 'SLBGA Board in Exile' (1993e: 1–14), reveal a long and sustained moment of constant upheaval and revolt in the banana industry. The main tactic was the no-cut strike, in which the power of the farmers as independent producers to starve the buyers of produce proved a critical weapon and frightened government officials with the possibility of collapse of the economy. The no-cut strikes were reinforced by the tactic of harassment of strike breakers and by the erection of road blocks to prevent the movement of trucks carrying produce to the various ports and collection centres. The peak of the banana revolts was a three-day strike that ended on 5 October 1993 and culminated in the killing by the police of two unarmed strikers, Julius and Randy Joseph.

At the time of the first skirmishes of the fatal three-day strike, the BSC, under the presidency of Abel Wilson, had organised a series of island-wide meetings to protest the banana profit levy and the 'inequitable distribution of the price paid by Geest to the Association', and to challenge 'squandermania and mismanagement' on the part of the association's directors (*The Voice* 1993a: 1). The refusal by the government to respond to demands led to the escalation of the strikes from the no-cut tactic to roadblocks using burning tires and fallen branches and other debris, which brought economic activity in the country to a standstill. Of particular concern on this occasion was the longevity of the strike, the widespread use of roadblocks and the direct confrontations with police by strikers, who defended and remounted roadblocks as quickly as they were dismantled by security personnel. Of specific concern to the authorities was the impact on the tourism industry, as the blocked roads and poor security situation frustrated inland travel, and tourists had to be airlifted between the island's two airports (see Slocum 1996: 135). Given the security and economic consequences of the strike, as well as the potential political cost to Compton and the UWP, the government resorted to a level of force that had not been witnessed since the 1950s. Thus, on 7 October 1993, two strikers, Julius and Randy Joseph, 'died when police opened fire on what they called a mob of striking banana farmers who attacked them with stones while clearing road blocks in the Dennery Valley' (*The Voice* 1993d: 1).

Significantly, the extreme nature of the government response to the strike served as a critical marker in beginning the process of delegitimation of the Compton administration. One commentator, asking rhetorically whether the bloodshed could have been avoided, painted the following picture of Compton's loss of face following the deaths of the strikers:

> [O]ne of the many questions being asked is whether the whole thing could have been prevented. Prime Minister John Compton made a half sub-missive, half belligerent speech to the nation on 'bloody Thursday', away from the defiance he had shown earlier in the week. What was particularly sad about the rather yielding parts of Compton's address to the nation was that he was conceding many of the complaints the growers had been making against the Banana Growers Association (SLBGA). He agreed that the management of the association was dismal; that the Association was bankrupt; that there had been waste and squandermania; that the dissolution of the board of directors was necessary; that restructuring of the SLBGA, and the banana industry as a whole was urgent.
>
> *(David Vitalis in* The Weekend Voice, *9 October 1993: 3)*

With the killing of Julius and Randy Joseph, it was clear that a fatal blow had been struck to the relationship between the government and the banana farmers, and that the politico-economic arrangements that had hitherto sustained the banana industry could not be easily recaptured.

The final story in the 1990s labour upheavals revolved around Compton's last attempts to destroy the BSC. Thus, further strikes followed the deaths of Julius and Randy Joseph, when Compton sought to criminalise the BSC, via an Act of Parliament. The resolution preceding the Act made clear the government's intention to make illegal any action designed to prevent lawful productive activity and as such was a thinly veiled attack on the leaders of the BSC, who had utilised the no-cut strike and the roadblock tactic to effectively frustrate banana production and export. In its preamble, the resolution made a clear link between the ongoing transitions in the global market for bananas and the government's determination to crush all domestic opposition to the preservation of the banana industry. Significantly, the resolution highlighted:

> [the ongoing] effects of the inauguration of the Single European Market on the preferential arrangements ... the fierce international competition to which the industry has been exposed, and the efforts by government to lobby the European Community for the preservation of these arrangements.
>
> (The Voice *1993a: 1)*

It also expressed concern that, 'there are some elements in St. Lucia bent on the destruction of the industry, unconcerned about the damage which this could cause to the economy of St. Lucia' (*The Voice* 1993a: 1).

This resolution would later metamorphose into Article 651, which, given its intent to make illegal any action that would obstruct a person in the lawful conduct of their duties, would lead to resistance from the trade unions, as they viewed the Act as outlawing the normal activities of trade unionism. This resistance to Article 651 therefore widened the banana revolts into a grand anti-Compton coalition and would form the main plank upon which the 1997 election would be contested.

The combined impact of all these developments meant that, by the mid 1990s, the politico-economic relations of bananas had come to an end. Throughout the period of these developments, a number of major developments took place in the industry, all pointing to the process of dissolution of the earlier banana economy. These include: the transformation of Geest from a privately owned firm to a public liability company; the withdrawal of Geest from banana production and marketing; the purchase by the Windward Islands governments of Geest's banana interests and the formation of WIB-DECO; and the removal, through the WTO, of the special trading arrangement that had protected and sustained the Saint Lucia banana industry, which opened Saint Lucian production to direct competition from US-owned Latin American producers.

On the basis of the weight of these developments, and given the revolt of the banana producers against the government, the electoral landscape of Saint Lucia was to be radically transformed. In the 1997 elections, the UWP was totally routed, managing to hold only one seat in the new parliament (see Midgett 1998). This electoral defeat had also followed upon the resignation of Compton as prime minister and head of the UWP in 1996, with clear evidence that the loss of support among his natural banana base was a critical factor in his decision. Although the UWP would later retake the government with Compton as prime minister in 2006, this was only to be short-lived, as the party would later lose the government in 2011, with Compton himself having passed away in 2007.

Conclusion: the end of peasant revolts in Saint Lucia

What was significant, however, was not the future electability of the UWP,[6] but the fact that the electoral system had been radically transformed in the entire period between 1960 and 1997, when Compton's banana–politics alliance had ensured the political domination of his party. Indeed, the key feature of the electoral politics of Saint Lucia after 1997 is the end of the certain domination of the UWP and the return of a moment of electoral fluidity. Of the five elections held between 1997 and 2016, the SLP has won three to the UWP's two. This lies in stark contrast to the experience between 1964 and 1997, when the UWP lost only one election and was in opposition for only two and a half years. Although other factors are present, the sharp break in the electoral patterns between 1964–1997 on one hand and 1997 to the present on the other can be traced almost directly to the impact of the banana revolts in breaking the internal political relations that had sustained the earlier electoral patterns.

More important, however, and quite apart from the impact of the revolts on the electoral outcomes in Saint Lucia, is the fact that the period following 1997 marks the end of the political economy of bananas in Saint Lucia. With the change in the global trade and economic relations, and with the years of tension, instability and conflict in the industry, the efforts of the SLP government, post-1997, were geared towards shifting the economy of the country away from bananas into tourism and services as the dominant sectors. One consequence of this, although never acknowledged as official policy, was the government's efforts to transform internal social relations to limit the capacity of banana producers to wield significant levels of political influence.

Thus, following 1997, the SLBGA was transformed into a private company – the Saint Lucia Banana Corporation (SLBC) – effectively ending government involvement in banana production, but also effectively bringing to an end an important element of cooperative production and economic democracy among a significant section of the working population in a major global industry. In addition, the SLP government facilitated the emergence of competing private banana companies through a process of 'privatisation', as the rivalry between the directors of the SLBC resulted in the emergence of new companies, greatly undermining the coherence and stability of the already fragmented industry. The continued unviability of these arrangements would lead eventually to the dissolution of the private companies themselves, including the SLBC, marking the end of the organised arrangements of agrarian producers as central players in the economics and politics of Saint Lucia.

By the first and second decades of the twenty-first century, therefore, it can be safely argued that the history of peasant revolts has come to an end in Saint Lucia, at least for the foreseeable future. With the main thrust of all governments since 1997 revolving largely around the development of tourism and services, and with the agricultural sector significantly diminished in both economic and political terms, Saint Lucia can be seen to have entered a new political economy that has brought to an end the era of peasant revolts.

The political implications of this are already beginning to be clear. Just as in an earlier period Saint Lucian electors exhibited preferences for personalities who had links to the banana industry, some of them being direct producers themselves, in the second decade of the twenty-first century the country elected as prime minister Allen Chastanet, whose background is in the hotel and tourism sector, a businessman by profession and an unapologetic neo-liberal with no links to the trade union movement or the agrarian sector. With his election, the country has been reoriented towards participation in the global economy on the basis of tourism, hospitality and entertainment as the main thrust. Any future worker revolts with political consequences on the scale of 1952–1957 or 1992–1997 will occur around institutions vital to the tourism industry and the urban sector, such as the air- and sea ports, the hotel plant themselves or the communications infrastructure relevant to the country's participation in the modern global political economy, or, perhaps more directly, the customs officers and the air traffic controllers, who, in Saint Lucia's current modes of insertion into the global political economy, are the groups most likely placed to effect national shutdowns as a weapon against entrenched capitalist interests.

Notes

1 The Roseau and Cul-de-sac Valleys were the two main sugar-producing regions in the 1940s and 1950s, and the theatre of peasant struggles in the last days of the dominance of sugar.
2 Allen Lewis, the brother of Saint Lucian Nobel Laureate W. Arthur Lewis and later Governor General of Saint Lucia who was one of the founders of the Saint Lucia Labour Party, serving as its president.
3 The 'American invasion' here refers to the construction of American military bases in the island during World War II, and the 'Castries reconstruction' refers to the reconstruction of the city of Castries after the 1948 fire (made famous in Derek Walcott's poem 'A City's Death by Fire'). Reference to coaling speaks to the role of the capital, Castries, as a major coaling port for refuelling in the era of steamships.
4 Compton would later become the first and longest-serving prime minister of Saint Lucia, dominating the politics of Saint Lucia between 1957 and 2007.
5 WIBDECO was formed following the exit of Geest from the Caribbean Banana trade and the sale of sections of the business to the Windward Island governments.
6 Indeed, the UWP would regain the government in April 2016.

References

Acosta, Y. and Casimir, J. (1985) 'Social Origins of the Counter-Plantation System in St. Lucia', in P.I. Gomes (ed.), *Rural Development in the Caribbean*, London: C. Hurst.
Adrien, P. (1996) *Metayage, Capitalism and Peasant Development in St. Lucia 1840–1957*, Kingston: Consortium Graduate School University of the West Indies.
Barrow, C. (1992) *Family Land and Development in St. Lucia*, Bridgetown: Institute of Social and Economic Research University of the West Indies.
Cabral, A. (1969) *Revolution in Guinea: An African People's Struggle. Selected Texts*, London: Stage 1.
Charles, G.F.L. (1994) *The History of the Labour Movement in St. Lucia 1945–1974: A Personal Memoir*, Castries: Folk Research Centre.
Frucht, R. (1967) 'Neither Peasant nor Proletarian', *Social & Economic Studies* 16(3): 295–300.
Jackson Commission Report. (1957) Report of the Commission Appointed to Investigate the Causes of the Stoppage of Work in the Sugar Industry during March and April in St. Lucia. Chairman D. Jackson.
Joseph, T.S.D. (2011a) *Decolonization in St. Lucia: Politics and Global Neo-Liberalism, 1945–2010*, Jackson: University Press of Mississippi.
Joseph, T.S.D. (2011b) 'Grace Augustine: Feminist Trailblazer or Defender of Colonialism? Unraveling the Contradictions of St. Lucia's First Female Legislator', in C. Barrow-Giles (ed.), *Changing Faces of Women in Caribbean Politics*, Kingston: Ian Randle.

Lewis, W.A. (1936) 'The Evolution of the Peasantry in The British West Indies' (unpublished manuscript).

Louis, M. (1982) '"An Equal Right to the Soil": The Rise of a Peasantry in St. Lucia 1838–1900', PhD dissertation, Baltimore: Johns Hopkins University.

Malone Commission Report. (1952) Report of the Commission of Enquiry into the Stoppage of Work at the Sugar Factories in St. Lucia in March 1952 and into the Adequacy of the Existing Wage Fixing Machinery in that Colony. Chairman C. Malone.

Midgett, D. (1998) 'The St. Lucia Labour Party Victory of 1997 and the Decline of Conservative Movements', *Journal of Eastern Caribbean Studies* 23(4): 1–24.

Mintz, S.W. (1979) 'The Rural Proletariat and the Problem of the Rural Proletarian Consciousness', in R. Cohen, P. Gutkind and P. Brazie (eds), *Peasants and Proletarians: The Struggles of Third World Workers*, New York: Monthly Review Press.

Public Records Office – Colonial Office Reports. (1952a) PRO CO/1031/267 – Extract from Windward Islands Political Report for January 1952.

Public Records Office – Colonial Office Reports. (1952b) PRO CO/1031/2809 – List of Persons Charged and Taken to Court between 3 and 26 April (27 April).

Public Records Office – Colonial Office Reports. (1954) PRO CO/1031/1528 – Windward Islands Intelligence Report – (27 January).

Public Records Office – Colonial Office Reports. (1960) PRO CO 1031/3422 – Note of Meeting Between Colonial Office and Van Geest (23 November).

Slocum, K. (1996) *Producing Under a Globalizing Economy: The Intersection of Flexible and Local Autonomy in the Work Lives and Actions of St. Lucian Banana Growers*, PhD dissertation, Gainesville: University of Florida.

Vitalis, D. (1993) 'Bloody Thursday: Could All this have Been Avoided?', *The Weekend Voice*, 9 October: 3.

The Voice of St. Lucia. (1957) 'Government Faces $120, 950 Strike Bill: Duty on Tobacco, Cigarettes Raised', Sunday 26 May: 2.

The Voice of St. Lucia. (1988a) 'Banana Protest', 26 October: 1.

The Voice of St. Lucia. (1988b) 'Levy, New Bill, Kick up Banana Storms', National Day Supplement, 9 December.

The Voice of St. Lucia. (1988c) '1988 – Year of Intense Activity', 10 December: 9.

The Voice of St. Lucia. (1993a) 'Banana Farmers Angry', 9 November.

The Voice of St. Lucia. (1993b) 'Banana Strike Looms', 21 September: 1–14.

The Voice of St. Lucia. (1993c) 'Growers Threaten New Strikes', 25 November: 1–14.

The Voice of St. Lucia. (1993d) 'Slain Farmers Buried', Tuesday 19 October: 1.

The Voice of St. Lucia. (1993e) 'SLBGA Board in Exile', 25 November: 1–14.

Wallerstein, I. (1974) *The Modern World-System*, New York: Academic Press.

The Weekend Voice. (1988) 'Politics goes "Bananas"', 29 October: 4.

Williams, O. and Darius, R. (1998) 'Banana, the WTO and Adjustment Initiatives in the Eastern Caribbean Area', *Eastern Caribbean Central Bank*: 100–111.

6

THE RETURN OF THE LEFT?

Post-crisis social movements, anti-austerity activism and social policy in the UK

Gregory White

The political challenge of the economic crisis

The economic crisis of 2007 presented a challenge to welfare states across Europe and beyond (Farnsworth and Irving 2017). It also presented a challenge to citizens, who experienced the brunt of the austerity agenda and subsequent tightening of welfare spending. If nothing else, the financial crisis demonstrated the resistance of economic theories and ideas – such as those prominent in financial capitalism.

> [Austerity] is not simply about expenditure cuts – it more accurately describes an intention towards, and reconfiguration of, economies and welfare states that cannot be measured or assessed simply by reference to social spending as a proportion of gross domestic product (GDP). While the intention is to dissolve the bonds of solidarity that characterised the post-war period of welfare state building, because for neoliberalism they have always represented constraints on freedom, it is the reconfiguration of the welfare state that is expected to achieve this outcome.
>
> *(Farnsworth and Irving 2017: 103)*

The current period of instability is indicative of a systemic crisis: '[it] shows how the capitalistic system is structurally unstable and how free market theory is not able to affront such instability' (Fumagalli and Mezzadra 2010: 247). During and after the crisis, an eruption of activity in civil society galvanised many across the political divide – those directly and indirectly affected by austerity. The social and political issues that arose because of the economic crisis are manifold. What started as a crisis born out of financial deregulation and excess quickly became an issue that had huge structural ramifications. Broadly, these ramifications can be outlined thus:

1   First, a crisis of confidence over the welfare state apparatus: what types of provision can be made for the citizen in a period of declining acceptance of social security? Moreover, what is the role of the welfare state, and how should it provide for those that require support?
2   Second, a democratic deficit, or renewal: methods of traditional, institutional engagement with the political system are not satisfactory and do not meet the demands of citizens. What types of engagement – that is, non-institutional – can be used to hold systems to account?
3   Third, the continuing economic crisis and working-class politics: social movements have had mixed success in tackling wider social policy questions, but, have not sufficiently challenged existing political structures. Which movements should take on the questions of social justice, regulation, redistribution, and so on, and represent the working class?

The first crisis has its roots in the political approval of governments, mainly on the right of the political spectrum, that have sought to decrease spending on welfare. The second follows from the first, in that citizens become increasingly disenfranchised in a political system that no longer represents popular opinion. There are concerns that the traditional methods of political engagement have not been representative, and, therefore, citizens have taken to other forms of organisation. Finally, the traditionally representative trade union movement has been unable to take up the legitimate grievances of the working class within the UK, primarily as a result of embedded structural issues, such as the existence of anti-trade union laws. The result is that there is now a vacuum in which effective political representation does not exist, formally or informally. In the absence of this representation, social movements are tasked with engaging with the socio-political challenges that arise as a result of heavy state retrenchment. This chapter aims to deal with the above crises and discuss which movements have attempted to manoeuvre into the vacuum of effective criticism that has, arguably, been left open by other political parties on the left of the spectrum and the trade union movement.

In response to this, there have been several key responses from civil society (in the UK), in recent years, from pressure groups, activist networks and social movements, aiming to address some of the fundamental questions posed by the crisis – that is, how to regulate financial institutions, how to redistribute resources *and* how to equalise society. This has been consciously coupled with activism on the issue of public spending and cuts to welfare. Although many concessions have been won on a national level, the wider issues of macro-economic stability – that is, the crisis caused by financial deregulation – have remained largely unchallenged, or at least the discourses have stagnated owing to a 'crisis of imagination'. As yet, few of the challenges from civil society, and social movements, have seriously disrupted or altered the economic structures that permit the uneven flow of capital. In this period of crisis, reform and piecemeal regulation, social struggle has become even more important in terms of presenting challenges to the current political and economic order. This chapter will focus on the current social policy challenges and how social movements have sought to disrupt and change the current economic system by campaigning on issues, and what successes and failures have marked their sudden ascendancy in the arena of political discourse.

Mapping the methodological terrain

Interviews conducted as part of a research project form the bulk of the investigation for this chapter. For the study to have both a historical context and contemporary relevance, the types of organisation and movement approached ranged from political parties to trade unions and non-aligned social movements.[1] The motivations for this approach were that, in aiming to achieve the richness of a data set that compares the objectives of separate organisations and movements, the chasm between *intent* and *outcome* can be more adequately assessed, and a more definite conclusion can be made on whether there are tangible and observable impacts on the social policy landscape as a result of the interventions of post-crisis social movements.

Data collection involved a process of semi-structured interviews with activists and organisers in social movements and trade union organisations. The process of semi-structured interviewing in this context provided a sound methodological basis on which to interrogate the aims and objectives of social movements and how their demands might translate into social policy ideas. In the post-crisis context of anti-austerity activism and the re-emergence of networked individuals across a variety of social movements, it was clear that a number of issues had to be addressed in targeting questions that allowed researchers to make sense of how ideas are formed and how information is disseminated. The narratives of movements can be disjointed and disorganised and, therefore, difficult to categorise in any meaningful sense.

Individuals were offered an opportunity to express their opinions on a range of topics, focussing on their own involvement, knowledge and understanding of austerity, engagement with social policy issues, strategies for interventions, and how decisions to act on a particular issue might be taken. Individuals were invited to interview between May and September 2015.

Reflections and observations on contemporary struggle

The findings presented a mixed picture of activism, organisation and protest action in a post-crisis environment. What stood out ultimately from the results is a rejection, at least from social movements, of the hierarchies that dominate left-wing political struggles within the UK. Moreover, there are signs of frustration with key elements of left-wing organisations that have failed to take on the challenge of sustaining protest activity against government austerity. The findings here represent a shift in thinking, in some respects, from the organised left. The post-crisis era of government austerity and increasing inequality has forced people to rethink strategies, practices and actions, and has, in many ways, ushered in a period of reflection on how activism contributes to debates in public social and political discourses. It has also, more importantly, demonstrated that the institutional arrangements and organisations orchestrating austerity *can be* challenged, and coherent – and alternative, progressive – visions for social policy are observable. The challenge, however, is linking the various actors on the left to advance a progressive alternative. The following will first investigate responses that look back to a period of institutional trade union organisation and contrast that to the current situation of radical politics in a post-crisis era. The discussion will analyse the interview responses that dealt with the visions for social policy as advanced by social movements. Finally, it will conclude by examining the decisions of social movements to act given all the above and explain how such movements are working with other similar struggles on the left and providing the most vocal challenge to government austerity.

Movements, unions and institutional politics

The issues that commonly appeared during interview related to the historical organising tendencies of trade unions in the UK, compared with the contemporary context. Some respondents chose to reflect on tensions between different union organisations and movements, which, in the context of the present crisis, gave weight to the argument that the left of the political spectrum – in the UK – had, in some cases, become embittered and fractious. Taking the issue of historical and contemporary trade union action, there was a sense from one respondent, a national trade union official linked to the TUC, with a background in regional and national organising, that the organisation of labour on a national scale does not compare to the levels of activism seen in the UK in the 1970s and 1980s:

> From my perspective, you look at Sheffield trades council, in comparison to the other trades around the country, and there's a large number of trades councils that are now defunct, that are not meeting at all. There's renewed interest in some of them, but it's very patchy on a national basis, it's not like it was 30 years ago when every town, city, local authority had a very vibrant trades council.[2]

For this reason, it can be said that there has been a shift in the organisation of the working class and in the mobility of action for organised labour. The tendencies for contemporary, militant political action in the UK simply do not reflect the achievements of the past decades; this is, of course, a result of successive governments' tackling union power and the ability to strike.

For some respondents, there was a sense of scepticism regarding the links between the Labour Party and the trade union movement. Changes in the direction of Labour Party affiliation with the main trade unions is perhaps one of many reasons why working-class organisation is so fragmented, and why protest actions are rarely sustained. Another respondent, a local trades council organiser with links to a regional TUC organisation, made it clear that the reasons for this are mainly due to a shift in attitudes within the Parliamentary Labour Party:

> At the macro level, I think the most significant issue is the Labour link. The Parliamentary Labour party has been ignoring the votes of its own conferences, ignoring the wishes of its own membership, at least 40 or 50 years now, going back to the 60s and 70s. Under Kinnock and Blair this became more and more egregious; inequality increasing practically every year under the new Labour government, Blair's failure to tackle the anti-trade union laws and all the rest of it …

The respondent added:

> I think it's difficult because already a lot of rank and file trade unionists, and certainly a lot of the best activists, are not Labour, they are members of the SP, the SWP or they're anarchists, or they're involved in other organisations. McCluskey spoke at our AGM about 2 or 3 months ago and he said I'm not a Labour loyalist, I'm not wedded to them for all time, but until a party comes along that's a credible alternative then I think we should stick with Labour.

The sense of difficulty over taking a position or choosing between two methods of engagement in many respects reveals the tendency to reluctantly put intellectual and practical weight behind the orthodoxies of institutional politics, despite the scepticism over how hierarchies between movements and parties reveal a tense relationship. Historically, the radicalism of actions taken by social movements has been supported, in large part, by assistance from the Labour Party and the labour movement more generally. For a DPAC member and local trade union organiser working in disability rights and a campaigning organisation, however, the loss of the radical element in the labour movement was the catalyst for the rise in social movement action:

> The disabled people's rights movement traditionally are voices through disabled people's organisations such as Inclusion London or any one of a number of others, but over the new Labour years got very much into … contract culture service delivery [and we] really lost the radical edge and

I think lost our way, and then that meant that the movement wasn't really prepared when the coalition government came along in 2010, when the cuts started to happen, there wasn't some kind of national coordinated response to that from disabled people: being targeted by the cuts and hit disproportionately and so [our movement] basically fit in that gap.

Given that radicalism is, largely, absent in contemporary Labour Party politics, social movements, to some extent, look towards the trade union and labour movement for support. Historical tensions, however, as the DPAC member and local trade union organiser explained, have strained the relationship and the spirit of collaboration:

[There have] been barriers between the disabled people's rights movement and the trade union movement and there's lots of reasons for that. One of the things I think you can trace it back to we're looking at the history of the long-stay institutions and when those were being closed down the trade unions were defending the workers of those places and for example denying that abuse was happening, and the DPRM doesn't forget. It can be there's that tension when, particularly if services are under-funded and haven't been meeting the needs of disabled people, disabled people have been warehoused or treated as products rather than humans within them, then obviously, there's a tension between the workers who are being seen to perpetrate the abuse or oppression, the unions who are defending them, and the disabled people.

In a similar vein to the previous respondent, the above recalls a reticence over social movements working with organisations with hierarchical and institutional arrangements – in this case, trade unions. The evidence would suggest here, then, that the relationship between social movements and the trade union movement appears strained. Another respondent, a former Occupy London activist and organiser with a background in formal legal work, shared their frustrations on this issue, and they cited a lack of consistency from the trade union movement when it came to the Occupy London protests of 2011 outside Saint Paul's:

In my experience [the unions] will press release and try and get something in their supportive media, such as the Morning Star, and then that will be it, it doesn't seem to then be followed up with anything more and their involvement with [our movement], back when we had lots of meetings, was about trying to learn from our perhaps more direct action tactics, and it's just not followed up from them because what they're going to have in the back of their mind is perhaps the fear of them facing legal action, being categorised as terrorists or something like that, there's a reluctance that needs to be dropped by people generally if they want to enact change.

In this instance, the formal engagements between the social movement and trade union organisations demonstrate a fractious relationship in which some actions taken in non-institutional activism are viewed with suspicion. From the view of another respondent, another former Occupy London activist and organiser with a background in environmental movement and climate change camps, the relationship between movements and unions was less of an issue in terms of activity, and more one of inconsistent communication:

> We've tried with the trade unions and had a little bit of contact, but it's very hard to get anywhere with them, but we have had some ... There were, way back at Occupy St Paul's, connections made, and I wasn't involved in that bit, but I know there were people that went out in support of striking workers, and we had a couple of trade union people come and speak at Occupy. I think ... there were a few people in Occupy who really wanted to make links with the trade unions, and there were probably a few trade union people who really wanted to make links with Occupy, but there weren't enough on either side for it really to happen in a big way.

On the point of jointly organising, the evidence from this respondent suggests that, despite efforts to collaborate, there were inevitable shortfalls in organising at scale. Given what has been revealed thus far about the nature of the relationships between organisations, it is reasonable to suggest that the point of contention is one regarding tactics and what is deemed as legitimate protest.

There were some interesting observations from another respondent regarding relationships between social movements and trade union organisations. The links that groups might have, by this account, might not always be as clear:

> It's not surprising that the most militant unions are the ones we get on best with, so we have very good links with the bakers, just because they're loud and they want action and are not afraid to take it and so are we. The trade unions we've got links with, both really good links, are the RMT and TSSA, which is the more conservative union, but we've got quite a lot in common, and so the cuts they are facing to the railways, to the underground have a direct knock-on effect on disabled people's ability to travel ... [These are] some of the unions which we have the best links with, kind of which you wouldn't really expect, considering what they do. We do a fair bit of work with unions that work in the voluntary sector, social care settings, which are Unison and Unite. Unison really don't like us, because we're too militant.
>
> *(DPAC member and local trade union organiser)*

Regarding the point of 'militant' action, there is nothing new or surprising about where social movements find common ground with radical trade unions. It fits the narrative of hierarchies in trade unionism, where militancy is viewed as a disadvantage. On the point of 'conservative' unions, this somewhat disrupts the picture of unity among groups that deploy a set of tactics in the field. Some movements might find common ground on certain issues and grievances, but disagree on the tactical behaviour of group actions. For the most part, this section has shown that there are tensions between movements and organisations. In terms of bringing together a cohesive response from the left, the terrain becomes more challenging. If the aim is to demand alternatives and influence policy, the above would suggest that there are obstacles – at least from an institutional perspective – in terms of developing coherent strategies to solve problems in the post-crisis environment.

Social movement ideas and objectives

The types of policy objective that social movements *might* espouse during the process of conducting interviews were perhaps less easy to discern, as activists were less willing to make specific links with policy aims. Although this was limited, there are a few examples of where issues of social policy were placed front and centre of an individual's critique. Overwhelmingly, it was clear that, in the case of Occupy London at least, the space provided was one that signified a collective activity, aimed at discussing shared grievances:

> The way I saw it was about a collective group of people ascertaining, or asserting, that enough was enough. For them, even though they were resolutely peaceful, something had changed in consciousness, and they were willing … to be defiant.
>
> *(The Former Occupy London activist and organiser*
> *with background in formal legal work)*

If the objective is to create spaces for citizens to express defiance on shared grievances, then much of the evidence – theoretical and empirical – would suggest that Occupy London succeeded in this regard. The point here, however, is to demonstrate that there were ideas about the direction of the movement. The practice of such an approach made it difficult, at least from the outside, to understand fully the demands of Occupy. One respondent gave an account of the ideas that spurred the movement, although qualifying it by highlighting the problem of overstretching – a criticism that has frequently been levelled at the Occupy movement in London:

> [Occupy] was trying to do a lot of things, one thing would definitely have been to get greater regulation of the financial industry, clamp down on tax evasion and avoidance, tax loopholes, reduce the power of corporations and of the financial sector, but also sort of more social kind of community based stuff as well like trying to help people with housing troubles, trying

to affect policy by changing attitudes towards sort of making it known that it's ridiculous that all the social housing has been sold off and that we've got loads of empty buildings and they're clamping down on squatting at the same time as the housing crisis, so supporting people in local communities, and that happened more towards the end of Occupy when we went and helped with libraries that were being shut down and things like that.

> *(The former Occupy London activist and organiser with background in environmental movement and climate change camps)*

The range of issues discussed here indicates that there was no one clear objective – at least for this respondent – that should be the focus of Occupy. It does, however, demonstrate the movement's willingness to engage with local issues – such as social housing – which is clearly important to, and a strength of, direct-action activism. It also reflects some of the discussions on what contributions social movements might make to a post-crisis narrative – engagement on 'tax avoidance' and 'corporate power' is certainly a part of that. The same respondent continued to give an account of engagement with similar grassroots activist networks:

> We engaged with loads of groups: UK Uncut, DPAC, local campaign groups like E15 housing, Barnet Library, a lot of small community grassroots stuff, as well as Reclaim the Power, anti-fracking groups, fuel poverty action, London Black Revs, more recently with Occupy Democracy. [There are] loads of groups Occupy has cooperated, coordinated with and networked with.

Discussion of the overlaps with similar campaigning groups presented a picture of multilateral support networks, focussing on cooperating and coordinating on the local and the proximal. In terms of ideas and objectives, the notion that there are social movements acting and coordinating together, on several grievances, provides an indication of how the boundaries of engagement are fluid.

The impact of the decision to act

Concerning movements' decisions to act upon a grievance, there were many interesting responses from interviewees. The decision to act takes the theoretical for social movements into the practical. In moving from organising either in person or on Internet forums, a decision is made by these movements that direct action is a viable and important method for communicating demands on specific issues. One of the respondents gave an account of their actions, which used a set of norms and beliefs as the foundation for any activity:

We respond in that situation, based on the underlying principles and values that [our movement] is based on which is the social model of disability, the idea that you know we work with the left and trade unions, that's what we try and do, and were coming from an anti-austerity position, and then in terms of like setting our plan of work, we try and have annual conferences we can't always, and so what we try and get is our members to say what the important things are that they want to focus on.

(The DPAC member and local trade union organiser
on disability rights)

Responding to events as they happen is an example of where social movements are adept at mobilising – especially where networks are well developed. The decision to act, in this case, is predicated on the grievance being related to anti-austerity. The respondent continued:

We're always trying to broaden out, but the problem is capacity, because we do try and work with anyone that we agree with, around basic points on anti-austerity. After the [2015] election, a lot of people's response was to kind of set up new things, and that meant a proliferation of different groups that we want to be involved in, and that we were relating to, but don't possibly have the time to be everywhere. What we're also seeing I think, we'll see a lot more industrial disputes, but with groups of workers rather than coming from the national leadership, you know you've got the RMT, which is great and coordinated, things like you've got the Sother-by's workers, you've got the PCS National Gallery, you've got pockets of workers that are taking really serious action and they want [us] to be involved, and to support them, because it means something to them which is exactly we want to do there.

As with the previous discussion on objectives, the crucial point here is that some social movements are flexible in their strategies for engagement. If there is a mutually agreed objective, then the decision to act collaboratively is a straightforward response. There are difficulties, of course, in deciding to act on an issue, and in some cases maintaining a level of momentum. One considera-tion for those involved in social movement action, as raised by the former Occupy London activist and organiser with a background in the environmental movement, is to view an aspect of a struggle as part of a wider set of actions that bring activists together:

One thing I've heard since the [2015] election and the horribly disappoint-ing result is people looking at, you know, how to go forward from here with another … with a view of five years more Tory rule, and about connecting with local communities at the sharp end of what's going on, both to support them, the people involved in grassroots stuff like at really basic level but also to ... help to inform those people about the fact that it, that they might not be able to see the bigger picture because they're concentrating so much on their own struggle, so about sort of bringing the bigger picture in and saying it's not just you it's the whole system, so therefore trying to inspire people to work more together.

By this account, part of the decision to act is based on an understanding that work undertaken on the local level should not be dismissed. The process of keeping momentum and focus in social movement activity is, perhaps, where much of the critical work should be undertaken in considering how and when to act.

Another significant issue raised by respondents was that of internal organising, and divergent views impacted the decision to act. In horizontal activist groups and community sites of action, there are often disagreements on the tactics involved in organising on an issue. Although this is certainly nothing new to social movement scholars, it does pose some questions for those engaged in social policy research, seeking to understand the efficacy of actions where tangible objectives – for example, influencing the direction of domestic economic policies – are not achieved because of directionless individuals or movements. The former Occupy London activist and organiser with a background in formal legal work made a very clear statement on this matter:

What I'm increasingly frustrated about is that people who organise certain protests will do the protest and for them that'll be it, there's not, they don't look at it in context of the protest being a tactic for wider objectives. For example, an occupation of St. Paul's outside should've been seen as a tactic and then progressing on to things to be worked and developed on ... So, what I want to see going forwards is for people to be thinking far more intelligently about how they enact change so perhaps a protest on the ground is only the first step.

The frustrations – often widely shared in direct-action activist groups and networks – underscore the importance of collective behaviour and activity. For this respondent, a lot of the work in following through on an initial decision to act did not materialise. There are, of course, many reasons for the failure of movement objectives, as is well covered in social movement theory literature. The respondent identifies a specific grievance: seeing protests as a tactic in the pursuit of wider objectives. In this context, the decision to act has limited impact, and the efficacy of interventions from movements is significantly diminished. The broader ramifications are that well-meaning social and direct action can fall short of influencing the political discourses that have been previously identified as being contentious.

Discussion

From the data presented in this chapter, a few general points can be made: (1) there are several points of contention on grounds of organisation and tactical objectives; (2) some views of those engaged in social movement activity reflect a wider discontent over actions that has resulted in activist fatigue; (3) the distance between people and networks is, in some cases, too great, resulting in ephemeral moments of action; (4) there are significant tensions between institutional and non-institutional actors that are hindering, if not preventing, meaningful dialogue. If there are to be challenges to institutional orthodoxies, they should be sustained and coordinated across organisations and movements, rather than inward-looking. Despite this, there is a more positive interpretation of the results: signs of collaboration between movements are emerging. In addition to this, the evidence suggests that social policy issues are firmly on the agenda. For researchers and scholars engaged in debates on social policy, it would be pertinent to refocus the present research agenda on the impact of social movements.

The literature focussing on the role of social movements and anti-austerity movements in the contemporary period has grown substantially, within and outside an academic context. As has been outlined previously, the extent to which there is a substantive discussion on how such movements are advancing social policy issues through their practices and actions has only been touched on lightly, if at all. On the weight of the evidence collected so far, and following from discussions in the previous chapter, there is a necessity to (re-)examine the possibilities of a new class struggle, given the failures of the democratic apparatus in contemporary British society and the hierarchical political arrangements of the contemporary trade union movement. The following will, therefore, suggest that the role of social movements has been reinforced in the post-crisis context as actors of change. A direct result of this is that matters of inequality and disparities in economic outcomes are open for discussion and criticism. In bridging the gulf between non-aligned citizens and committed activists, the surge in such activity provides an insight in to how the left might envisage moving forward for a wider class struggle and a broader and less hierarchical labour movement.

There are a few main points in the literature that need to be given attention if we are to understand the (re-)emergence of social movements as part of a broader mosaic of political upheavals after the economic crisis. The first, as discussed, is to view such interventions through the lens of a class dynamic, or cleavage. Second, the notion of radicalism should be restated – especially in terms of anti-capitalist activity – by way of understanding the demands of social movements as coherent political alternatives. Finally, we need to address the question of democracy *within* social movement activity, as without such a grounding it would be difficult to consider the effectiveness of long-term interventions. On these questions, there have been several recent pieces of work by academics that aim to clarify our understanding (Fanelli and Brogan 2014; Della Porta 2015; Della Porta and Mattoni 2015). A unifying aspect of the literature is the position taken on the role of class in explaining the rise of recent protest activity:

> In all of these mobilisations, a new class – the social precariat, young, unemployed, or only part-time employed, with no protection, and often well-educated – has been singled out as a main actor ... Precariat is characterised by a sum of insecurity on the labour market, on the job, on the work, on income.
>
> *(Della Porta 2015: 5)*

Re-examination of notions of class is essential to understanding the thrust of contemporary social movement activity. In this chapter, actors from different networks and groups – some of which fit the above definition – have been discussed as part of the broader anti-austerity patchwork of activity. The most recent understanding of class activity has been reinvigorated by the emergence of new groupings, such as the precariat (Standing 2011). It can be argued that many of those attending the demonstrations described – as has been evidenced by this chapter – fit the mould of a 'social precariat'. As has been indicated throughout this investigation, historical notions of class have been set against the appearance of individuals and groups that do not fit a traditional analysis. In drawing attention to this aspect of post-crisis social movement analysis, it is clear that the traditional modes of organising through institutional means bear less significance to the wider and more nebulous interpretations of mobilisation that have emerged recently.

On the second point, we turn to notions of radicalism and the contribution of post-crisis social movements to the development and furthering of alternative narratives. This chapter has identified from respondents that there are elements of militancy and direct action that are viewed by contemporary protest groups as advantageous to the spreading of radical and alternative narratives. The literature on this topic confirms some of the findings, but also provides nuance. In terms of Occupy London, as an example, there have been a significant number of investigations into the standpoints of the movement, which have, in the past, suffered criticism for their coherence. More recently, the notion of an anti-capitalist Occupy movement in London has been downplayed:

> In our interviews ... activists expressed some anti-capitalist sentiments but they are articulated at best a very shallow critique of the elements of the prevailing socio-economic system, echoing much of what might be described as romantic anti-capitalism ... [Occupy] was a critique mostly on a moral level, on issues such as bankers' bonuses or the privileged tax regime enjoyed by big corporations.
>
> *(Sotirakopoulos and Rootes 2015: 184)*

Although not entirely the consistent with the sense of radicalism exuding from Occupy London, it should be emphasised that the encampment and online presence were part of a wider set of anti-elitist narratives made popular after the economic crisis of 2007–2008. The somewhat complicating juxtaposition is that one of the primary images shared globally of Occupy London was that of a banner that stated: 'capitalism is crisis'. The ostensible disconnect between theory and practice can be summarised thus: Occupy London maintained an image of radicalism, but was in fact a reformist movement.

Nevertheless, the summary above should not detract from what some elements of the movement aimed to achieve by way of promoting a radical image. Recent studies have made assertions consistent with the evidence presented not only in this chapter, but also throughout this study:

> the main issues of the movement are policy reform, governance, and regulation (especially in the financial sector), and there are also major concerns regarding the environment and all aspects of social reproduction, wherein housing, education, and health care are key.
>
> *(Dowling et al. 2012: 613)*

Indeed, taking such positions that challenge the narrative of government austerity – and articulating progressive views on social policy issues – can be understood as a part of a broader radical attitude that characterised a period of contention, post-economic crisis.

The final point to address is that of democracy within social movement activity. As a rule, this investigation has been interested in the ideas that emerge from movement activity, and how they can be interpreted as demands and interventions in social policy. That said, it would be negligent not to engage in an understanding of the sociological aspects of social movement activity that have been present in many recent investigations. This chapter has made several points in terms of thinking about democracy *and* democratic structures in post-crisis social movement activity: (1) the organisation of resources is a key factor in considering how movements decide to act on a grievance; (2) the capacity for intersecting actions and activities (between social movements) is a considera-tion, but is limited by the availability of resources; (3) a strong set of values and beliefs is the cornerstone of any action and, as such, should be taken as the principle factor in deciding to act. The literature on this subject is very clear, and equally so are the recent innovations of both theoretical interventions (Della Porta 2015) and the practical applications of social movement activity. With understanding of such innovations, the following model of participation and deliberation can be used as a lens through which to view the actions of social movements:

(a) *Preference (trans)formation*, as deliberative democracy requires the transformation of preferences in interaction;

(b) *Orientation to the public good*, as it draws identities and citizens' interests in ways that contribute to the public building of public good;

(c) *Rational argumentations*, as people are convinced by the force of the better argument;

(d) *Consensus*, as decisions must be approvable by all participants;

(e) *Equality*, as deliberation takes place among free and equal citizens . . .

(f) *Inclusiveness*, as all citizens with a stake in decisions to be taken must be included in the process and able to express their voice;

(g) *Transparency*, as a deliberative democracy is an association whose affairs are governed by the public deliberation of its members'.

(Della Porta 2015: 166)

The model outlined above is one recent example of how we can view the interventions of post-crisis social movements as innovators in the modern democratic state. The evidence both from the literature and presented in this chapter confirms that there were coherent methods of direct democracy being deployed in social movements, which enabled alternative narratives (against the prevailing economic conditions) to be expressed and disseminated.

Conclusions

The literature and evidence in this chapter on post-crisis social movements within the UK have made several points: the first is that the re-emergence of contentious politics had forced the broad left to reconsider its position and formulate a sustained and meaningful critique of the crisis (Della Porta 2014). The apparent lack of a coherent message – one that can be used to critique neo-liberal arguments and ideas of reconstructing capitalism – had distracted attention away from the actions of individuals and groups. Media narratives indeed sustained this line of argument – that the new protest groups had no single, clear message – which became especially true of attempts to assess the Occupy movement. The second point raised by the literature indicated some of the potential structural issues: those within certain movements had fallen, or were falling, out of activism or into a level of fatigue. The absence of immediate, material gains from active organisation was inducing a sense of despondency. For social movement studies, this is well-covered terrain: the theoretical and spatial distance between people and networks, at some point in active struggles, becomes too great to sustain any possible challenge to existing social and political structures. Although the structural aspects of social movements have not been the focus of this investigation, it is clear that we cannot make any claims about the successful dissemination of ideas from social movements without considering their organisational limitations. The findings from this research equate in many respects to the existing literature, but also add to it in terms of viewing the demands of social movements as progressive and coherent visions of social policy.

Although it would be untenable to suggest that this chapter has conclusively answered questions on social movement demands and social policy outcomes, there is clearly a spread of evidence to suggest engagement on such issues from *outside* the traditional policy formation framework. We can begin to make links between organisation on the left and the transfer of ideas. The approach in this chapter also makes it clear that the demands of post-crisis social movements in the UK are indeed relevant to the work that is undertaken to understand social problems and the crisis of the contemporary British welfare state. This chapter, therefore, makes a key contribution by demonstrating that the plurality in contemporary political anti-austerity activity *does not* rely on – and indeed is suspicious of – institutional actors and structures in the formation of social policy objectives. Indeed, non-institutional actors and movements in the post-crisis context are organising and formulating ideas in the spaces where organised labour movements – funded by political parties on the left – used to hold a firm ground. The implications for social policy are, then, that social and political discourses aimed at influencing and informing new policy arrangements are no longer the preserve of state and institutional actors. Although there is some evidence to suggest that social movements and non-institutional actors have become subsumed into the institutional sphere – that is, professionalisation of protest – the investigations broadly demonstrate that the location of class struggle is no longer fixed and is not governed by the rigid labour organisations that characterised the 1970 and 1980s.

The visions for social policy, radical or otherwise, are actively informed by movements that have no recognisable constitution or discernible organisation. Key to this is the point that labour movements, which have historically shaped the domain of many social policy issues, are now characterised by a cosmopolitan, flexible, transnational culture. The anti-austerity movements of the post-crisis period (2011 and onwards) demonstrate this clearly, and this chapter makes links between movement interventions, protest actions and policy objectives. It should be made clear, however, that any contributions of this sort should not be overstated. The work of Piven and Cloward (1977) should be viewed as totemic in linking protest movements, public policy and political outcomes. It is through the lens of their critical work that this chapter can, in part, be viewed, and indeed it is indebted to it.

In terms of the broader political climate, much has changed since the inception of this particular research project, and indeed many of the movements discussed have either become inactive or have disbanded. In the process, however, several other grassroots protest movements have begun organising on issues directly related to social policy – and some have been mentioned in this concluding section. The present conditions for the British welfare state, however, could not be worse, and the various aspects of security afforded to citizens that provide well-being are on the decline. In the face of such a dire political context, it is the social movements and protest groups that have consistently defied expectations and continued to organise. The (re-)

invention of anti-austerity protest activity in the UK after the economic crisis of 2007–2008 has provided some much-needed respite and critical thought, but, as examined, it has yet to find a foothold and mainstream recognition in wider political and policy discourses. This chapter has sought to provide some acknowledgement of these demands, and it is with this that ongoing research in social policy should recognise the sustained action of these movements and take seriously their objectives.

Notes

1 Organisations that have contributed to the study in some form: UK Uncut, Occupy London, Unite the Union, Unison, the Labour Party (England & Wales), Disabled People Against Cuts (DPAC), the Trade Union Congress (TUC), and National Campaign Against Fees and Cuts (NCAFC).
2 Interviews for this paper were conducted between May and September 2015. Participants referenced in this paper are drawn from the following organisations: DPAC, NCAFC, Occupy London, and the TUC. A total of n = 7 are referenced. The age range of participants was 20–40 years old. The positions held included coordinator, activist, communications specialist and branch representative.

References

Della Porta, D. (2014) *Social Movements in Neoliberal Europe (Online)*, Eutopia, at: http://eutopiamagazine.eu/en/donatella-della-porta/speakers-corner/social-movements-neoliberal-europe

Della Porta, D. (2015) *Social Movements in Times of Austerity*, Cambridge: Polity Press.

Della Porta, D. and Mattoni, A. (2015) *Spreading Protest: Social Movements in Times of Crisis*, Colchester: ECPR Press.

Dowling, E., Feigenbaum, A., Pell, S. and Stanley, K. (2012) 'Occupy London', *South Atlantic Quarterly* 111: 608–615.

Fanelli, C. and Brogan, P. (2014) 'Austerity, Labour, and Social Mobilizations: Rebuilding Trade Union and Working Class Politics', *Studies in Social Justice* 8: 113–117.

Farnsworth, K. and Irving, Z. (2017) 'The Limits of Neoliberalism? Austerity Versus Social Policy in Comparative Perspective', in B. Jones and M. O'Donnell (eds), *Alternatives to Neoliberalism: Towards Equality and Democracy*, Bristol: Policy Press.

Fox-Piven, F. (2015) 'Neoliberalism and the Welfare State', *Journal of International & Comparative Social Policy* 31(1): 2–9.

Fumagalli, A. and Mezzadra, S. (2010) 'Nothing Will Ever Be the Same: Ten Theses on the Financial Crisis', in A. Fumagalli and S. Mezzad (eds), *Crisis in the Global Economy: Financial Markets, Social Struggles and New Political Scenarios*, Los Angeles: Semiotext(e).

Halvorsen, S. (2012) 'Beyond the Network? Occupy London and the Global Movement', *Social Movement Studies* 11(3–4): 427–433.

Pickerill, J. and Krinsky, J. (2012) 'Why Does Occupy Matter?', *Social Movement Studies* 11(3–4): 279–287.

Piven, F. F. and Cloward, R. A. (1977) *Poor People's Movements: Why They Succeed, How They Fail*, New York: Pantheon.

Shannon, D. (2014) 'Snapshots of the Crisis, Austerity and the Movements Against', in D. Shannon (ed.), *The End of the World as We Know It? Crisis, Resistance, and the Age of Austerity*, Oakland: AK Press.

Sotirakopoulos, N. and Rootes, C. (2015) 'Occupy London in International and Local Context', in D. P. Donnatella and A. Mattoni (eds.), *Spreading Protest: Social Movements in Times of Crisis*, Colchester: ECPR Press.

Standing, G. (2011) *The Precariat: The New Dangerous Class*, London: Bloomsbury.

7

SOCIAL MOVEMENTS, MEDIA ACTIVISM AND PARLIAMENTARY ORGANIZATION

A brief history of Podemos

Marcello Gisondi

Introduction

On the evening of 25 May 2014, a small chanting crowd reunited in the square of the Reina Sofía Museum, in Madrid. The chants 'Que sí nos representan!' (They do represent us!) and 'Sí, se puede!' (Yes, we can!) welcomed the appearance of a 35-year-old ponytailed professor, Pablo Iglesias (born 1978), and of his comrades Íñigo Errejón (1983), Carolina Bescansa (1971), Juan Carlos Monedero (1963) and Teresa Rodríguez (1981). Podemos (We can), the electoral platform they had founded four months before, had just obtained an astonishing success in the European elections: 1,253,837 votes on a national scale, resulting in 7.98 per cent of the Spanish electorate and five European MPs. But Iglesias himself looked, rather than happy, resolute:

> Perhaps for many people, this result is a success. But I want to tell you that we are not satisfied. Starting from tomorrow, we'll work to establish a decent government in this country, and we'll get rid of the *Casta*. We'll work ... to accomplish a Europe of dignity and democracy, where no financial power is more important than the interests and the will of the people.
>
> *(Domínguez and Giménez 2014: 14)*

It is with this challenging spirit that Podemos has become one of the strongest progressive forces in Europe and the most unpredictable manifestation of radical politics for several decades.

In just three years, and often in alliance with independent regional forces, Podemos has gained the municipalities of cities such as Madrid and Barcelona and 71 MPs in the Spanish Congress of Deputies and it has repeatedly been the first party in the key regions of Catalonia and Basque Country. Moreover, it has transformed the Spanish political chess-board, breaking the de facto two-party system dominated by the Socialist (PSOE) and Conservative (PP) parties since the transition to democracy in the late 1970s. How could these quick successes and profound transformations be possible? If we want to understand the history of Podemos, we must focus on the small group of activists and academics that created it. Therefore, I will give an account of the biographies, political trajectories and publications of Podemos's founding members, as well as the party's discourse, campaign materials, electoral data and media coverage. This prosopography will be divided into four sections, to shed light on the period from the end of the 1990s to the summer of 2017.

Late 1990s to late 2000s: from anti-globalisation movements to the Bolivarian experiences

The political trajectories of Podemos's founders are various, but some of the most influential started in the transnational movements against neo-liberal globalisation of the late 1990s. During his Erasmus term in Bologna (October 1999 to July 2000), Iglesias joined the Italian Tute Bianche (White Overalls), whose civil resistance techniques emulated the Zapatista movement in Chiapas. In 2008, he completed his PhD thesis on *Multitud y acción colectiva postnacional: un estudio comparado de los desobedientes: de Italia a Madrid 2000–2005* (Multitude and post-national collective action: a comparative study of the disobedient movement: from Italy to Madrid 2000–2005). This work shows some key features of the future intellectual milieu of Podemos. On the one hand, it reflects on civil disobedience, political communication, recent Latin American emancipation movements, the relationship between grassroots activism and parliamentarian representation, the contrasts between traditional, radical and mainstream left-wing forces, and the will to transform radical politics into mainstream common sense. On the other hand, it is evidence of the centrality of Madrid, the involvement in Spanish academia from an outsider position, a transnational European education, and contamination between activism and scientific research.

Madrid is the key spot for the birth of Podemos. Like Iglesias, Monedero or Errejón, most of the people involved in the project from its beginning were born in the Spanish capital. That is the case, for instance, with Luis Alegre (1977), Rita Maestre (1988), Pablo Bustinduy (1983), Sarah Bienzobas (1985), Miguel Vila (1984), Jorge Lago (1976), Germán Cano (1971), Miguel Ardanuy (1991), Emilio Delgado (1976), Miguel Bermejo (1988), Raquel Huerta (1988), Miguel Urbán (1980), Eduardo Fernández Rubiño (1991), Jesús Gil (1989), Raúl Camargo (1978), Miguel Bermejo (1988) and Jorge Moruno (1982). Others, such as the Galician Carolina Bescansa – whose signature joins that of Iglesias in the legal registration of the party on 11 March 2014 – were born elsewhere but moved to Madrid to study in one of the city's universities. That is the case, for instance, with the Extremaduran Ana Domínguez (1980), the Manchegan Diego Pacheco (1986), the Asturian Tania González (1982) and Segundo González (1988), the Leonese Pablo Fernández (1976), the Andalucian Noelia Vera (1985), the Basque Eduardo Maura (1981) and Nagua Alba (1993), and the Buenos Aires-born Ariel Jerez (1966).

Radical youth movements from Madrid such as Movimiento de Resistencia Global (MRG) draw inspiration from the experience of the 'Italian disobedience', but the transnational collective actions also strengthened the relationships with the activists based in Barcelona. In Bologna, Iglesias met the Catalan Gemma Ubasart (1978), future Podemos secretary for plurinationality. Also, in the June 2001 protests against the World Bank in Barcelona, he met Ada Colau (1974), who would later become a leader of the Plataforma de Afectados por la Hipoteca (Platform for People Affected by Mortgages) and, in 2015, the mayor of Barcelona thanks to an electoral coalition supported by Podemos. Iglesias learned several lessons from the global movements, which were not in line with most leftist traditions. Above all, any political movement that wants to act effectively must be able to handle its media image and create its narrative. The movement, therefore, needed recognisable spokespersons, whose primary function was to deal with the press and the police. The goal of the rallies was to raise the level of symbolic conflict without being politically isolated from public opinion. But, after initial successes, the events in Genoa during the July 2001 anti-G8 rallies opened up a crisis for the transnational 'civil disobedience' movements.

However, Madrid's section of MRG continued its actions. It contributed to organising the 2003 rallies against the Iraq war. In 2004, when Aznar tried to deny the link between the Atocha terrorist attack and the participation of Spanish troops in the Iraq war, MRG and thousands of people gathered in front of the PP headquarters in Madrid, responding to an appeal spread via SMS. Years later, it would become clear that the SMS originated in the Faculty of Political Science, and that at least five future Podemos members contributed to making it go viral (Rivero 2015: 65–67). A younger generation of activists mixed with that of Iglesias and created the group Arde Madrid (Iglesias Turrion 2015: 261), which lasted until the global action against the G8 meeting in Scotland, in July 2005. One year later, in the summer of 2006, some of the members of Arde Madrid created the students' organisation Contrapoder.

Among the founders of Contrapoder was Íñigo Errejón, who had also participated in the global movements. Like Iglesias, Errejón comes from a family with a leftist tradition. In his youth, nevertheless, he joined not only anarchist or Marxist groups but also scout organisations. Indeed, there is an echo of Baden-Powell's motto – 'Leave this world a little better than you found it' – in Errejón's conception of political activism in Contrapoder: 'When I leave student activism, I have to leave it better than I found it, stronger, better organized, with a greater cultural organization, more people and more prepared'. Contrapoder was an attempt to go beyond the limits of grassroots movements that can only survive when people's mobilisation is high: 'we must build spaces where memory, group identity and structures can be preserved, spaces that generate political education, that function as interchangeable experiences' (Domínguez and Giménez 2014: 87).

Iglesias and Errejón's personal and political friendship arose from these experiences and reflections. Both animated Madrid's leftist milieu and shared the idea that activism and scientific research must go hand in hand, and that there cannot be complete neutralism in the study of politics. During his PhD, Iglesias interviewed Errejón as a primary source on the global movement (Iglesias Turrión 2008: 67). In the thesis's acknowledgements, he praised the 'rare intellectual complicity' with his friend (Iglesias Turrion 2008: 26). Errejón cited a book edited by Iglesias as one of the readings that inspired his PhD research (Errejón Galván 2012: 43). In his thesis's acknowledgements, he also described Iglesias as a 'comrade of sharp mind and Bolshevist will, as well as a permanent intellectual trigger'. Also, he foretold: 'When we met we were on opposite sides, but it didn't take long to understand that we came from the same place and ought to take care of each other because we had still a long road to walk together' (Errejón Galván 2012: 10). Besides writing papers together, Iglesias and Errejón were mentors of Juventud Sin Futuro (JSF – Youth Without a Future), which was formed at the end of 2010 and involved former members of Contrapoder (Domínguez and Giménez 2014: 25). Both Contrapoder and JSF were mostly composed of students based in the Complutense campus of Somosaguas.

Complutense University, indeed, played a fundamental role in the development of Podemos. Most of the people and ideas that gave birth to Podemos come from the Faculties of Philosophy, History, Psychology and, especially, from the Faculty of Political Science and Sociology. Many members of Podemos, such as Maestre, Huerta, Bermejo and Ardanuy, had been students in the faculty. The dean, Heriberto Cairo, supervised both Iglesias's and Errejón's PhDs. Monedero, Jerez, Bescansa, Iglesias and others are, or have been, professors and researchers in the faculty. But only a few of Podemos's members hold a stable position in Spanish academia, whereas most could only obtain short-term contracts or research grants in foreign universities. Many other members of the party, who did not pursue an academic career, were forced, because of Spain's economic crisis, to look for a job outside the country. These precarious conditions, both within academia and in the greater job market, may well have played a role in the decision to get involved in such an ambitious political project. Some, such as Bustinduy, have even described Podemos's birth as the main reason for their decision to return to Spain (Guedán 2016: 211).

However, the most significant experience that has influenced the project belongs to South America, where, as Iglesias stated, 'they taught us how to win' (La Barraca 2015). Iglesias, Errejón and Alegre were members of the Fundación Centro de Estudios Políticos y Sociales's executive board (CEPS – Centre of

Social and Political Studies). The foundation, created in 1993, promoted cultural and political exchanges with the 'Bolivarian' governments:

> We believe that Latin America has become the most interesting laboratory for political and social transformation, triggering the hopes of many peoples around the world. We think that the value of Latin American experiences is not limited to that region, rather it can be useful to generate social transformations in Europe and the State.
>
> *(CEPS n.d.)*

Many members of the foundation spent periods of research in Latin America and worked as advisers for local governments or as election observers. Iglesias visited Venezuela and Bolivia. Alegre and his academic mentor Carlos Fernández Liria (1959) were awarded the Premio Libertador al Pensamiento Crítico 2010 by the then foreign affairs minister of Venezuela, Nicolás Maduro (Aporrea 2011). Monedero, whose bond with CEPS was loose, was, for several years, an advisor of President Hugo Chávez and other high institutions in Venezuela, and Bescansa was in the country to conduct opinion polls for the 2006 presidential elections on behalf of CEPS (Perdomo Velázquez 2006). Errejón, however, received the greatest influence from the Bolivarian milieu. Within CEPS's activities, he visited Bolivia for the first time in 2006 to work with the country's Constituent Assembly, then Ecuador and Venezuela (Errejón Galván 2012: 9; Guedán 2016: 69). His PhD thesis, *La lucha por la hegemonía durante el primer gobierno del MAS en Bolivia (2006–2009): un análisis discursivo* (The fight for hegemony during the first MAS government in Bolivia 2006–2009: a discursive analysis), analysed the country's political evolution through the perspective of Ernesto Laclau and Chantal Mouffe's discourse theory. This theoretical but praxis-oriented approach would later be the core of Podemos's populist hypothesis.

End of 2008 to end of 2013: La Tuerka and the 15-M

In late 2008, a group of professors, including Iglesias, Monedero, Bescansa, Jerez, Fernández Liria and Domínguez, formed *La Promotora de Pensamiento Crítico*. They tried to translate academic discussions into mainstream language, organising roundtables with prominent guests to hold discussions with students and activists on the main issues of national history and international politics, often after watching movies. One of the biggest events, presented by Errejón, was the visit to the Complutense of the president of Bolivia, Morales, on 14 September 2009, with Iglesias and Maestre intervening as representatives of CEPS and Contrapoder. On 20 May 2009, in a public debate on *The Left at the Left of the PSOE*, Iglesias coordinated the discussion in the Faculty of Political Sciences, acting simultaneously as chairman and television host. The format imitated the television show *59 Segundos*, forcing the scholars to adapt their arguments to a more immediate discussion. These roundtables attracted the attention of Paco Pérez, founder of the local television channel TeleK, which was based in the workers' neighbourhood of Vallecas (Domínguez and Giménez 2014: 25; Guedán 2016: 121). Pérez offered Iglesias and his team the chance to host a political talk show, and the chance was immediately taken. The weekly talk show, *La Tuerka de los Jueves*, made its debut in November 2010. TeleK broadcast the show via a low-quality digital terrestrial television (DTT) channel, but the clips were also uploaded on to YouTube.

From the early 2000s, DTT technology had opened up new communication possibilities for independent media groups in Spain. The *derecha cavernícola* ('cavemen's Right') seized these opportunities: with this expression, Podemos's key figure, Jorge Moruno, described the extreme right-wing channels, commentators and arguments that had questioned the dominant political correctness and opened a new field of political communication. These right-wing actors tried to legitimise in public debate controversial claims on themes such as abortion or civil rights, pushing against the PP's agenda from the right. Criticising the Spanish Left for its claims of 'moral and cultural superiority', Moruno urged it to get involved in this field of dirty communication: 'The postmodern cavemen understood better than the Left that in a digital economy the creation of common sense depends on its diffusion in all means of communications' (Domínguez and Gímenez 2014: 185–186). *La Tuerka*, he declared, is an attempt to reverse this cultural defeat.

Largely based on voluntary technical work by students and activists, *La Tuerka* empowered the work of translating academic-rooted political analysis into mainstream language. Also, it opened the floor to people not associated with the Left at all. Local and minor members of the PP, as well as conservative journalists, regularly participated in the show. This strategy served two purposes: on the one hand, it provided more pluralistic discussions and, on the other, it taught Iglesias, Monedero, Errejón, Urbán, Moruno and others how to maintain control of television debates in the face of aggressive arguments from non-politically correct guests. Clips and videos circulated through social media, multiplying the audience. This success enabled *La Tuerka* to serve another purpose, that of offering solid radical arguments on mainstream social and political issues to a wide range of people, thus informing their understanding of these themes. Iglesias affirmed provocatively: 'People believe they are militants in political parties or organisations, but that isn't true: people are militants in the media' (Domínguez and Giménez 2014: 15).

La Tuerka rapidly became bigger and more professional, but TeleK's technical equipment did not guarantee stable transmission, or a proper set, and so, in September 2012, the show moved to Canal 33. The programme also attracted international attention. In late 2011, the Iranian government had launched HispanTV, a news channel based in Madrid, inaugurated by President Ahmadinejad and broadcast to the entire Spanish-speaking world. In autumn 2012, Iglesias was offered the role of host of a new talk, show similar to *La*

Tuerka, which he accepted. *Fort Apache* began its run in January 2013 and became one of the most followed programmes on HispanTV. As of July 2017, Iglesias was still hosting the show, but his decision to collaborate with a media group linked to the Iranian government has been harshly criticised. Accusations of using Iranian money to fund Podemos, coming from right-wing commentators, have proven to be baseless, and Iglesias's response to left-wing criticism has been that 'politics consists in riding on contradictions' (La Tuerka 2012).

In December 2013, *La Tuerka* moved to its current location, the newsroom of the newspaper *Público*. Moreover, since spring 2013, Iglesias's radical positions and acquaintance with the medium brought him invitations to other DTT shows, namely those hosted by the 'cavemen's Right'. The *La Tuerka* group, and Moruno in particular, supported him in preparing for his appearances with data and arguments, making his interventions extremely sharp and his presence sought after. Even in the most hostile contexts, Iglesias appeared polite and comfortable, but also determined and combative. His irony and provocations created a distinct character that guaranteed an increase in the shows' audiences. Mainstream media noticed him, and prime-time talk shows such as *La Sexta Noche* began to invite him. Since mid 2013, Iglesias has made regular appearances on *La Sexta*, gaining definitive access to a national audience.

Among the viewers of these shows was the teacher and trade unionist Teresa Rodríguez, the future leader of Podemos Andalucía. Watching Iglesias on talk shows, she said, was like watching 'a football match where your team, which always loses, suddenly starts to score goals. He was able to describe, firmly but with style, what ordinary people say, in a way that was inclusive of the viewers' (Coll, Fernández and Fernández 2016: 57). Rodríguez was a long-time militant in the Trotskyist organisation Izquierda Anticapitalista (IA). Founded in 2008, IA had developed an extensive network of activists throughout the country. In Madrid, it counted on members such as Jaime Pastor (1946), Camargo, Urbán and Alegre, as well as on the sisters Clara (1982) and Isa Serra (1989), who would play a significant role in the development of the feminist and youth areas of Podemos. Urbán and Alegre participated in the collective ownership of the bookshop La Marabunta, one of the meeting points of IA in Madrid and the place where most of the preparatory discussions for the creation of Podemos would take place.

However, IA was not as big, nor as bureaucratized, as Izquierda Unida (IU), the main Spanish radical party from which it had split in 2008. IU was established in 1986 from the ashes of the Spanish Communist Party, and Podemos's members have had a tight but often conflictive relationship with it. In the early 2000s, Monedero was an advisor to IU's leader, Gaspar Llamazares. In late 2011, Iglesias and Errejón produced videos and speeches for IU's leader, Cayo Lara, but their attempt to renew the party's strategy and communication style failed, mostly because of Lara's weak image and IU's mistrust of the newly emerging social forces (Rivero 2015: 128–130).

These forces showed up in mid 2011, when the 15 May movement (15M), better known outside Spain as the *Indignados*, changed the face of Spanish society. From the beginning of the year, JSF and the hacktivist platform Democracia Real Ya! (Real democracy now!) had been denouncing the terrible consequences of the economic crisis for the younger generations and the neo-liberal turn of the Zapatero government. On 15 May, both groups called for a mobilisation in Madrid, not under any political banner, with the anti-élite mottos '¡Que no nos representan!' (They don't represent us!) and '¡Que se vayan todos!' (Kick them all out!). At the end of the rally, many people decided to spend the night in the Puerta Del Sol square. By 17 May, the square had turned into a camp, and more camps formed in Barcelona and other major cities. The actions were non-violent, and the 15M gained incredible support from the population. According to a CIS survey in June 2011, 76.2 per cent of the Spanish population showed interest in the 15M movement, and, among them, 70.3 per cent positively evaluated its claims and actions. Also, this support was, at least in the first months of the movement, 'transversal' (Urquizu 2016: 24). This word, more commonly used in Spanish and Italian than in English:

> gives expression to the idea of a democratic practice that looks for commonalities without asserting universalism: notions of difference are seen as encompassing, not replacing, equality. According to Cynthia Cockburn and Lynette Hunter, 'Transversal politics is the practice of creatively crossing (and redrawing) the borders that mark significant politicised differences'.
>
> *(Errejón Galván and Mouffe 2016: 75)*

The 15M attracted the sympathy of people who traditionally voted for parties from the whole right–left spectrum. After the first month, the movement left the squares and turned into neighbourhood assemblies and public sector *Mareas*, citizens' groups defending public schools or hospitals. However, 15M's main achievement was a change in the common perception of social reality. Nevertheless, its refusal of political representation weakened the movement's effective power.

In the November 2011 general elections, indeed, the PP obtained the strongest absolute majority in Spain's democratic history, exposing the greatest contradiction of the 15M experience: the socially widespread questioning of neo-liberal capitalism opened the gates to the political triumph of a party that relies on economic neo-liberalism. In the same electoral round, IU obtained 6.92 per cent, a good result considering the party's history, but a weak one for the historical moment. IU's leadership mistrusted the possibilities offered by 15M, which many leftists considered naive. IU started a process of renewal but renounced the general change of strategy suggested by, among others, Iglesias and Errejón.

Podemos's future members, instead, actively participated in 15M, and *La Tuerka* gave it extensive media coverage. At the beginning of Podemos's experience, some commentators described it as the *Indignados* Party. This definition is incorrect. There are, of course, numerous connections between the two phenomena, and Podemos could not have appeared if the *Indignados* had not opened up a new, transversal political space. But Podemos's relationship with 15M can be better understood as osmosis between two separate organisms. Also, we could say that this image explains Podemos's relationship with most of the previous experiences. Indeed, before Podemos's creation, its members belonged to several political groups. However, Podemos is not the thread that connects all these movements, platforms and parties, like pearls on a necklace. Rather, in an osmotic process, it interchanged people, ideas and practises with them, carrying on some of their deeds, but also renouncing some of their basic principles, as in the case of 15M's mistrust of leadership. So, even when Podemos absorbed these groups, as in the case of IA, they partially preserved their identity and often diverged from Podemos's strategy.

At the beginning of February 2013, Bescansa and Jerez published an article summarising the results of their investigations. Their surveys proved that the general political consensus born with the *Transición* to democracy of the late 1970s had broken down, although this fact had not yet manifested in a general election. At the same time, they insisted, a 'cognitive mobilisation' had started: 'there have been intergenerational convergences among the non-politicised people and the politicised of different ideological traditions, which have even overtaken the traditional identity division between Left and Right' (Bescansa and Jerez 2013).

These ideas were discussed at IA's 2013 summer school, where Urbán and Iglesias imagined a new political project: an electoral force to run for the 2014 European elections, built using a bottom–up approach to link citizens' movements and radical parties. Moruno immediately joined the project, somehow inspired by the idea of creating a 'Spanish Syriza' aggregating all regional leftist forces. Camargo also joined the initial trio and began the development of an online platform that would serve as the tool to acquire membership of the movement (Guedán 2016: 40). Iglesias and Urbán tried to convince IU's and IA's leaders to open up their electoral lists and create a common platform to include representatives and ideas from civil society and social movements. IA finally agreed to get involved in the project, even if some militants remained critical of it. IU's leaders, on the contrary, offered nothing more than a spot on the lists for Iglesias, which he refused. During late 2013, Iglesias and Urbán also dialogued with well-known regional leftist leaders such as Colau, the Andalucian trade unionist Diego Cañamero (1956) and the leader of the Catalan Procés Constituent, Teresa Forcades, but none eventually got involved in the project (Rivero 2015: 134–138). The idea of 'Spanish Syriza' vanished, but the movement kept growing.

By the end of December 2013, while Iglesias's fame allowed him to debate on television with PSOE's secretary general Rubalcaba, the morning meetings in La Marabunta had grown with the participation of Alegre, Fernández Rubiño, Vila, Luis Giménez (1989), Brais Fernández, Bienzobas, Andrea Raboso, Paula Ortega, Andrés Barrágan and David G. Marcos. Errejón, Monedero and Bescansa showed scepticism but also got involved in the project. The name 'Podemos' was created in a car, from chat between Iglesias, Moruno, Urbán and Camargo (Rivero 2015: 139). All these people, mostly friends, were soon joined by the largest Madrid group, mentioned above. Even if the boundaries between the groups were not clearly defined, and some activists did not belong to any, Podemos was essentially founded by Iglesias and the Complutense/*La Tuerka* people, on the one hand, and Urbán and IA on the other.

January 2014 to June 2016: the populist assault of the skies

At the beginning of 2014, the 15M mobilisations had lost momentum, but some groups began to formulate a transition from social movements to the electoral struggle. On 17 January, Podemos emerged from this milieu with the manifesto *Mover ficha: convertir la indignación en cambio político* (Move a piece: turn indignation into political change) and was launched at a press conference at the Teatro del Barrio, in the neighbourhood of Lavapiés, Madrid. Aiming at the forthcoming European elections, Iglesias described Podemos as a citizens' electoral movement – not a party – based on transparency, interested not in uniting the Left but in ending corruption, reversing economic austerity and bringing rising social demands into the political arena. Podemos's members would later describe these quixotic moments as incredibly uncertain and emotional. The acquisition of the 50,000 signatures required to consider the project viable was completed in less than 48 hours, even if the website podemos.info, the only tool to acquire membership, had gone down a few hours before the press conference.

In February, the last attempts to create a common platform with IU failed (Rivero 2015: 142), but a crowded meeting in Madrid's Palafox theatre demonstrated that Podemos was able to proceed autonomously. In its early months, Podemos focused on creation of the militants' *Circulos* (Circles), development of the digital life of the movement and definition of the electoral campaign. The local *Circulos*, developed at a municipal or regional level, often included participants from the post-15M assemblies. There were also sectoral *Circulos*, dedicated to specific issues such as economics, feminism or migration. This division somehow reproduced on a national scale the structure of the thematic workgroups of the 15M squares. The movement was growing quickly all over the country, and the election manifesto was being discussed online: among its programmatic points were a debt audit and exiting Nato. Because of Podemos's low visibility during the campaign, even the most radical demands were not scrutinised by public opinion. The mainstream media's polls did not even consider Podemos, but the meetings were more and more crowded, the social media pages multiplied exponentially, and the *Circulos* arose all around the country. In a Zaragoza meeting, Iglesias and Urbán met the local *Circulo's* spokesperson, Pablo Echenique (1978), an Argentina-born physicist destined to become the leader of Podemos Aragon. Other new faces, not related to the Madrid groups, began to acquire popularity, such as the Murcian Lola Sánchez (1978). The prominent anti-corruption judge Carlos Jiménez Villarejo (1935) offered to run in the primary elections, announcing that, if elected, he would leave his seat to the next candidate. However, the political and media strategy was decided in Madrid. The founders divided into several teams (legal, audio-visual, press, etc.): all of the teams were formed of both IA members and Complutense/*La Tuerka* people, except for the electoral campaign one, which included only the latter (Rivero 2015: 146).

The 'hypothesis Podemos' was the result of the intellectual research of the previous years. Iglesias's focus on political communication, influenced by Toni Negri, Alegre's reading of Marxism from a civic republican perspective (Alegre and Fernández Liria 2010), Monedero's attempt to imagine a twenty-first-century socialism beyond the reform/revolution dichotomy (2013) and Bescansa's exper-tise on polls and understanding of socio-political identities were all part of the hypothesis. These perspectives had some references in common, namely Antonio Gramsci and his concept of hegemony. However, it was Errejón who most profoundly embraced Gramsci's legacy, reinterpreted through Laclau and Mouffe's discourse theory. Since 1985's *Hegemony and Socialist Strategy*, the two authors had recognised the decline in socialist ideology and the rise of new emancipation struggles such as feminism, environmentalism and LGBT move-ments, claims that did not fit in the traditional interpretation of class struggle. As the class was less and less identifiable using traditional categories, the forces that wanted to challenge the rising neo-liberal hegemony had to adopt a new strategy. Laclau refined it in 2005's *On Populist Reason*, re-signifying the concept of populism in an emancipatory sense. The debate on the history of populism is tangled, although recent studies clarify the 'semantic drift' that led 'to a pejorative understanding of the term' after the Second World War (Jäger 2017: 310). For Laclau 2005: 117), however, populism is not 'a *type* of movement – identifiable with either a special social base or a particular ideological orientation – but a *political logic*' based on the alliance of different social demands against the establishment, under the hegemony of one of them. A central concept in Errejón's reading of Laclau is the idea of transversal politics: an approach capable of tying together different social demands in a 'chain of equivalences', highlighting their commonalities without denying their differences. Once in the political struggle himself, Errejón tried to adapt this populist logic to the Spanish context.

From Laclau's perspective, charismatic leaders acquire a central role. In Podemos's case, this was played by Iglesias, who, thanks to the television, had accumulated what Bescansa called a consistent 'media capital'. Polls conducted before the elections showed that 50 per cent of the Spanish population knew

Iglesias, but only 8 per cent knew Podemos (Domínguez and Giménez 2014: 122–129). Therefore, Podemos decided to put Iglesias's face on the ballot paper rather than its logo, a choice that reinforced his charismatic leadership but was criticised by the Left. The 15M had broken traditional political identifications: Podemos's discourse, therefore, substituted the Left/Right dichotomy with the people/élite one, without denying its members' leftist record. Podemos's older members, who had other intellectual sources than discourse theory (i.e. Fernández Liria, Cano, Maura or Lago), partially embraced Errejon's transversal populist perspective, even though others, such as Monedero, remained very critical of it. In this sense, it is safe to say that Podemos is – or was, in its early stages – a populist organisation.

This transversal strategy worked incredibly well in the European elections, and, despite being unknown to most of the Spanish voters, Podemos obtained five seats. For the first time since the end of the *Transición*, the sum of PP's and PSOE's votes did not reach 50 per cent of the total. The particular electoral system of the European elections, with only one national college, avoided the dispersion of Podemos's votes, which would have been inevitable with the fragmented proportional system that serves in Spanish general elections. The results gave Podemos a media and political boost: a CIS survey in June showed that the movement attracted sympathisers from across almost all of the political spectrum.

Podemos scheduled its first *Asamblea Ciudadana* (Citizens' Assembly) for the following autumn. About 7,000 people attended the convention in the Palacio Vistalegre, and 107,488 voted online. Many newcomers from the *Círculos* such as Echenique or Lola Sánchez, who had been elected a European MP, joined the IA group of Urbán and Teresa Rodríguez in the candidature *Sumando Podemos*. They confronted the candidature *Claro Que Podemos*, led by the so-called *Grupo Promotor*: Iglesias, Errejón, Monedero, Bescansa and Alegre. *Sumando Podemos* proposed to open a constituent process within the movement, dividing its leadership into three spokespersons and empowering the *Círculos*. *Claro Que Podemos*, in contrast, asked for confirmation of Iglesias as leader and Errejón as the political strategist, with the goal of winning the 2015 general election. Therefore, the party needed a hierarchical 'electoral war machine' (Errejón), because 'the sky isn't taken by consensus, it is taken by assault' (Iglesias). The system to elect the representatives of Podemos's principal organs, namely the *Consejo Ciudadano Estatal* (CCE – Citizens' State Council), was incredibly unfair to minorities. Iglesias reinforced his team's candidature by saying he would leave the role of secretary general in the case of defeat, and *Claro Que Podemos* gained all the seats of the CCE in a quasi-plebiscite. This audacity caused discontent among 15M and IA activists, who had been forced to dissolve their party to join the renewed Podemos. The open citizens' movement of the beginning of 2014 had turned into a hierarchical party by the end of the year. As a consequence of both the centralization of power within the party and its increased visibility in Spanish society, issues such as exiting Nato were nuanced. Famous economists Vicenç Navarro (1937) and Juan Torres (1954) composed, on behalf of Podemos's leadership, a neo-Keynesian plan, less radical than the militants' manifesto, but aimed at revitalising the Spanish economy through an energy transition financed with massive public investments.

On 31 January 2015, Podemos held a huge rally in the Puerta del Sol. Iglesias's speech made extensive references to patriotism, a theme usually associated with the Right in Spain, re-signifying it progressively. Also, after having campaigned with Tsipras, Iglesias complimented the Greek comrades of Syriza, who had just won their national elections. In these moments, Podemos reached its peak in the polls, resulting in it being the first party in Spain, and 2015 seemed to be *El año del cambio* (The year of change). By that time, however, Spanish parties and institutions had begun a renewal to strike back against a force that seemed capable of severely affecting the country's establishment. One week after the European elections, King Juan Carlos I had abdicated in favour of his son Felipe IV, and shortly afterwards the PSOE held primary elections to replace the old leader, Rubalcaba, with the younger Pedro Sánchez. Furthermore, in February 2015, the Marxist economist and Iglesias's friend Alberto Garzón (1985) was chosen as IU's leading candidate for the forthcoming general elections.

Only the PP, despite its numerous corruption scandals, did not change leaders or structure. But – some months after the president of the Sabadell Bank, Josep Oliu, had expressed the need for a 'right-wing Podemos' – Ciudadanos (C's), a minor neo-liberal party born in 2006 but always confined to Catalonia, came on to the national scene as the *cambio sensato* (sensible change). Campabdal and Miralles (2015) explained C's' quick rise in the polls by its ambiguous relationship with the media and entrepreneurial élite. Towards Podemos, in contrast, the mainstream media showed a fierce attitude. While the party was leading the polls, Monedero was accused of tax evasion and Errejón of breaching a research contract. The accusations had no legal consequence, but the media kept using them against Podemos's leaders and fomented rumours, always proven wrong by the judicial authorities, of secret funding from Venezuela.

However, the party had internal problems too. As Monedero's divergence from Errejón's populist strategy escalated, he resigned from the CCE, creating a fracture in the *Grupo Promotor*. In February, the primary elections for choosing the candidates for the *Autonomias* (regions) showed renewed support for the ex-IA members, now identified as *Anticapitalistas*. Echenique and Teresa Rodríguez won in Aragon and Andalusia, respectively. In the community of Madrid, Alegre won by a minimal margin over Urbán. Bescansa stated that the confrontation was between 'a Podemos to win and a Podemos to protest', a dichotomy that generated bitterness among the *Anticapitalistas*.

As a consequence of the appearance of C's, the attacks from the outside and the contrasts within the party, in early spring 2015 Podemos had already lost the lead in the polls. With its young leader, Albert Rivera (1979), C's undermined

Errejón's transversal strategy because it attracted people who asked for a democratic renewal but identified Podemos as a far left party. Indeed, the Andalucian and Catalan *Autonomias* elections, held in March and September, were a defeat for Podemos, despite the enthusiastic expectations the party had attracted.

Meanwhile, however, the Spanish renovation forces had found new nourishment. Several cities saw the birth of grassroots candidatures for the 24 May 2015 administrative elections. During the Vistalegre convention, Podemos had declined to run by itself for the elections as such, but joined the coalitions of this renewed *municipalismo* with excellent results. With Barcelona en Comú, Colau became mayor of the Catalan capital. The *anticapitalista* Kichi González (1975) won with Ganemos Cádiz. Ahora Madrid, with the support of the PSOE, elected as mayor the prominent judge Manuela Carmena (1944). These successes opened a discussion regarding Podemos's alliances. Overall, the civic coalitions' results had been better than the results obtained by Podemos alone in the elections for the *Autonomias* held on the same day. The possibility of supporting some PSOE administrations revealed a critical issue of Podemos's strategy – namely, whether it considered the socialists to be trembling allies or enemies in disguise. Podemos postponed the general problem but issued practical guidelines aimed at sustaining the PSOE only if that excluded the PP from local governments. Moreover, in some coalitions, Podemos had run together with IU, whereas, in other places, the conflicts had prevailed. They shared many ideological points but saw each other as competitors, and their formal relationship remained undefined.

In the first half of 2015, Iglesias based his strategy on the possible rise of a southern European alliance against German-led economic austerity. Therefore, when the troika ignored the outcome of the Greek referendum of 5 July, Podemos had to change its discourse. Tsipras's forced surrender demonstrated the impossibility of a single national government renouncing austerity, if not breaking with the EU institutions. From that moment, Greece disappeared from Podemos's speeches, and Iglesias affirmed that a situation like the Greek one could not occur 'in the fourth economy of the euro zone'.

Rajoy announced the general elections for 20 December 2015. At the beginning of the campaign, Podemos was not in a good state. The Catalan defeat of September, the inability to create a common platform with IU, the Greek defeat and the apparent recovery of the Spanish economy were all factors against Podemos's growth. At the beginning of its experience, Podemos could contend the left-wing space with PSOE and IU and carry the banner of democratic renewal against the PP. But the development of C's had split the political spectrum into four sectors: Podemos had to contend with the old/new cleavage with C's, and the left/right one with PSOE and IU. Moreover, if the conflicts among the party's two souls were temporarily silent, there were also conflicts between Madrid and the regional emanations of Podemos, displeased with the candidate selection process.

Yet, the 'electoral war machine' was efficient both in its grassroots mobilisation and its centralised strategy. Together with its *confluencias* – regional allies such as the Catalan En Comú Podem, the Galician En Marea and the Valencian Compromís – Podemos obtained 5,212,711 votes, 20.66 per cent of the total, and 69 seats, corresponding to 19.71 per cent of the total 350. PP, PSOE and C's won, respectively, 123, 90 and 40 seats. IU was penalised by the peculiar Spanish proportional system, obtaining only two seats for its 926,783 votes. For the first time in the post-Franco era, Spain had a hung parliament.

Meanwhile, faithful to the task of creating a new hegemony in Spanish society, Podemos had launched several cultural and social projects. In late spring 2015, Podemos set up the foundation Instituto 25 de Mayo para la Democracia and the review *La Circular*, both under the direction of the sociologist Lago, and in July the first summer school was organized in Madrid. The first *Moradas* opened in Madrid and Bilbao, not only as spaces for militants but also cultural centres open to citizens. Also, the party launched *Impulsa* – a project to economically sustain social initiatives, proposed by ordinary people or non-profit organisations, and chosen by Podemos's members voting on the online platform. These projects aimed at creating a constant osmosis between Podemos and the society around it.

These initiatives became possible because of the economic growth of Podemos: the crowdfunding and donations, the inexpensive electoral campaigns and reimbursement of part of the elected members' wages allowed Podemos to be independent of bank loans. This achievement is of primary importance in a country where most parties are deeply indebted to banks. The economic growth, however, strengthened the professionalisation of the party. Alongside the high number of members elected to public office, the number of *liberados* (advisors or employees) increased as well. Rodríguez López (2016: 168) calculated that five or six thousand people belonging to Podemos and its allies may be now involved in the 'industry of representation'. Nevertheless, if some of the party's political decisions have been taken with a hierarchical approach, its financial and economic transparency is a model.

However, the bureaucratisation increased internal conflicts. In March 2016, several members close to Errejón resigned from Podemos's *Consejo Ciudadano* of the community of Madrid. The aim of the *Errejonistas* – as the press began to call them – was to provoke a step back by Alegre, secretary general of the community of Madrid and Iglesias's trusted man. In so doing, the *Errejonistas* would weaken the position of the *Pablistas* – Iglesias's followers – inside the party. But Alegre did not resign, and the *Anticapitalistas* supported the *Pablistas*. Iglesias reacted by removing Sergio Pascual (1977), Errejón's trusted man, from the key position of *Secretario de Organización*; the fundamental role of coordinating the development of the party in the territories was assigned to Echenique. The Complutense/*La Tuerka* group split into *Pablistas* and *Errejonistas*, with the *Anticapitalistas* remaining the third minority faction.

These internal struggles reflected ideological and strategic differences. With no clear majority in Congress, the parties had difficult negotiations. A de facto alliance between Podemos and IU was ongoing in congressional discussions, but Errejón thought that strengthening the bond with IU would definitively situate Podemos on the Left, nullifying it possibilities to reach the national government. He advocated for continuing the transversal strategy, which implied a dialogue with the PSOE. Iglesias conducted confrontational negotiations with Sánchez, with a harsh attitude towards the PSOE that Errejón did not back up. Sánchez signed a deal with C's, whose neo-liberal economic policies were opposite to those of Podemos, and then asked for Podemos's support. Podemos called an internal referendum on its platform: 88.23 per cent of the 149.513 voting members refused to support a government based on the PSOE–C's deal, and 91.79 per cent were in favour of a government formed by PSOE, IU, Podemos and its *confluencias*, led by Sánchez and indirectly supported by the Basque and Catalan nationalist parties. The PSOE could not ask for the support of separatist forces, and, therefore, after six months of unsuccessful negotiations, new general elections were called for 26 June 2016.

July 2016 to July 2017: back to the Left

Podemos and IU agreed to run together as Unidos Podemos (UP) to avoid the waste of votes that affected both in the previous elections. Most polls predicted that UP would overtake PSOE. UP's campaign, therefore, aimed at 'seducing' former socialist voters. The results, however, were disappointing. UP obtained the same number of seats that Podemos and IU had received in December – 71 – but with 5,087,538 votes: more than 1 million votes reverted to abstention. PP, PSOE and C's obtained, respectively, 137, 85 and 32 seats. The parliament was in a stalemate again, but the reinforced Rajoy pushed Sánchez to form a grand coalition government, which the latter resisted. The older PSOE leaders then forced Sánchez to resign as secretary general in a sort of internal coup and allowed PP to form a cabinet with the support of C's. After resigning, Sánchez revealed in an interview that the Prisa group, owner of *El País*, had put pressure on him to avoid forming a government with Podemos. Anyway, Podemos's ambition to lead a progressive government definitively failed.

As the new Rajoy government began its course, Iglesias called a new convention in Vistalegre for February 2017, where three main candidatures competed. Urbán and Rodríguez led *Podemos en Movimiento*, which did not present a candidate for secretary general. Despite the harsh treatment received after the 2014 convention, the *Anticapitalistas* remained loyal to Podemos. With a strong presence in the territories, but with no members in the CCE, they could not achieve Urbán's aim of distributing 'all the power to the *Circulos*'. Their claim for the new convention was to hybridise the party with social movements and reverse its bureaucratisation. Errejón led *Recuperar la Ilusión*, but refused to run for secretary general. His team included most of the Complutense people from the 2014 campaign. Errejón's political strategy relied on the assumption that the transversal 'populist moment' was still open and Podemos should avoid going back into leftist identitarianism. Nevertheless, he maintained that the need for an 'electoral war machine' was over, and, therefore, Podemos ought to democratise its structure, reducing the weight of its leadership. Iglesias, the only strong candidate for secretary general, led *Podemos Para Todas*. The *Pablistas* included elected representatives who had emerged from social struggles, such as deputy Alberto Rodríguez (1981), well-known figures such as Echenique and Navarro, and long-time communist militants such as Manuel Monereo (1959). Iglesias's closest entourage counted on his former comrades from the *Juventudes Comunistas* (Communist Youth), Juan Manuel del Olmo (1982) and Rafael Mayoral (1974), and on younger militants Ramón Espinar (1986), Ione Belarra (1987) and Irene Montero (1988), people who had joined Podemos after the European elections but soon acquired important roles. Iglesias stated that the crisis of institutional hegemony opened up by 15M had ended, the electoral blitzkrieg planned in the first Vistalegre convention had failed, and, therefore, Podemos should abandon the transversal populist strategy. Instead, the party should back labour struggles to reinforce the leftist block that constituted a consistent part of its electorate.

The months before the convention were Podemos's most difficult moment. The confrontation between *Pablistas* and *Errejonistas* became so harsh that the *Grupo Promotor* fell apart. Errejón forced his campaign messages, including Iglesias's pictures in *Recuperar la Ilusión*'s posters. Monedero had left all charges but firmly supported Iglesias from the media. Bescansa urged a joint candidature of the two leaders, but was crushed in their clash: she and leading economist Nacho Álvarez (1977) decided to leave the CCE. Alegre defined Iglesias's closest circle as a 'clique of conspirators' attempting to destroy the party. He was backed up by Fernández Liria, whose article Iglesias commented on with 'disgust', while Urbán called for a peaceful resolution.

Around 9,000 people attended the Vistalegre II convention, and 155,190 voted online, with an election system based on points and, again, unfair to minorities. Iglesias announced that he could only lead Podemos if his team were to obtain the majority in the CCE. *Podemos Para Todas, Recuperar la Ilusión* and *Podemos en Movimiento* received, respectively, 50.78 per cent, 33.68 per cent and 13.11 per cent of the votes, resulting in 37, 23 and 2 seats. Iglesias's victory meant a left turn for the party and a weakening of the *Errejonistas*. Errejón's position of political secretary was terminated, and Montero substituted him as deputies' spokesperson. Nevertheless, Podemos did not split, and perhaps that is enough to show that it is not the usual radical left party.

Paradoxically, Podemos united the Spanish radical Left from the outside, without the apparent will to do so. Revising the surveys and electoral results, one may argue that Errejón's populist strategy could only have worked if C's had not appeared (Padoan 2017). Since early spring 2015, indeed, the transversal support of Podemos, facilitated by the discrediting of the traditional parties, diminished significantly, although the party continued to be the first option among the younger generations and in the biggest cities. As of July 2017, it is not easy to foretell which strategy Podemos will adopt in the future, nor how other parties will confront it. C's is supporting the PP government, whose corruption cases escalate day by day. The PSOE has held new primaries, and Sánchez has been chosen again by the militants over the apparatus's candidate. In June 2017, Podemos presented a *Moción de Censura* (Motion of no confidence) against the PP government, which did not succeed but demonstrated that Rajoy's government is far from stable. Meanwhile, the governments of municipalities such as Madrid and Barcelona, where Podemos plays a key role, are demonstrating that it is possible to reduce debt and implement social expenditure at the same time. These deeds were underlined in an article by Errejón and Iglesias (2017), which somehow publically shows their reconciliation. In the long run, they maintain, the possibilities of a 'government of change' in Spain depend on whether the PSOE decides to turn towards Podemos or remain anchored to the PP–C's axis.

In the meantime, great tasks await Podemos if it wants to fulfil its principles: democratising the 'electoral war machine', cultivating a ruling class taken from younger generations and social struggles, feminizing politics and continuing the work of cultural hegemony to carry Spain towards a fairer country in the difficult context of EU austerity. It is a long and uncertain path, but Podemos has shown it can walk on the most difficult terrains.

References

Coll, A., Fernández, B. and Fernández, J. (2016) *Anticapitalistas en Podemos*, Barcelona: Sylone.

Alegre, Z. L. and Fernández, L. C. (2010) *El Orden de 'El Capital'. Por Qué Seguir Leyendo a Marx*, Madrid: Akal.

Aporrea. (2011) 'Este Lunes Entregan Premio Libertador al Pensamiento Crítico', *Agencia Venezolana de Noticias*, 5 December, at: www.aporrea.org/actualidad/n194218.html (accessed 29 July 2017).

Bescansa Hernández, C. and Jerez Novara, A. (2013) 'Coyuntura Fluida y Nuevo Sujeto Constituyente', *eldiario.es*, 9 February, at: www.eldiario.es/zonacritica/Coyuntura-fluida-nuevo-sujeto-constituyente_6_99100110.html (accessed 29 July 2017).

Bienzobas, S. and Padilla Estrada, P. (2013) 'No Nos Vamos, Nos Echan', *Libre Pensamiento*, n. 77, Winter, at: http://librepensamiento.org/wp-content/uploads/2014/03/LP-77_web4.pdf (accessed 29 July 2017).

Campabadal, J. and Miralles, F. (2015) *De Ciutadans a Ciudadanos. La Otra Cara del Neoliberalismo*, Madrid: Akal.

CEPS Fundación. (n.d.) *Somos*, at: https://web.archive.org/web/20160211074828/http://ceps.es/index.php?option=com_content&view=category&layout=blog&id=35&Itemid=60 (accessed 29 July 2017).

Domínguez, A. and Giménez, L. (eds) (2014) *Claro Que Podemos*, Barcelona: Los libros del lince.

Errejón Galván, I. (2012) *La Lucha por la Hegemonía Durante el Primer Gobierno del MAS en Bolivia (2006–2009): Un Análisis Discursivo*, PhD thesis, Madrid: Universidad Complutense, at: http://eprints.ucm.es/14574/, (accessed 29 July 2017).

Errejón Galván, I. and Iglesias Turrión, P. (2017) 'De Madrid al Cielo', *20 minutos*, 25 July, at: www.20minutos.es/opiniones/pablo-iglesias-inigo-errejon-madrid-cielo-3098575/ (accessd 29 July 2017).

Errejón Galván, I. and Mouffe, C. (2016) *Podemos: In the Name of the People*, London: Lawrence & Wishart.

Guedán, M. (ed.) (2016) *Podemos. Una historia colectiva*, Madrid: Akal.

Iglesias Turrion, P. (2008) *Multitud y Acción Colectiva Postnacional: Un Estudio Comparado de los Desobedientes: De Italia a Madrid (2000–2005)*, PhD thesis, Madrid: Universidad Complutense, at: http://eprints.ucm.es/8458/ (accessed 29 July 2017).

Iglesias Turrion, P. (2015) *Politics in a Time of Crisis*, London: Verso.

Jäger, A. M. M. (2017) 'The Semantic Drift: Images of Populism in Post-War American Historiography and Their Relevance for (European) Political Science', *Constellations*, 24(3): 310–323.

La Barraca Producciones. (2015) 'Podemos: 130 Días Para la Historia', *YouTube video*, 9 December, at: www.youtube.com/watch?v=lg7HznCOBf4&feature=youtu.be&t=21m50s (accessed 29 July 2017).

Laclau, E. (2005) *On Populist Reason*, London: Verso.

La Tuerka. (2012) '"Hacer política es cabalgar contradicciones" Pablo Iglesias sobre la Realpolitik', *YouTube video*, 25 December, at: https://youtu.be/mZrmo_u0Tps?t=9m6s (accessed 29 July 2017).

Monedero, J. C. (2013) *Curso Urgente de Política Para Gente Decente*, Barcelona: Planeta.

Padoan, E. (2017) '"Part of the Elite"? Anti-Austerity Populism and Trade Unionism in Italy and Spain', Paper presented at the 24th Conference of the Council for European Studies, *Sustainability and Transformation*, Glasgow, 12 July.

Perdomo Velázquez, A. (2006) 'Según Profesora de la Complutense Ventaja de Chávez Sobre Rosales es Irreversible', *Agencia Bolivariana de Noticias*, 24 November, at: www.aporrea.org/energia/n86985.html (accessed 29 July 2017).

Rivero, J. (2015) *Podemos*, Barcelona: Planeta.

Rodríguez López, E. (2016) *La Política en el Ocaso de la Clase Media*, Madrid: Traficantes de Sueños.

Urquizu, I. (2016) *La Crisis de Representación en España*, Madrid: La Catarata.

8

TWENTY-FIRST-CENTURY BRITISH ANTI-CAPITALISM

Joseph Ibrahim

Introduction

This chapter charts the wave of anti-capitalism that has swept Britain in various forms and involving different groups, from the 1990s through to the first decade of the twenty-first century. Two major ideologies dominated the British anti-capitalist movement between 2001 and 2005 – anarchism and socialism. Although it would be simplistic to claim that all anti-capitalist activists fell into one of these two ideological camps, it is the case that variants of these major ideologies provided the guiding strategy for many activist groups. What is more, the anti-capitalist collective action frame extended beyond groups that were anti-capitalist and led to a developing critique by groups who connected with the anti-neo-liberal action frames and themes of social justice. The wave of British anti-capitalism morphed into newer movements and networks, which then led to a veritable ideological division between what could be categorized as anarchist- and socialist-influenced movements and networks. For example, the anarchist networks Reclaim the Streets (RTS) and Earth First! UK (EF! UK) gave rise to spin-off groups such as Critical Mass, the WOMBLES, the Social Centres Movement, the Squatters' Movement and the Dissent! network. The Socialist Workers Party initiated the anti-war movement in 2001 and 2003 in the form of the Stop the War Coalition (StWC) and Globalise Resistance (GR) in 2001. In 2011, following the financial crash of 2007–2008, a new global movement emerged in the form of Occupy; again, this was replete with ideological division but it contained a lot more diversity and variation. Following the collapse of Occupy as a political force in the UK circa 2012, a new upswing of activism took place in the form of the campaign group Momentum, which aligned itself with the left of British parliamentary politics.

The purpose of this chapter is to provide a potted history of twenty-first-century British anti-capitalism and show how, as an ideology, it has taken a new form of critique, which has extended into parliamentary politics on an anti-austerity platform. By drawing on data from activist websites, documents and archives, as well as previously published material from my own and activist accounts (see Ibrahim 2013, 2015), this chapter can be divided into two main sections. First, it provides the context of and background to a new wave of anarchist anti-capitalism that emerged in the 1990s through to 2005. Second, it then moves on to discuss the rise of the socialist wave, including GR and other mass movements heavily influenced by socialism and anti-imperialism, particularly StWC. At the same time, this section of the chapter also makes some observations about where British anti-capitalism is at the end of the second decade of the twenty-first century. Here, the chapter outlines how anti-capitalist ideas influenced a new model for social justice within the campaign group Momentum.

Anarchist Britain: a new wave of anti-capitalism

Although anti-capitalism has existed as long as capitalism, as an oppositional phenomenon, social movements come in waves or cycles of contention, dependent on grievances, resources, political opportunities and the emergence and spread of political cultures, identity and ideas (Melucci 1996; Tarrow 2011). The particular wave discussed here charts the main groups from the 1990s through to 2005. This new wave of British anti-capitalism started in the early 1990s with anarchist networks such as EF! UK and RTS. These networks were the initiators of a wave of British anti-capitalist activism that led to spin-off groups and inspired other networks to emerge in the pursuit of social justice. To make sense of this wave, this chapter charts it ideologically and chronologically.

EF! UK and RTS initiated the new wave of British anti-capitalism in the 1990s, which was on an upswing. This spawned the anti-road-building movement and carnivals against capitalism. To provide some detail on who EF! UK are, their website states:

> The general principles behind Earth First! are non-hierarchical organization and the use of direct action to confront, stop and eventually reverse the forces that are responsible for the destruction of the Earth and its inhabitants. EF! is not a cohesive group or campaign, but a convenient banner for people who share similar philosophies to work under.
>
> *(Earth First! n.d.)*

It is important to distinguish it from the US network that started in 1979, as the UK one emerged later, in 1991, with an explicit non-violent ethos:

In the UK it was successfully started in 1991, and quickly grew, developing its own distinct character. Initially the biggest campaigns were around imports of tropical timber and anti-roads campaigns, though there were numerous smaller campaigns. Genetic crops, international solidarity, peat and climate change have been other strong campaigns over time.

(Earth First! n.d.)

RTS London emerged around the same time as EF! UK, and they are inextricably linked. Activists involved in one network were often involved in the other. This is not to say they are the one and the same, but there was a good degree of overlap and interconnection, both in terms of their ideologies and the style of their action repertoires. Ideologically speaking, they are anarchical networks and are anti-consumerist, with a clear message on ecology. As the RTS website states:

RTS was originally formed in London in autumn 1991, around the dawn of the anti-roads movement. With the battle for Twyford Down rumbling along in the background, a small group of individuals got together to undertake direct action against the motor car. In their own words they were campaigning: FOR walking, cycling and cheap, or free, public transport, and AGAINST cars, roads and the system that pushes them.

(Reclaim the Streets n.d.)

Part of the action repertoire of both RTS and EF! UK was the use of satire, spoof newspapers, subvertising and culture jamming. These methods of protesting indicate that they were influenced by earlier 'anarchical' movements such as the Situationist International. Of course, it would be too simplistic to define these groups as purely anarchists, both conceptually and empirically. Conceptually, because anarchism is such a broad-church ideology that to classify them as such runs the risk of losing nuances of the different variants that were active within and alongside these networks. Empirically, because some activists who belonged to these networks would not want to define themselves as anarchists or have *any* ideological labels attached to themselves; in fact, some actively avoid it. That said, we need to make sense of the overarching principles that guided and influenced these groups to understand them as a social movement. Therefore, anarchism in the broadest sense was the driving ideology behind these two networks, either explicitly or implicitly. Moreover, the activists I encountered during my research were predominantly 'anarchical' in their outlook and the political values they held (Ibrahim 2013, 2015) – that is, rejecting all forms of power, striving for freedom and equality, organizing towards mutual aid and arguing against capitalism, as they perceived it as an economic system of domination. Furthermore, referring to an ideology as a guiding framework for these activists helps us to understand the distinction between their world-view and other groups – for example, socialist-influenced groups, who also emerged later as part of this new wave of anti-capitalism and who, although anti-capitalist, have very different alliances and action repertoires from anarchical groups.

A brief chronology of actions by EF! UK and RTS includes the anti-road-building protests such as against the M3 extension at Twyford in 1992, Bath Easton bypass in 1993, and the Newbury bypass in 1996. EF! UK was more than just anti-road building, however: the activists were challenging neo-liberal capitalism generally, and, although these actions seemed local, they were anything but. In fact, they had a philosophy of 'think globally, act locally', with an explicit connection between the two informed political actions. As Plows outlines:

> The First EF! National actions were rainforest related, with mass demonstrations outside Harwood importers; super quarries in the UK, such as Whatley Quarry, were also the site of mass actions. Activists stopping the bulldozers at Twyford, Newbury and other road protests quickly became aware of how construction companies they were opposing were linked to destructive construction projects globally.
>
> *(Plows 2004: 99)*

RTS, who were also part of this wave, held actions between 1995 and 2001. There was a considerable overlap of the activist base between the EF! UK and RTS networks. RTS were known for organizing street-party protests, festivals, carnivals and parties on motorways. Their political contention was very similar to EF! UK's They framed their arguments against growing neo-liberal globalization and the growth in power of supranational institutions that create free trade agreements that benefit the wealthy and encourage an increase in the flow of objects and subjects, leading to an incessant consumerism that, in turn, leads to an ever-increasing search for cheap resources (including oil, which arguably leads to war), exploitation of labour in low-wage economies and pollution from the transportation of 'cheap' goods facilitated by free trade agreements, leading to the destruction of the planet and climate change.

The impact of free trade policies implemented by supranational institutions has been felt acutely in South American countries since at least the 1980s (Walton and Seddon 1994). EF UK! and RTS were aware of these effects and, in the 1990s, they became involved in the larger network, the People's Global Action (PGA), which worked with the Zapatistas in Mexico on humanitarian projects and organized the two *encuentros*. The encuentros were a call by the Zapatistas against neo-liberalism and for humanity. This was a defining moment for the wider alternative globalization movement, as it brought together a number of social movements who networked together, first in 1996 in Mexico and then in 1997 in Spain (Kingsnorth 2004; Maecklebergh 2009). The Zapatistas essentially created a master collective action frame with which anti-neo-liberal groups could identify, thus creating transnational solidarity.

Following on from the encuentros and continuing with an explicit anti-capitalist politics, the City of London, UK, came to a standstill on 18 June 1999 when British anti-capitalist networks launched what was termed a 'Carnival Against Capitalism'. It was actually an international day of protest that was planned to run alongside the G8 summit in Cologne, again in keeping with an anti-neo-liberal political position – the slogan of the day was 'our resistance is as transnational as capital'. This was a coordinated action involving different networks; as well as RTS and EF! UK, Corporate Watch distributed leaflets detailing the locations of financial institutions in London's Square Mile. Samba bands played, and the radical cycle network Critical Mass cycled through the city. Their aim, not dissimilar to EF! UK's and RTS's, was to draw attention to the motor car, pollution, the demand for oil and, arguably, the wars it causes, the damage to human life and the environment, and the cycle as an alternative mode of transport – not to mention the dangers cyclists encounter riding around the City of London, especially during rush hour.

A spoof newspaper, *Evading Standards* (a play on words of *Evening Standard*), was produced and distributed the day before, informing city workers that a financial meltdown was occurring. The City of London came to a standstill as all these coordinated sets of events took place. The event became known as J18, and, after this, there were a number of global days of protest against supranational institutions that also used a shorthand abbreviation relating to the date of the event. There was N30, on 30 November 1999, to coincide with the Seattle protests against the WTO summit. This was probably the biggest event, involving a number of groups, including trade unions and organized labour, environmentalists as well as aid organizations. A British contingent as well as European activists attended S26 (26 September 2000) in Prague, Czech Republic, against the IMF and the World Bank. The next event was one of the most controversial, where feelings of animosity towards elites ran high after an Italian Black Bloc activist, Carlo Giuliani, was shot and killed by Italian police in Genoa during the anti-G8 protests in July 2001. This was a notable protest event for activists of the wider anti-capitalist movement because of the violence meted out against activists by the Italian police. Not only was an activist shot and killed, but activists were also beaten and arrested when they were not protesting but residing in community centres and other spaces that were regarded as safe. Neale (2002) and Notes from Nowhere (2003) document some of the accounts from activists who were there. Neale (2002) states that, following the death of Carlo Giuliani, a mass demonstration took place that brought 300,000 people out on to the streets.

British anarchist groups were present at the events mentioned above and, building on the alliances they made, also started to connect with and or morph into other social groups/networks and reform according to different political foci. A distinctive anarchist squatters' movement formed in 2003, and, linked to this, a nationwide autonomist social centres movement came into being in the UK circa 2003. A new network, following on from EF! UK and RTS, formed in

2005, called the Dissent network. A little later, No Borders, a network that aims to support migrants and asylum seekers and has a distinctive anarchist edge, also emerged. These were significant developments for the anarchist networks in the UK and highlight important political activity within the wider context of British anti-capitalism. I will now unpack each of these new turns to provide a detailed analysis of what their actions and aims were.

Squatting has a long history in the UK, from the early Peasants' Revolt in 1381, through to movements such as the Diggers in the seventeenth century; even in the mid twentieth century, after World War II, a squatters' movement emerged because of homelessness. In response to the UK housing crisis during the 1960s, a new wave of squatting emerged again. However, it was not until the 1970s that an explicit anti-capitalist squatters' movement developed, with a wave of actions by a range of diverse political groups, which included both Trotskyists and anarchists. This was a different movement from earlier family squatters' movements: the 1970s activists framed their actions as a political rejection of the current housing system and did not want to work with the local councils to seek agreements with them to stay. Therefore, squatting is not exclusively an anarchist phenomenon.

However, when the UK Squatting Archive (1998) from 1998 to 2003 is analysed, the squatters' movement is distinctly an anarchist one and included activists from EF! UK and RTS. For example, the Manchester chapter of Earth First! was the main point of contact for the well-known anarchist 'OKasional squat café', which was based in Manchester in 1998. The UK network of squatters, just like the anti-road-building networks, sought to mobilize outside official institutions. This sometimes led to many debates within anarchist circles, and, although it was sometimes necessary to engage with official institutions, the general position was that they would try and not seek permission from or engage with the local authorities.

To some extent, this new wave of squatting was influenced by the earlier social centres movement in various parts of Europe, most notably in Italy, since the 1970s and certainly at the turn of the century. In Italy, social centres were to be found in abandoned buildings, including factories and military barracks. Autonomist activists squatted in these industrial and military wastelands and made them into free spaces, often holding events of a social and political nature, including films and legal advice sessions (for example, for refugees and migrants), holding public and political meetings to discuss the future of the community's needs and wants, sometimes to raise awareness about important political issues around the world, organizing book fairs and access to computers and selling refreshments.

Linked to squatting and the onset of autonomist politics and free spaces in Italy was the creation of autonomist activist groups and social centres in the UK; circa 2001, the new British autonomist group, The WOMBLES (The White Overall Movement Building Libertarian Effective Struggles) was established. These groups were influenced by the Italian autonomist groups Tute Biance and

Ya Basta. The action repertoires of these groups at demonstrations include wearing white overalls and heavy padding to confront riot police on demonstrations (Bircham and Charlton 2001). The idea is to protect themselves from anti-riot weaponry while trying to break through police lines that are perceived to be protecting political and/or corporate elites. Alongside this, the UK autonomist social centres movement also emerged around 2003. The social centre movement in the UK occupied or rented certain disused or low-rent buildings. The centres host not-for-profit activities and offer a free political and social space. In Leeds, for example, a social centre – The Common Place – was set up that sold light refreshments and vegan food, and it had computers and a small library for people to use. Many of the events held were political in nature, such as films from around the world about the struggles of other groups campaigning for autonomy – for example, the Zapatistas. Indeed, fundraising events for the Zapatistas were held, and some of the activists involved would visit Mexico and help with humanitarian projects.

The political-ideological composition of social centres was predominantly anarchist in terms of the people who set them up, organized events and generally worked in them, voluntarily, of course. However, the general attendance to events was very mixed and included a number of different people from a wide section of the cities' communities. Ideologically speaking, it was also the case that the distinction between, say, older anarchist groups and the newer autonomist groups was less clear than, for instance, in parts of Europe, where there can be serious political rivalry. The social centres, based on my research, showed there to be much overlapping activism and friendship between those who would describe themselves as anarchists and autonomists (Ibrahim 2015). In this sense, social centres were political hubs where like-minded activists shared political ideas and resources and planned actions. Indeed, it was in social centres that regular meetings were held in the run-up to summit-meeting protests

The Dissent! network was one such example. After its formation at an EF! UK meeting in 2003, social centres would hold organizational meetings for the network to plan actions. Dissent! brought together a range of anarchist, autonomist and various libertarian groups to organize for a few days of action against the G8 summit meeting to be held in Gleneagles, in July 2005. The Dissent! network has roots in older networks such as EF! UK, RTS and the PGA network, which was established in 1996 at the Zapatista encuentro. The network is open and is explicitly anti-authoritarian. It does not have a membership list, but is open to those willing to subscribe to the hallmarks of the PGA. These are as follows:

1. A very clear rejection of capitalism, imperialism and feudalism, all trade agreements, institutions and governments that promote destructive globalization,
2. We reject all forms and systems of domination and discrimination including, but not limited to, patriarchy, racism and religious fundamentalism of all creeds. We embrace the full dignity of all human beings,

3. A confrontational attitude, since we do not think that lobbying can have a major impact in such biased and undemocratic organizations, in which transnational capital is the only real policy-maker,
4. A call to direct action and civil disobedience, support for social movements' struggles, advocating forms of resistance which maximize respect for life and oppressed peoples' rights, as well as the construction of local alternatives to global capitalism,
5. An organizational philosophy based on decentralization and autonomy.

Smith (2005: 161)

When the Dissent! network mobilized for the Gleneagles protests, the protestors settled in an eco-camp near Stirling and organized their actions from there. The camp was a similar political set-up to the Zapatista idea of a barrio (a neighbourhood). This is an example of how Dissent! was aligned with autonomist politics and even anarchist notions of mutual aid. Activists were expected to help with the running of the camp, including cooking and cleaning, and abide by consensus-based decision-making. Dissent! very much had the hallmarks of anarchical living, albeit temporary.

The main actions of Dissent! were to mobilize through affinity groups against the G8 in Scotland, on 2–6 July 2005. The main actions that week included disrupting the Make Poverty History (MPH) march on Saturday 2 July by joining the demonstration and holding placards that stated 'Capitalism Respects Acceptable Protests' (CRAP). The political message here was that MPH was allowed to proceed because it very much supported the New Labour government and the G8 policies towards Africa, which would not bring about an end to poverty. The next action included a flash mob in Edinburgh city centre at approximately 12 p.m. on 4 July named *The Carnival of Full Enjoyment*, and action then moved on to the actual summit meeting on Wednesday 6 July at Gleneagles.

The protests on 4 July were very much in the style of surrealism, akin to situationism, which had been part of the RTS action repertoire for sometime. This was to draw attention to their ideological perspective, which views capitalism as an economic system that encourages citizens to live to work. The idea of the carnival is to subvert and overturn this idea: instead of seeking employment, one should embrace *full enjoyment*. This involved a samba band marching in the city centre and a number of other activists coming from different directions with stereos playing music.

The police surrounded the first set of activists, which caused a blockage on Princes Street, as there were approximately 11 police vans. Activists came in from different directions, and then the police found themselves between and among activists and citizens (the latter who were going about their normal, everyday business) in the middle of Princes Street. The protests continued for a number of hours, and later riot police were called in, as some protesters started to become more violent, throwing objects at the police. Later in the day, the protests dispersed, but only after the police had kettled various groups of protestors and made a number of arrests. The majority of the protest went on until early evening, around 6 p.m. (Ibrahim 2015). Alongside the Edinburgh protests, there was the Faslane nuclear base blockade. Faslane is home to the Trident submarines. From activist accounts, there was a significant overlap between Dissent! and peace activists – CND and Trident Ploughshares. Although these groups are distinct in terms of their politics and activist base, there was coalescence around the ideas of being anti-war and against the expense of such weapons. This action and cooperation resulted in the closure of the base for most of the day (Harvie et al. 2005).

The next significant set of actions by Dissent! took place on 6 July, the day of the summit meeting, which was framed as a global day of protest. Activist writings from Harvie et al. (2005) detail that the aim was for activists to mobilize at Gleneagles, where the G8 summit was taking place, and, as per the title of the book that outlines Dissent! actions, to Shut Them Down! The following account of events on that day is taken from the aforementioned book. The Dissent! activists started mobilizing from the convergence centres that they were staying in at around 3 a.m., on 6 July. One particular location was an eco-camp in Stirling, about 20 miles from the Gleneagles summit meeting. A number of activists travelled to the Ochil hills to light fires, which were named 'Beacons of Dissent!' The idea was that these fires could be seen by the elites in the Gleneagles hotel as a sign of protest and dissent. Other contingents and affinity groups from the Stirling eco-village/convergence centre left to blockade the M9, which becomes the A9 road to Gleneagles. The aim of this was to try and block the roads for delegates who were attending the summit meeting.

Although there was an overall plan to blockade roads to Gleneagles, this was loosely planned, and there was no central direction, which fits with anarchist politics. Therefore, affinity groups planned and carried out their own actions and would meet up with other groups or remain separate if they wanted to. Activists from the Edinburgh and Glasgow convergence centres also started to leave at a similar time, with the intention to blockade hotels where delegates were staying. According to activist accounts, the Sheraton hotel in Edinburgh was targeted, and the Japanese delegates who were staying there were delayed. Later, when the police had cleared the blockade and the Japanese delegates were en route, anarchists crashed two cars on the Forth Bridge, which delayed the Japanese delegates even further. Because of the blockades on the M9, the Canadian delegates never reached Gleneagles that day (Trocchi et al. 2005: 86). At Gleneagles itself, a perimeter fence was erected as a barrier to activists. A range of activists – not only those who were part of Dissent! – broke through the fence and then ran up to the inner fence that denoted the red zone. More police were flown in by Chinook helicopters; they made arrests and pushed the activists back in to the 'safe zone' (Gorringe and Rosie 2008: 199).

Dissent! is significant not just in its own right as an anarchist anti-capitalist network, but also as a response to a renewed and growing socialist contingent that also engaged in anti-capitalist politics and protest. The anarchist networks reigned supreme as *the* anti-capitalists during the late 1990s and early 2000s (Carter and Morland 2004) and even gained a certain symbolic dominance for some time (Ibrahim 2013). However, a socialist challenge emerged, which meant that, at certain events – summit meetings, protests and general anti-capitalist rallies – socialist groups with an altogether different politics also started to mobilize around broad anti-capitalist issues with trade union groups, whereas anarchist groups tended to neglect the political potential of working with trade unions. These socialist groups, in particular, were those who opposed the war in Afghanistan and later Iraq, trade unions, and left of UK Labour parliamentarians unhappy with the move to the right following the electoral success of New Labour.

The socialist challenge

Although socialist groups were active when the new wave of anti-capitalism emerged at the turn of the century, they were not really part of it. In some ways, their action repertoires were seen as outdated, and they were not involved in mobilizing for the summit meetings or other protest events (Carter and Morland 2004). However, in 2001, this changed for two main reasons. First, there were a number of left-wing activists with socialist or social democratic views who wished to contest the worst excesses of neo-liberal capitalism and the democratic deficit created by supranational political institutions, but who did not fit in with the ideological views of the anarchist groups or their actions. This led to the emergence of newer socialism-influenced organizations that were coalitions from a range of left-wing activist groups. These included GR and the Socialist Alliance. These groups were made up of the Socialist Workers Party, Workers Powers, some green activists, trade unionists and independent activists (the last were unaffiliated to any political group). Second, the UK government, along with the US, went to war in Afghanistan following the terrorist attacks of 9/11 in 2001, and it seemed Iraq would also be targeted as a rogue state soon. Within socialist ideology, there is a strong anti-imperialist discourse, and in reference to this the subsequent wars in Afghanistan and Iraq were framed as imperial wars. In particular, the reasons for war on Iraq (that Saddam Hussein, then president of Iraq, had chemical weapons and was a threat) were considered to be a ruse in order to invade the country and capture oil resources (Reza and Rees 2003). The invasion of Afghanistan led to the creation of the StWC, and then, when it seemed Iraq would be next, the movement grew to produce the largest demonstration in the history of the UK – even estimates from conservative sources put the number at 1 million (Syalm et al. 2003).

According to my research (see Ibrahim 2013, 2015), it is the case that GR was created to build alliances between different activists groups that were anti-neo-liberal but did not fit into the anarchist collective-action frame. It was also developed to move away from the tactics and strategies of older socialist groups that were based around arguments of class struggle. This is not to diminish the importance of class struggle, but rather to re-evaluate the way in which post-industrial economies have led to a fragmented class identity through precarious and temporary working conditions. Thus, GR appealed to a different activist constituent that was anti-capitalist and left-wing, but not anarchist. GR emerged from a series of conferences held around the UK with keynote speakers including George Monbiot (a longstanding environmental campaigner and *Guardian* columnist). Interestingly, he was also dissatisfied with anarchist politics at the turn of the century, but wanted to raise concerns about the environment, social justice and the problems with neo-liberalism (Monbiot 2000).

Following on from the conferences, it seemed that GR had a political appeal amongst socialists, social democratic activists and trade union activists, based on attendance and the political mood at their meetings. After these conferences, GR set up an office in Brick Lane, in East London, and headed a multitude of campaigns and mobilizations from there. The structure of GR was very different to the anarchist groups mentioned. It had a steering committee and a defined membership base. It held regular meetings and forums to decide on actions for upcoming events. It seems from its website that there have been no updates since 2014. However, at the start of the twenty-first century, GR was very much a presence during British anti-capitalist mobilizations. It had a high profile and presence and attended and or helped organize numerous events. These included being part of StWC from 2001, the first European Social Forum (ESF) in Florence in 2002, the ESF in 2004, which was held in London, and the G8 Alternatives in Edinburgh during the G8 summit meeting, in July 2005. It brought attention to a range of contentious issues such as the arms trade, environmental degradation by corporations, and unethical corporate practices and poor working conditions for employees in 'sweat-shops'. As well as international events, it also brought attention to local issues in London, one being low pay for workers in Canary Wharf who were campaigning for union rights and a living wage (Globalise Resistance 2004). It was GR's ability to connect with a wider social base through a wider range of social issues that brought about a challenge to the anarchist dominance of the British anti-capitalist politics in the twenty-first century. The formation of GR and StWC within months of each other led to some ideological competition and conflict between them and the anarchists. The latter accused the former of being merely front groups for the long-standing socialist organization the SWP (Schnews 2001a, 2001b).

Although both GR and StWC had or have a clear relationship with the SWP and, to some extent, overlapped in terms of membership base and issues, both organizations appealed to a much broader activist and citizen base than the socialists. The activist base and affiliations of GR have been outlined above.

The StWC was even broader still. The SWP was instrumental in setting it up, but a range of different people were involved from a number of different groups, including left of New Labour politicians (Jeremy Corbyn and George Galloway); the first president of StWC was the late left-wing political activist and former Labour MP, Tony Benn. On the steering committee, together with SWP activists such as Lindsey German and John Rees, was Andrew Murray of the Communist Party (CP). This is noteworthy as the SWP and CP are in reality political rivals and have very different views. However, these were put aside because of the anti-war collective action frame they share. In addition, the StWC also developed links with the long-standing peace group CND and the religious group the Muslim Association of Britain, for the demonstration in London on 15 February 2003.

StWC was also a key part of the anti-G8 mobilization in Edinburgh and Gleneagles, in July 2005. It, along with other groups, formed the G8 Alternatives. This protest coalition was distinct from both the MPH campaign and the Dissent! one mobilizing at the same time. It included around 200 speakers from a number of different groups – for example, the SWP, the Scottish Socialists, George Monbiot, George Galloway of the Respect Party, Caroline Lucas of the Green Party and activists from GR. It helped mobilize thousands of activists throughout the week, from Friday 1 July to Wednesday 6 July. A number of rallies and talks were held throughout Edinburgh during this time. On the morning of 6 July, the day of the summit meeting, attempts by the Edinburgh contingent to reach Gleneagles were thwarted when the police cancelled the pre-booked coaches. This led to an impromptu demonstration in the centre of Edinburgh by thousands of activists who were waiting for the coaches but discovered they had been cancelled. Activists also discovered that trains to Gleneagles had also been cancelled. The coaches were later reinstated, but not before the people waiting for transport took to protest in the centre of Edinburgh, which resulted in traffic coming to a standstill for most of the day. Some of the activists did manage to reach Gleneagles after some coaches were reinstated, but others decided to stay and carry on demonstrating in Edinburgh.

The broadly speaking socialist anti-capitalist contingent, which included the SWP, GR, StWC and the various groups that were part of the mobilization in Gleneagles, the G8 Alternatives, filled a political gap in British left politics. It included those who were anti-war, pro-trade union, anti-New Labour and pro-environment. Although it could be argued that the anarchist anti-capitalist networks are some of these things, their ways of politically organizing are not always understood or accessible to the wider activist populace or indeed the general public. By contrast, the socialist contingent reached a broader populace by working more closely with anti-Blairite trade unions and protesting against the wars in Iraq and Afghanistan, which connected with a significant British public.

From 2001 to 2005, then, British anti-capitalist groups were mobilizing regularly, and thus an upswing was happening. Yet, although contentious politics is ongoing, it rises and falls according to numerous factors encapsulated within the contentious politics framework of external opportunities, mobilization of resources and cognitive mechanisms (Tarrow 2011). From 2005 to 2009, British anti-capitalism was on a down-swing, and levels of contention in terms of mobilization were evident – the flash mobs and large-scale demonstrations subsided. However, another cycle emerged after the financial crash of 2007–2008, and groups started to become more visible again. A case in point was the Climate Camp movement in April 2009, in the City of London, against the G20. The political focus was against climate change and against the banking crisis. The effects of the financial crash of 2007–2008 started to be felt from 2009 onwards, and, by September 2011, another upswing of contention against neo-liberalism emerged in full flow, in the form of the Occupy Movement. The Occupy Movement was, of course, heavily influenced by the Arab Spring and Spanish Indignados earlier in the same year (Kerton 2012).

Over the last 7 years, the effects of austerity policies have started to be felt by sections of the population. These include education cuts to, for example, the Education Maintenance Allowance, the trebling of tuition fees for higher education, the introduction of the bedroom tax and, more recently, the imposition of universal credit. These policies have mobilized a new generation of activists who are not necessarily explicitly anti-capitalist, but who are anti-neo-liberal and anti-austerity. In response to this, we have seen an electoral challenge through the election of Jeremy Corbyn as Labour Party leader and an increase in membership of the Labour Party, from 388,000 in December 2015 to 552,000 as of January 2018 (Audickas et al. 2018). The campaign group Momentum has managed to mobilize young voters and connect with them effectively through social media, which has led to an increase in parliamentary seats for the Labour Party, and, as a consequence, the sitting Conservative government lost its majority. Although the Labour Party is not anti-capitalist in the same sense as the early mobilizations discussed, it is addressing and raising some concerns that challenge the neo-liberal orthodoxy that has been in place for more than 25 years. To this end, some aspects of the social justice claims that were apparent within the anti-capitalist movement have extended into a discourse that translates into a social democratic and parliamentary political framework for change.

Conclusion

This chapter has detailed the main actions, alliances, political formations and ideological compositions of the twenty-first-century British anti-capitalist movement. The anarchist and anarchical mobilizations emerged in the 1990s and carried on well into 2005; the new socialist and socialism-influenced political mobilizations emerged in 2001 and were galvanized primarily by the wars on Afghanistan and Iraq. The former emerged to challenge the incessant consumerism of capitalist Britain and, in true anarchist style, sought to subvert the status quo, using flash-mob tactics that often took the authorities and corporations by surprise.

It seemed, during the early 2000s, that the only real anti-capitalists were the anarchists; however, there were many groups and citizens on the left who wished to raise awareness about different causes, or at least in a different way, but not in the old way as some of the long-standing socialists had always done, particularly the A to B march. Britain then saw a new wave of socialism-influenced groups, primarily GR and StWC, which drew attention to the use of sweat-shop labour, low-pay Britain and environmental harm from corporations. The main difference between issues is the action and position on the wars against Afghanistan and Iraq. Although anarchists would probably agree with the anti-war stance, they were not really active on this issue.

Both ideological camps have been active throughout the twenty-first century, but, after 2005, there was a veritable down-swing, and the protests noticeably declined. That said, it is arguable that, after the financial crash of 2007–2008 and the subsequent austerity policies, a new generation of activists has established a new anti-neo-liberal master frame that argues against austerity and for social justice. The main difference between turn-of-the-century anti-capitalism and this new left movement, in the form of Momentum and some of the current grassroots activists of the Labour Party, is that they are seeking parliamentary representation. If austerity and cuts continue in their current form, we may well see a newly elected government that promises to address some of the concerns of the next generation of activists.

References

Audickas, L., Dempsey, N. and Keen, R. (2018) *Briefing Paper Number SN05125 Membership of UK Political Parties*, London: House of Commons Library.

Bircham, E. and Charlton, J. (2001) *Anti-Capitalism*, London: Bookmarks.

Carter, J. and Morland, D. (2004) *Anti-Capitalist Britain*, Cheltenham: New Clarion Press.

Earth First! (n.d.) 'What is Earth First!', at: https://earthfirst.org.uk/actionreports/whatisef.html (accessed 16 February 2018).

Globalise Resistance. (2004) 'Canary Wharf Demonstration', at: www.resist.org.uk/global/social-forums/esf-london-2004/canary-wharf-demonstration/ (accessed 8 May 2018).

Gorringe, H. and Rosie, M. (2008) 'It's a Long way to Auchterader! Negotiated Management and Mismanagement in the Policing of G8 Protests', *British Journal of Sociology* 59(2): 187–205.

Harvie, D., Milburn, K., Trott, B. and Watts, D. (2005) *Shut Them Down! The G8, Gleneagles 2005 and the Movement of Movements*, Leeds and New York: Autonomedia.

Ibrahim, J. (2013) 'The Struggle for Symbolic Dominance in the British Anti-capitalist Movement Field', *Social Movement Studies* 12(1): 63–80.

Ibrahim, J. (2015) *Bourdieu and Social Movements*, London: Palgrave.

Kerton, S. (2012) 'Tahrir, Here? The Influence of the Arab Uprisings on the Emergence of Occupy', *Social Movement Studies: Journal of Cultural & Political Protest* 11(3–4): 302–308.

Kingsnorth, P. (2004) *One No, Many Yeses*, London: Free Press.

Maecklebergh, M. E. (2009) *The Will of the Many: How the Alter Globalization Movement is Changing the Face of Democracy*, London: Pluto Press.

Melucci, A. (1996) *Challenging Codes*, Cambridge: Cambridge University Press.

Monbiot, G. (2000) 'Streets of Shame', *The Guardian*, 10 May.

Neale, J. (2002) *You Are G8, We Are 6 Billion: The Truth Behind the Genoa Protests*, London: Vision.

Notes from Nowhere. (2003) *We Are Everywhere: The Irresistible Rise of Global Anti-Capitalism*, London: Verso.

Plows, A. (2004) 'Activist Networks in the UK: Mapping the build up to the Anti-Globalization Movement', in J. Carter and D. Morland (eds), *Anti-capitalist Britain*, Cheltenham: New Clarion Press.

Reclaim the Streets. (n.d.) 'The Evolution of Reclaim the Streets', at: http://rts.gn.apc.org/evol.htm (accessed 16 February 2018).

Reza, S. and Rees, J. (2003) *Anti-Imperialism: A Guide to the Movement*, London: Bookmarks.

Schnews. (2001a) 'Monopolise Resistance? – How Globalise Resistance would Hijack Revolt', at: www.schnews.org.uk/monopresist/monopoliseresistance/index.htm (accessed 9 May 2018).

Schnews. (2001b) 'Monopolise Resistance- The SWP Try to Hijack Anti-War Protests', at: www.schnews.org.uk/sotw/monopolise-resistance.htm (accessed 9 May 2018).

Smith, A. (2005) 'The International Mobilisation to Gleneagles', in D. Harvie, K. Milburn, B. Trott and D. Watts (eds), *Shut Them Down! The G8, Gleneagles 2005 and the Movement of Movements*, Leeds and New York: Dissent! and Autonomedia.

Syalm, R., Alderson, A. and Milner, C. (2003) 'One Million March against War', *The Daily Telegraph*, at: www.telegraph.co.uk/news/uknews/1422228/One-million-march-against-war.html (accessed 14 May 18).

Tarrow, S. (2011) *Power in Movement*, Cambridge: Cambridge University Press.

Trocchi, A., Redwolf, G. and Alamire, P. (2005) 'Reinventing Dissent! An Unabridged Story of Resistance', in D. Harvie, K. Milburn, B. Trott and D. Watts (eds), *Shut Them Down! The G8, Gleneagles, 2005 and the Movement of Movements*, Leeds and New York: Dissent! and Autonomedia.

UK Squatting Archive. (1998) Available at: www.wussu.com/squatting/#links (accessed 16 February 2018).

Walton, J. and Seddon, D. (1994) *Free Markets and Food Riots*, Oxford: Blackwell.

PART III
The state and leftist parliamentary politics

9

PREJUDICE ON THE DOORSTEP

Labour activists talk immigration

David Bates

Introduction

In the early autumn of 2016, a spate of highly publicised interventions by senior Labour politicians highlighted deepening divisions in the Parliamentary Labour Party (PLP) on the question of immigration. In a collection of essays published by the Fabian Society in September, the former shadow chief secretary to the Treasury, Rachel Reeves, argued for stronger immigration controls and an end to free movement in light of the popular vote for 'Brexit' three months earlier. She later warned that her constituency of Leeds West was like a 'tinderbox' waiting to 'explode' if the issue was not adequately addressed. Later that week, however, Labour leader Jeremy Corbyn used his keynote speech at party conference to defend freedom of movement and defy calls for his party to commit itself to a cap on immigration. In the following months, the tension between Corbyn and many of his backbenchers on the issue would resurface continually, both before and after the general election of June 2017.

This chapter explores the rhetorical aspects of such debates through the accounts of a handful of Labour activists and councillors from the north-east of England, who describe their own encounters with the issue of immigration in constituencies that voted by a majority to leave the EU. How, for example, do activists talk about immigration and the outpouring of racism that occurred across Britain in the months that followed the referendum? What do they think their party's response should be to the widespread hostility towards immigration that surfaces in opinion polls? What are their experiences of talking about immigration with voters? Critical discourse analysis (CDA) is employed to explore how activists and councillors position themselves in relation to public opinion, the national media and debates in the PLP.

In a number of ways, it can be seen how Labour's current divisions over immigration are not unprecedented, with contemporary discourses bearing remarkable similarities to those from the mid to late twentieth century. However, although senior Labour politicians can be seen at times to draw on 'Powellite' discourses that construct immigration as a threat to the privilege of the 'white working class', the talk of activists and councillors is marked by a 'common sense anti-racism' (Benwell 2012) that emphasises the racial heterogeneity of the working class but also attempts to 'deracialise' immigration as an issue of Labour Party policy. In this respect, current discourses around racism and migration in the Labour Party are perhaps more complex and contradictory than ever. Activists attempting to bridge the gap between their own anti-racist beliefs and the right-wing drift of public opinion in recent years do so by highlighting the wider benefits of achieving electoral power, although it is notable how 'public opinion' is constructed in ways that involve the strategic silencing of certain voices. Drawing on theories of race and racism from cultural studies and sociology (Gilroy 2004; Lentin 2016; Virdee 2014), the chapter also ponders the question of whether it is possible for Labour to engage in a meaningful 'conversation' about immigration without also addressing the legacies of colonialism and empire that are woven into the fabric of British culture and society. Beginning with the EU referendum campaign and its aftermath, the following analysis offers some tentative answers.

Making the white folk angry: racism, migration and Brexit

The result of the referendum on the UK's membership of the European Union in June 2016 shook the country's political establishment to its core. Within hours of the vote to 'leave' being announced, Prime Minister David Cameron had announced his intention to resign, and the value of the UK's currency plummeted to its lowest point in decades. Labour Party leader Jeremy Corbyn, meanwhile, faced days of mass resignations from shadow cabinet colleagues in protest at his handling of Labour's campaign to remain in the EU, and was formally challenged over his leadership just a few weeks later.

In the weeks and months after the vote for Brexit, reports of racial and religious hate crime soared by 41 per cent (BBC News 2016). The issue of immigration had played a key role in the referendum campaign – during which a Labour MP, Jo Cox, was murdered by a far-right nationalist – and, in the aftermath of the vote, researchers were quick to identify immigration as a key issue for many of those who had voted to leave the EU. As Goodwin and Ford (2017: 21) observed, 'by the time of the EU referendum, immigration had been at the top of the political agenda for well over a decade, something which had never happened before in British politics'. The topic duly became the focal point of Theresa May's first substantial speech as new prime minister at the Conservative Party conference in September, with May arguing that the benefits of 'high immigration' were 'close to zero', and that immigration had exerted negative pressure on wages, public services and social cohesion.

Such was the context for the fresh arguments that surfaced in the Labour Party that autumn over whether the principle of free movement embodied in EU membership was electorally sustainable in Britain following the popular vote to leave. Wider divisions over immigration had riven the party since the general election of 2010, when Prime Minister Gordon Brown had privately denounced as a 'bigot' one voter who raised concerns about incoming migrants from Eastern Europe. The rising popularity of the United Kingdom Independence Party made immigration a source of mounting concern to Labour under the leadership of Ed Miliband, between 2010 and 2015, particularly given its support among former Labour voters (Goodwin and Ford 2013). In October 2014, a leaked party campaign document urged Labour activists that, in conversing with UKIP supporters, their focus should be on 'moving the conversation on to issues where we have clear policy which tackles the problems people are worried about, whether they express those concerns through the prism of immigration or not' (Labour Party 2014: 23). This prompted accusations of evasion and denial that bolstered the party's determination to appear 'tough' on immigration in the run-up to the general election of 2015, when Miliband's leadership team repeatedly criticised the Coalition government's failure to reduce the number of migrants entering the country and called for stronger border controls and curbs on new migrants' access to welfare benefits.

Race, migration and discourse

It is significant that many of the debates described above hinge upon how the party is seen to 'talk' about immigration. Numerous media articles written by MPs and activists in recent years have made reference to the party's need to 'talk', 'discuss' and 'converse' about an issue that has dominated Labour politics for more than a decade. As long ago as 1999, for example, Labour Prime Minister Tony Blair could be found briefing aides on the need to be 'tough' on crime and asylum: 'These may appear unlinked to patriotism but they are: partly because they are toughness issues; partly because they reach deep into British instincts' (Watkins 2004: 16). In fact, language itself has long been considered a key feature of 'race relations' in British politics. Moore (2013: 355), for example, has pointed to the rhetorical continuities between Enoch Powell's 'rivers of blood' speech in 1968 and Margaret Thatcher's comment in 1978 that British people felt 'swamped by people with a different culture'; Moore points out that such rhetoric was echoed in 2002 by Labour education minister David Blunkett, who claimed that some schools in Britain were in danger of being 'swamped' by asylum seekers. Rachel Reeves's recent comments to the effect that her 'white working class' constituents might riot if immigration was not curbed are only the latest to draw on a form of 'Powellite' rhetoric that attributes the existence of racism to the very presence of migrants in Britain (Barker 1981).

Much of the research on racism in Britain and Europe since the Second World War has focused accordingly on the role of language or 'discourse' in reproducing racist ideas and discriminatory practices (Augoustinos and Every 2007; van Dijk 1987, 1993; Wetherell and Potter 1992). Following the 'linguistic turn' in the social sciences in the 1980s, the operations of racism were increasingly seen to be discursive, with Stuart Hall (1992), for example, describing 'race' itself as an 'organising category of those ways of speaking, systems of representation, and social practices (discourses) which utilise a loose, often unspecified set of differences in physical characteristics' – such as skin colour – as 'symbolic markers' in order to differentiate groups of people (1992: 298). This was based on an understanding that 'race' had no scientific basis, and skin colour was no more indicative of biological group difference than hair colour or eye colour. The idea of race was, therefore, seen to be socially and culturally constructed, albeit materially constituted through the racial ordering of the world from colonialism onwards.

Discursive studies of immigration in the tabloid media have consistently highlighted the prevalence of discourses that racialise migrants and minorities and invoke the language of invasion and war to describe the arrival of newcomers (Gabrielatos and Baker 2008; Lynn and Lea 2003). Gilroy (2004: 98), for example, has noted the 'obsessive repetition of key themes – invasion, war, contamination, loss of identity' in discussions of immigration, which he attributes to 'post-colonial melancholia':

> That structure of feeling governs the continuing antipathy toward all would-be settlers. Later groups of immigrants may not, of course, be connected with the history of empire and colony in any way whatsoever. However, they experience the misfortune of being caught up in a pattern of hostility and conflict that belongs emphatically to its lingering aftermath.
>
> *(Gilroy 2004: 110)*

Indeed, even contemporary references to the 'white' working class can be seen to bear traces of this imperial nostalgia, with Eastern European workers excluded from symbolic formations of whiteness in much the same way as English and Irish workers themselves were once seen to be a race apart from the white Victorian bourgeoisie. As Bonnett (2000) and Virdee (2014) have carefully detailed, English workers were only gradually invited to identify themselves as 'white' and British as part of a campaign to popularise empire and prevent the emergence of a revolutionary, internationalist proletarian class consciousness. It is noted that the Labour Party and the wider labour movement (including trade unions) played a key role in this process, and, as Virdee (2014: 99) observes, only in the aftermath of the Second World War were the working classes fully brought into a racialised white nationalism in which 'the state, employer and worker' were united in a shared sense of white, British superiority.

Methods

The following research draws on CDA of interviews with Labour Party members and councillors from the north-east of England who discuss their own views and experiences of racism, migration and party political activity in contemporary British politics. As such, the analysis focuses on the interviewees' use of language to construct 'versions of the world, of society, events and inner psychological worlds' (Potter 2011: 188), with discourse here understood as 'language in use'. The methods adopted for analysing the talk of interviewees is influenced by both CDA and discursive psychological approaches that focus on 'what people are doing with their talk' (Goodman 2014: 147). Discourse is understood as being 'socially constitutive as well as socially conditioned – it constitutes situations, objects of knowledge, and the social identities of people and groups of people' (Fairclough and Wodak 1997: 258). That is to say, it is through language that people understand themselves as well as the world around them; language is seen 'not merely as representative of the world, but as constituting, defining and characterising it' (Khosravinik 2015: 59).

CDA is concerned with the analysis of discourse from a critical political perspective, and, as Wodak and Meyer (2001: 2) comment, CDA is 'fundamentally concerned with analysing opaque as well as transparent structural relations of dominance, discrimination, power, and control as manifested through language'. In this way, CDA practitioners draw on the epistemology of critical realism to argue that 'discourses should be examined in relation to social structures, including the power relationships that are responsible for occasioning them' (Bryman 2008: 508). Critical analyses of racist discourse, for example, have shown how, 'through discourse discriminatory, exclusionary practices are prepared, promulgated, and legitimised' (Wodak and Reisigl 1999: 172). Although most CDA studies of migration and racism have focused on 'elite discourse' – that is, the discourse of politics, journalism, business, academia and other spheres where socially powerful groups are to be found – the focus here is primarily on how immigration and racism are constructed in the non-elite political discourse of Labour Party members and activists in a single parliamentary constituency in the north-east of England. Engelbert (2014: 435) has observed how Labour Party members' discourse can be understood 'for its relatively autonomous rhetorical ability to play an important role in justifying and legitimising a party's contested political narrative'. In the following analysis, the focus is on how members justify, challenge and rework existing political narratives about immigration and racism that are a common feature of the elite discourse described above. Analysis focuses on such features as stake or interest management (Engelbert 2014), common-sense anti-racism (Benwell 2012), prejudice denial or mitigation (Condor et al., 2006), and other linguistic features suggestive of the 'norm against prejudice' and a 'norm against racism' (Goodman 2014). In examining the use of these strategies, the analysis seeks not only to understand how racism and immigration are constructed, but also to 'unpack the ideological underpinnings of discourse that have been naturalised over time so deeply that we begin to treat them as common, acceptable and natural features of discourse' (Khosravinik 2015: 51).

The interviews featured here took place between September 2016 and May 2017 and were conducted mostly in person at locations chosen by the interviewees. Eight individuals were interviewed in total, with interviews typically lasting between 30 and 45 minutes, and interviewees were chosen on the basis of their extensive involvement in party campaigning in recent years – these individuals belonged to a core of around 20 activists who had been most active in their constituency Labour Party in recent years, mostly before the 2015 general election. Interviewees answered a small set of pre-prepared questions that focused on their background as members of the Labour Party, their experiences of encountering the issue of immigration during political activity, and their views on how both the party itself and activists more generally should respond to current concerns around the subject of immigration. Interviews were conducted in a dialogic, conversational manner in which the researcher would offer his own comments, where appropriate, in order to prompt further discussion; as Roseneil (1993: 199) has observed with reference to her own ethnographic work, this kind of mutual exchange of stories was not only felt to be 'ethically desirable' but also 'added to the richness of the interview material'.

It should also be noted that the researcher was known to some of the interviewees before the interviews took place, primarily through joint involvement, to varying degrees, in local Labour politics. The use of a researcher's own experiences, hobbies or employment history to inform research is well established in social research, and some of its advantages are spelled out by Costley, Elliot & Gibbs (2010: 3): 'Not only do you have your own insider knowledge, but you have easy access to people and information that can further enhance that knowledge'. This approach was also undertaken with an understanding that such interviews produce 'situated knowledge' that is 'inscribed by, and not separate from, its social location and context' (Gunaratnam 2003: 60). In fitting with the analytical approach adopted, the relevance of that social location and context have been highlighted wherever it is deemed to be especially significant.

Analysis

On close inspection of the talk uttered by Labour Party members during interviews, a number of interesting themes emerge, revealing much about the ideological assumptions underpinning contemporary political debates on immigration and racism, as well as the ideological dilemmas facing party activists who are committed to both anti-racism and majoritarian democratic politics. Interviewees emphasised their commitment to anti-racism in various ways, drawing on subtly different interpretations of what constitutes racism, with some invoking their own migrant identities to challenge or rework dominant narratives that frame immigration and free movement in a predominantly negative way. Often this went hand in hand with attempts to 'deracialise' the issue of immigration and mitigate some expressions of hostility towards immigration while unreservedly condemning others. Such themes are explored below through examination of three substantial stretches of talk, each from separate interviews with a different individual, highlighting some of the discursive strategies that were common among interviewees. The first focuses on how attempts to deracialise immigration can be seen to rest on notions of racism as primarily being a matter of skin colour prejudice. The second focuses on how speakers distinguish between different forms of racism, some of which are more objectionable than others. The third and final extract focuses on how activists manage the balance between anti-racist beliefs and their commitment to electoral politics, given the rightward shift of public opinion on this question. Throughout these sections, certain themes recur, such as the shared assumption that more 'talk' on immigration is needed, as well as the implicit importance attached to maintaining the norm against prejudice.

Extract 1 – it feels like it's a race issue

Although the topic of racism figured prominently in the talk of most respondents, it was notable that differing conceptions of racism were articulated. The first extract is from an interview with a female Labour councillor from a largely urban, socially deprived council ward, who made the following comments in response to a question on how often immigration had been raised as an issue during her time as an elected councillor or as a campaigner across the wider parliamentary constituency.

Most notable here are the speaker's attempts to disentangle the issues of Brexit, race and immigration. 'Race' is taken to mean 'skin colour', and the speaker is careful to foreground her own racial identity as a 'first generation immigrant' who is privileged as a result of being 'white'. This acknowledgement of white privilege was one of the few examples where interviewees hinted at a deeper and more institutional understanding of racism, rooted (as the speaker goes on to suggest) in the historical practices of colonialism and imperialism that imbued white skin with symbolic meaning in such a way as to dominate and exclude those who did not belong to the 'white' race. The racialisation of skin colour and its institutionalisation in UK immigration control has been discussed at length by scholars who identify the period between 1962 and 1981 as the period in which the phrase 'immigrant' became synonymous with the phrase 'Black' (Miles and Phizacklea 1984; Smith and Marmo 2014; Solomos 2003). The speaker's implication is that immigration continues to be racialised in this way, given that she is a 'first generation immigrant' who is not subjected to racism because she is white. What this particular discourse of racism overlooks, however, is the way groups who are ostensibly 'white' can also be racialised (Dawney 2008; Fekete 2001).

Extract 1

---

1   I know from speaking to people who've been doing the doorstep recently that it has

2   been coming up (0.2) And it is a difficult question (.) Erm (.) I think what I find most

3   frustrating is the fact that the Brexit won't actually do anything it won't have any

4   impact on immigration they're two separate issues (.) Especially because a lot of

5   migrants actually come from without of the EU zone (.) Erm (.) And it's quite a

6   sensitive subject for me anyway because my dad's an immigrant (.) Erm and on my

7   mother's side her parents were also immigrants as well so I'm basically a first

8   generation immigrant myself (.) Erm (.) And I get quite angry with people because it

9   does actually feel like it is a race issue (0.3) People don't have a problem with me

10 being a first generation immigrant because I'm white (.) Erm if I had brown skin it

11 would be a different matter and I'm very aware of the fact that I have privilege

12 because I am white (.) Erm (.) but immigration has been around a very very long time

13 (.) erm (.) going back thousands of years (.) Erm (.) we are a mongrel country even

14 our language basically I think someone described it as English basically is erm beat

15 up other languages and roots into the pockets for spare grammar (.) Is how English

16 has been described (.) That's rather apt (.) And as well we used to be an empire we

17 spread across the globe a lot of people who are non erm European stock were brought

18 here against their will (.) erm which is something that has always been brushed over

19 erm but some have obviously come over for a new life and new opportunities and

20 things like that but there is a significant amount of people non-whites who were

21 brought over as slaves in this country (.) Erm and so I think it's really hard I think

22 for people to try and separate the two issues the race issue and the immigration issue

23 because they are separate (.)

Interestingly, the speaker's comment that it 'feels like it's a race issue' suggests that those who are hostile towards immigration are concerned primarily with non-white immigration, and this seems to be the main justification for the speaker's anger. The implicit suggestion is that, if people were concerned about the numbers of all immigrants – including white ones like herself – then this would be more reasonable. This is further demonstrated in the speaker's observation that, 'it's really hard I think for people to try and separate the two issues, the race issue and the immigration issue, because they are separate'. In this sense the speaker is demonstrating what Condor et al. (2006) observe is a tendency for speakers to defend 'the absent other' from charges of racism, in this stance suggesting that it is 'difficult' to disentangle the two issues, given the historical legacy of imperialism and colonialism in the UK. This is also an example of 'discursive deracialisation' – described by Goodman (2014: 149) as 'the removal of race from debates that could (at least potentially) be viewed as about race'.

In this example, the speaker inserts race into the discussion only to subsequently put forward the suggestion that concerns around immigration should not necessarily focus on race as skin colour. Much of her talk – like all the interviewees – bears traces of what Benwell (2012: 360) describes as common-sense anti-racism, in which 'speakers appear to need to establish their enlightened anti-racist credentials and dispel any possibility of being deemed racist', a stance that characterises 'a particular kind of educated, liberal, white, western consciousness in relation to issues of immigration, particularly in a British context'. Benwell observes that a number of linguistic features can be used to indicate such common-sense reasoning, some of which can be seen in this extract. For example, the speaker uses aphorisms to highlight the status of British culture as hybridised ('We are a mongrel country ... English basically beat up other languages and roots into the pockets for spare grammar'), as well as extreme case formulations to emphasise her opposition to the colour-based racism of colonialism and empire ('something that has always been brushed over'). The speaker is also careful to foreground her own subjectivity throughout the interview, even identifying herself partially with the oppressed group in line 7. In arguing that it is this history of racism, with its institutionalisation in the form of colonialism (which has 'always been brushed over'), which makes it 'difficult' for people to separate the issues of race and immigration, she is careful to leave open the possibility that the majority are open to reason on this question. Yet this suggestion that racism can be excised from wider concerns about immigration perhaps points to the way that 'that which is conceived as "real" racism is externalised from the ordinary business of politics' (Lentin 2016: 37). As with other interviewees, racism is somewhat narrowly conceived as something extreme and exceptional, even when it is held to be central to current debates around immigration.

Extract 2 – we've got to find a way of saying it

The second extract is from an interview with a senior councillor and campaigner from a strong Labour-supporting family. In these comments, the speaker has been asked what the Labour Party could do to address people's concerns on the issue of immigration.

One theme that emerges from this stretch of talk, common to the other interviews, was the importance of 'talking' about immigration using the appropriate

---

Extract 2

---

1 I can't distil it down like into a sentence but I think the difficulty we have (.) I think

2 what we've got to say to the masses I mean you know (.) the out and out racists who

3 have a Ku Klux Klan outfit in the wardrobe I don't think they'll ever be engaged but

4 the bit in the middle (.) the masses who have these worries these fears and they

5 rightly or wrongly think the problem is immigration (.) I think we have to talk to

6 them because if we look at all the evidence of the polling that's the constituent and

7 we represent (.) And we've got to find a way of saying it (.) Now I think I think one

8 thing we could do because I sort of understand why I think in the last years of

9 Labour since 2010 I think there was a lot of what I was hearing where it was don't

10 mention this don't mention the economy and I think we should have engaged on the

11 economy (.) When you look at Gordon Brown's record on the economy second to

12 none (.) And when you look at the national debt under Labour, second to none, you

13 know you know (.) We were dealing with a global cr- (.) And the other thing don't

14 mention immigration (.) And of course we had the incident with Gordon Brown and

15 bigot and all of that (.) But I think we have to engage because locally for example we

16 see at SITA we see industrial action because labour is coming in from the continent

17 under the flag of convenience and the undercutting the terms and conditions of our

18 local workers (.) So as a trade unionist that's not me saying Poles and Spanish go

19 home that's me saying we welcome Spanish but we have rates for the job and we've

20 got to pay people the going rate for the job (.) And I think it's a consequence of

21 globalisation that Labour hasn't got right …

---

language: 'We have to talk to them … We've got to find a way of saying it … Don't mention this … That's not me saying …' This seems to be predicated on an understanding of prejudice against migrants being mundane, ordinary and perhaps even superficial rather than deeply rooted; certainly, the speaker suggests that the majority of those who are hostile to immigration are not irrational or extremist – a point emphasised with humour in the extreme case formulation in lines 2–3 ('the out and out racists who have a Ku Klux Klan outfit in the wardrobe') – but are rather open to reasoned debate. Indeed, a key feature of this interview was the speaker's strong condemnation of racist utterances – allied to an identification of himself as descended from African slaves, in spite of his whiteness – but also an insistence that racist attitudes were in many ways an understandable, if misguided, response to socio-economic inequalities. Indeed, the speaker divides those who are hostile to immigration into two categories: the 'out and out racists' and 'the masses who have these worries, these fears'. He is careful not to be overtly judgemental of the latter group – who 'rightly or wrongly think the problem is immigration' – indicating that he is willing to approach such conversations with an open mind, an act of concession that may strengthen his position when he attempts to make a counter-argument.

The speaker's suggestion for how the party addresses itself to such people focuses on how the issue can be talked about and framed. As Fairclough and Fairclough observe about arguments for action:

> Ways of describing the situation, of explaining its causes, or of narrating a sequence of events are usually contributing premises to an argument for action, whose conclusion will be supported by certain ways of describing, narrating and explaining, but not others.
>
> *(Fairclough and Fairclough 2012: 30)*

In this case, the speaker frames the issue by drawing on a specific local example where a multinational corporation is accused of 'undercutting the terms and conditions of our local workers' by bringing in workers from abroad. He is careful, however, to follow this with a clarification that draws on an aspect of his identity distinct from being a Labour councillor: 'So as a trade unionist that's not me saying "Poles and Spanish go home". That's me saying "We welcome Spanish but we have a rate for the job"'. This is a means of stake or interest management whereby the speaker is able to call for action to uphold the 'going rate' as a trade unionist rather than as a Labour activist, thus presenting such calls as garnering support from beyond the confines of the Labour Party. Importantly, his proposal that 'we' ensure that the appropriate rates are paid to all workers does not in itself exclude European workers, although the suggestion is that it may discourage companies from hiring European labour in the first place if the reason for their employment is the undercutting of domestic pay rates. In this way, the speaker is able to address concerns about immigration without referring to immigration controls in a formal sense, thereby preserving the principle of free movement.

In some respects, the speaker can also be seen to draw on the tendency observed by Condor et al. (2006: 459) for speakers to 'defend not only themselves, but also others, from charges of prejudice', which in this extract takes the form of 'defending the reputation of absent others, including groups with which the speaker identifies'. Condor et al. also observe that, in doing this, speakers may not adopt 'a single, or consistent, footing throughout a stretch of talk', instead moving from one social identity to another (in this case from Labour activist, to councillor, to trade unionist). The speaker's stake in defending these absent others is linked to his position as an elected councillor accountable to constituents: 'Look at all the evidence of the polling, that's the constituent we represent'. The shifts of footing from councillor, to activist, to trade unionist then allow the speaker to frame this discussion in ways that acknowledge voters' concerns but also address them from a 'deracialised' perspective.

Extract 3 – everyone can't live in the same place

Despite their anti-racist credentials, rarely did interviewees refer to people with concerns about immigration in terms that suggested they were a threatening 'Other' worthy of outright condemnation. Most of the interviewees articulated the view that such concerns were worthy of serious engagement and did not always constitute racism in their own right. Extract 3 is from an interview with a female Labour activist and refugee rights advocate who made the following remarks in response to a question about what Labour's position on immigration should be, and about current divisions among senior Labour politicians on this issue.

Once again, it can be see how immigration 'talk' is seen to be key: 'a united message ... conversations happening ... what people want to hear ... no point in saying ... let's row back on words like "control"'. An interesting feature of this account, however, is the significant concessions that are made after the speaker declares that she believes in 'free movement', whereby she then appears to be arguing against free movement. Engelbert (2014: 435) has commented that the discourse of Labour Party members 'should be understood for its relatively autonomous ability to play an important role in justifying and legitimising a party's contested political narrative'. Here, the speaker displays significant rhetorical agency in arguing for a compromise between her own principles and the views of voters. This leads her to critique her own initial declaration on free movement in light of debates in the Labour Party over whether the defence of freedom of movement should be jettisoned following the EU referendum. As Engelbert (2014: 442) points out, 'being explicitly seen to pander to the view of critical others after having made a proposition ... can in fact strengthen or bolster the initial proposition'. Drawing on Antaki, it is argued that concessions act as a 'protective flag' that signals that the speaker is rational, open-minded, acknowledges opposing arguments and cannot be accused of being biased or unreasonable. Interestingly, however, the speaker does not return to the initial proposition in this instance, but instead arrives at a rather different proposition about immigration being based on the needs of the national economy.

It could be that the initial statement in favour of free movement is a gesture aimed at attaining a degree of positive self-presentation. Interestingly, in the speaker's list of what is entailed by free movement – 'people should be able to go where they're most comfortable and most happy and where they can work' – it is notable that one of the features (the ability to work) is very different from the others (feeling comfortable and happy), one being about the ability to be economically productive and the others being about the physical and emotional

---

Extract 3

1　Let's get a united message and okay that's probably the most difficult thing to get a

2　united message on, but I don't see the conversations happening anywhere across the

3　party to make sure there is any sort of two sides coming together with that. I mean I

4　believe in free movement, I believe that people should be able to go where they're

5　most comfortable and most happy and where they can work, you know, at some point

6　you have to start being realistic and also that's what people want to hear you say.

7　You can believe something and then have to take in, let's be realistic here, but it's up

8　to us to decide what is our realistic. That's where some people might struggle but

9　you have to face up to these difficult questions. There's no point in saying I think

10　everyone should be able to live where they want. That's going to annoy people

11　because it's not true is it, everyone can't live in the same place, so how do you deal

12　with it. Let's row back on words like control and think about it differently and use

13　words like need. So where do we need people? You know, what skills are people

14　bringing? Let's talk about need, let's talk about skills, let's ditch the other word, you

15　know, the words of division, and talk about things that are practical.

---

welfare of the individual. As Fairclough (2000) astutely observes, lists in political discourse are often used to indicate the equivalence of very different things, and it is possible that the inclusion of 'work' in this list is to emphasise that the 'right' to migrate is based on the condition of employment in the destination country.

The speaker then draws on the generalising formulation 'you know' to indicate the common-sense nature of her concession to the argument that freedom of movement is unrealistic ('you have to start being realistic') and that voters share this view ('that's what people want to hear you say'). Her overall argument is one that also surfaces among Engelbert's interview respondents, namely that 'idealistic' propositions are 'problematic because of their discarding of a wider and more important issue: the general interests that would be served with Labour's return to power' (2014: 447). Although the speaker's key claim is a reasonable one – that is, a compromise must be found between what is right in principle and what is necessary to win power – this nevertheless entails certain ideological presuppositions being naturalised, particularly the idea that free movement is unrealistic. This is particularly evident when the speaker discusses in further detail what free movement may entail. Her comment that 'there's no point in me saying I think everyone should be able to live where they want' is justified on the grounds that it would 'annoy people' and that it is 'not true', because 'everyone can't live in the same place'. These extreme case formulations seem designed to concede the point that freedom of movement should be eased off Labour's political agenda, even drawing on what Antaki (2003) describes as the discursive use of absurdity in the speaker's suggestion that 'everyone' would want to live in the same place.

The speaker then shifts the argument from one that is based on rights to one that is framed through the prism of economic functionalism: 'where do we need people?' The use of the pronoun 'we' is particularly interesting and can be taken to be a national identification. This perhaps draws on discourses often found in migrant rights advocacy that emphasise migrants as 'assets' to the countries in which they arrive, although, as Moore (2012) points out, these often seem to be underpinned by conceptions of individual economic value that are a hallmark of neo-liberal ideology. In this way, it can be seen how some ideological assumptions come to be naturalised in the talk of political activists, even while other aspects of the consensus on migration are challenged.

Discussion and conclusion

The key points of this analysis suggest that Labour activists exercise a significant degree of rhetorical agency in their talk about immigration, both challenging and reworking aspects of elite discourse on this issue. None of the activists drew on the kind of Powellite rhetoric found in the speeches of some senior Labour politicians in recent years, although to varying degrees they were willing to concede certain points to voters with concerns about high levels of immigration. Each of the speakers displayed a form of anti-racist common sense that distanced them explicitly from forms of racism centred on skin colour, but, although there were some references to Britain's colonial history in the talk of Labour members, racism was 'most commonly explained in terms of its manifestation as a behaviour, action or attitude rather than as the expression of systemised racial logics with complex and multi-routed underpinnings' (Lentin 2016: 36). There was a general reluctance to link wider concerns around immigration explicitly with the issue of racism, embodied in some attempts to 'deracialise' immigration and construct the issue of numbers as a legitimate concern. In this sense, there were traces of what Goodman (2014) has described as the 'norm against racism', in which accusations of racism are only reserved for the most extreme circumstances. Racism was thus understood largely as a form of anti-social behaviour rather than as something deeply rooted in Britain's history and political culture.

The fact that the speakers were willing to make concessions to arguments against immigration was directly linked to their identity as Labour Party members whose orientation to 'public opinion' was perceived as key to winning power for the overall good. As such, these various concessions – such as acknowledging that people's concerns were rooted in real material conditions, or that immigration controls were necessary, or that free movement was 'unrealistic' – were seen not only as a means to an end but also as an important democratic principle in their own right. As Fairclough and Fairclough (2012: 81) point out, such considerations are a key feature of political argumentation: 'Among people's reasons for action are reasons that express various external (structural, institutional) constraints on what they can do'. Yet these concessions also serve to naturalise certain ideological perspectives that may dominate and exclude powerless groups whose rights are 'traded away' in the pursuit of electoral compromise. This view also tends to see 'public opinion' on immigration as static and immovable, rather than fluent, complex and contradictory; as Hall (1988: 273) observes, 'politics does not reflect majorities, it constructs them'.

In this respect, much of the talk generated in the interviews conforms to an existing consensus in which immigration is distanced from race, the existence of immigration controls is accepted by all sides, and open borders and free move-ment are seen as taboos (Smith and Marmo 2014; Tyler 2006). Although the benefit-scrounging migrant of the racist imagination has repeatedly been found to be a myth (Migration Observatory 2015), it continues to underpin common assumptions that Britain would be 'overwhelmed' if its borders were more liberal. It is worth noting, however, that even this perspective is historically contingent: Labour's previous commitment to open borders within the British Commonwealth, for example, was based on an understanding that 'the flow of migrant labour to Britain ... corresponded closely with fluctuations in the demand for labour in Britain' (Miles and Phizacklea 1984: 41). In the early 1960s, Labour leader Hugh Gaitskell commented, in opposing restrictions on Commonwealth migration: 'The rate of immigrants into this country is closely related ... to the rate of economic absorption' (Smith and Marmo 2014: 32). Labour's position on this issue changed only when it was faced with a political backlash against 'coloured' immigrants, rooted in the racism of Britain's colonial legacy and championed by Conservative and Labour politicians alike (Joshi and Carter 1984).

Although some political scientists argue that public views of immigration are responsive to variations in immigrant numbers and type, and that policymakers are generally sensitive to such shifts in public opinion (Jennings 2009; Ford et al. 2015), critical sociological and cultural approaches have sought to examine the role of power and ideology in the processes through which perceptions of immigration are socially and culturally constructed (Hartmann and Husband 1974). The role of elite discourse, it is argued, is crucial in providing the public with explanatory frameworks for understanding such issues. Labour activists interviewed for this research also agreed that the importance of constructing a coherent narrative was key. Is it possible, however, to engage in a meaningful discussion about immigration without also addressing the post-colonial melancholia that so pervades British politics and culture and shapes perceptions of 'the outsider'? Seventeen years ago, the Parekh Report famously called for a 're-thinking of the national story' that accounted for the national, cultural, sexual and class-based heterogeneity of Britain's history and the formation of its constituent national identities (Commission on the Future of Multi-Ethnic Britain 2000). More recently, Virdee (2014, 2017) has argued for a similar rethinking of British working-class history, focusing on the Irish Catholic, Jewish, Asian, African and Caribbean workers who 'were the linchpin – the key mediating agent – that helped to align struggles against racism with those against class exploitation' at key moments in the formation of the English working class (2017: 16). Such an approach perhaps has lessons for those who wonder what Labour's current narrative should be.

References

Antaki, C. (2003) 'The Uses of Absurdity', in H. Van den Berg, M. Wetherell and H. Houtkoop-Steenstra (eds), *Analysing Race Talk*, Cambridge: Cambridge University Press.

Augoustinos, M. and Every, D. (2007) 'The Language of "Race" and Prejudice. A Discourse of Denial, Reason, and Liberal-Practical Politics', *Journal of Language & Social Psychology* 26(2): 123–141.

Barker, M. (1981) *The New Racism*, London: Junction Books.

BBC News. (2016) 'Race and Religious Hate Crimes Rose 41% after EU Vote', at: www.bbc.co.uk/news/uk-politics-37640982 (accessed 19 April 2017).

Benwell, B. (2012) 'Common-sense Anti-racism in Book Group Talk: The Role of Reported Speech', *Discourse & Society* 23(4): 359–376.

Bonnett, A. (2000) *White Identities*, Harlow: Prentice Hall.

Bryman, A. (2008) *Social Research Methods*, 3rd edn, Oxford: Oxford University Press.

Commission on the Future of Multi-Ethnic Britain. (2000) *The Future of Multi-Ethnic Britain*, London: Profile Books.

Condor, S., Figgou, L., Abell, J., Gibson, S. and Stevenson, C. (2006) '"They're not Racist ..." Prejudice Denial, Mitigation and Suppression in Dialogue', *British Journal of Social Psychology* 45(3): 441–462.

Costley, C., Elliot, G.C. and Gibbs, P. (2010) *Doing Work Based Research Approaches to Enquiry for Insider-Researchers*, London: Sage.

Dawney, L. (2008) *Racialisation of Central and East European Migrants in Herefordshire*, Sussex Centre for Migration Research – Working Paper No 53, Brighton, UK: University of Sussex.

Engelbert, J.M. (2014) 'Rhetorical Agency in Ideological Dispute Party Members Discursive Legitimisation of Contested Political Narratives', *Journal of Language & Politics* 13(3): 434–452.

Fairclough, N. and Wodak, R. (1997) 'Critical Discourse Analysis', in T.A. van Dijk (ed.), *Discourse as Social Interaction*, London: Sage.

Fairclough, N. (2000) *New Labour, New language?* London: Routledge.

Fairclough, N. and Fairclough, I. (2012) *Political Discourse Analysis*, London: Routledge.

Fekete, L. (2001) 'The Emergence of Xenoracism', *Race & Class* 43(2): 23–40.

Ford, R., Jennings, W. and Somerville, W. (2015) 'Public Opinion, Responsiveness and Constraint: Britain's Three Immigration Policy Regimes', *Journal of Ethnic and Migration Studies* 41(9): 1391–1411.

Gabrielatos, C. and Baker, P. (2008) 'Fleeing, Sneaking, Flooding: A Corpus Analysis of Discursive Constructions of Refugees and Asylum Seekers in the UK Press 1996–2005', *Journal of English Linguistics* 36(1): 5–38.

Gilroy, P. (2004) *After Empire*, London: Routledge.

Goodman, S. (2014) 'Developing an Understanding of Race Talk', *Social & Personality Psychology Compass* 8(4): 147–155.

Goodwin, M. and Ford, R. (2013) *Revolt on the Right*, Abingdon, UK: Routledge.

Goodwin, M. and Ford, R. (2017) 'Britain After Brexit: A Nation Divided', *Journal of Democracy* 28: 17–30.

Gunaratnam, Y. (2003) *Researching Race and Ethnicity*, London: Sage.

Hall, S. (1988) *The Hard Road to Renewal. Thatcherism and the Crisis of the Left*. London: Verso.

Hall, S. (1992) 'The Question of Cultural Identity', in S. Hall, D. Held and T. McGrew (eds), *Modernity and its Futures*, Cambridge, UK: Polity Press.

Hartmann, P. and Husband, C. (1974) *Racism and the Mass Media*, London: Davis-Poynter.

Jennings, W. (2009) 'The Public Thermostat, Political Responsiveness and Error-Correction: Border Control and Asylum in Britain, 1994–2007', *British Journal of Political Science* 39(4): 847–870.

Joshi, S. and Carter, B. (1984) 'The Role of Labour in the Creation of a Racist Britain', *Race & Class* 25(3): 53–70.

Khosravinik, M. (2015) *Discourse, Identity and Legitimacy*, Philadelphia: John Benjamins.

Labour Party. (2014) *Campaigning Against UKIP*, London: Labour Party.

Lentin, A. (2016) 'Racism in Public or Public Racism: Doing Anti-racism in "Post-racial" Times', *Ethnic & Racial Studies* 39(1): 33–48.

Lynn, N. and Lea, S. (2003) '"A Phantom Menace and the New Apartheid": The Social Construction of Asylum Seekers in the United Kingdom', *Discourse & Society* 14: 425–452.

Migration Observatory. (2015) 'Election 2015 Briefing – Why Do International Migrants Come to the UK?' at: www.migrationobservatory.ox.ac.uk/resources/briefings/election-2015-briefing-why-do-international-migrants-come-to-the-uk/ (accessed 19 April 2017).

Miles, R. and Phizacklea, A. (1984) *White Man's Country*, London: Pluto.

Moore, K. (2012) '"Asylum Crisis", National Security and the Re-articulation of Human Rights', in K. Moore, B. Gross and T. Threadgold (eds), *Migrations and the Media*, New York: Peter Lang.

Moore, K. (2013) '"Asylum Shopping" in the Neoliberal Social Imaginary', *Media, Culture & Society* 35(3): 348–365.

Potter, J. (2011) 'Discursive Pyschology and the Study of Naturally Occurring Talk', in D. Silverman (ed.) *Qualitative Research*, 3rd edn, London: Sage, 187–207.

Roseneil, S. (1993) 'Greenham Revisited: Researching Myself and my Sisters', in D. Hobbs and T. May (eds), *Interpreting the Field*, Oxford: Oxford University Press.

Smith, E.B. and Marmo, M. (2014) *Race, Gender and the Body in British Immigration Control*, Houndmills, UK: Palgrave Macmillan.

Solomos, J. (2003) *Race and Racism in Britain*, 3rd edn, Basingstoke, UK: Palgrave Macmillan.

Tyler, I. (2006) 'Welcome to Britain: The Cultural Politics of Asylum', *European Journal of Cultural Studies* 9(2): 185–202.

van Dijk, T.A. (1987) *Communicating Racism*, Newbury Park: Sage.

van Dijk, T.A. (1993) *Elite Discourse and Racism*, Newbury Park: Sage.

Virdee, S. (2014) *Racism, Class and the Racialized Outsider*, London: Palgrave.

Virdee, S. (2017) 'Some Thoughts on the Theory, History and Politics of Race and Class, or, Why Class Analysis Must Take Race Seriously', in O. Khan and F. Shaheen (eds), *Minority Report: Race and Class in post-Brexit Britain*, London: Runnymede Trust.

Watkins, S. (2004) 'A Weightless Hegemony: New Labour's Role in the Neoliberal Order', *New Left Review* 25: 5–33.

Wetherell, M. and Potter, J. (1992) *Mapping the Language of Racism*, London: Harvester Wheatsheaf.

Wodak, R. and Meyer, M. (eds) (2001) *Methods of Critical Discourse Analysis*, London: Sage.

Wodak, R. and Reisigl, M. (1999) 'Discourse and Racism: European Perspectives', *Annual Review of Anthropology* 28: 175–199.

10

REVIVING POPULAR SOVEREIGNTISM

The French radical left and the nation-state

Enrico Reuter

Introduction

The amorphous revolt against the ongoing 'crisis' of global capitalism in the Western world seems to come primarily from the political right, with a few notable exceptions in southern Europe (Rendueles 2017). Whether it is Brexit, the election of Donald Trump as president of the United States or the rise of populist parties across Europe, dissatisfaction with depressed living standards and the insecurities of life due to generalised competition manifests itself often in support for parties that seek to restore (former) national glory, to protect citizens and communities from free trade and the pressures of an international division of labour, and to regain control over borders to reduce immigration while rolling back multiculturalism (see Geiselberger 2017 for diverse interpretations of politics during 'the great regression'). In short, the promoted response to the shortcomings, vagaries and interdependencies of global capitalism in its contemporary neoliberal form appears to be a return to the sovereign nation-state, with a supplement of xenophobia and cultural regression. In light of this increasingly influential narrative, it may not be surprising at first sight that the political left struggles to capture this spreading popular anger, given its propensity to advocate openness and internationalism while keeping its critical distance from attitudes that could be mistaken for nationalism.

However, a closer inspection of historical and current political movements and parties of the radical left quickly leads to the conclusion that the relation between left-wing progressivism and the nation-state is more complex and ambiguous, notably in the case of France where a leftist version of patriotism, driven by a strong attachment to republican ideals and the universal reach of these values, has established itself for centuries both culturally and politically, albeit in changing guises.

It is, hence, the aim of this chapter to shed some more light on to this conflictual relation, to assess how the two most prominent exponents of French left-wing radicalism – the social movement Nuit debout and the political movement La France insoumise, with its candidate for the presidential election in April 2017 Jean-Luc Mélenchon – have situated themselves with regards to the question of national sovereignty. It will be argued that in particular the latter has attempted to create a new form of popular sovereigntism, understood as a political project to foster domestic democratisation and continuous popular participation in combination with a reaffirmation of French national sovereignty on the international level, notably within the European Union (EU). In other words, by locating the metaphysical '*ultimate* source of political power' (Davies 2017: 24, emphasis in the original) in the French populace, while using the state as conduit to channel actual political power and as an instrument to implement an ambitious programme of social, ecological and cultural change, this strand of the French radical left seeks to offer a progressive answer to the current challenges of democratic governance.

To explore this answer, I will proceed in three steps. The first section outlines how substantive parts of the French left have historically developed their programme and political strategies within an intellectual framework of sovereigntism, with a strong ideological attachment to the nation-state as indispensable and a primary tool for the realisation of the left's policy objectives. Second, in the main section of the chapter, I will explore the latest incarnation of popular sovereigntism in Nuit debout and La France insoumise, to highlight this doctrine's contents, coherence and limits. Finally, the chapter will attempt to draw more general conclusions regarding the role of nation-states and the potential of this renewed popular sovereigntism in the context of global capitalism and multilevel governance, seeking to underline both the intrinsic limitations of this approach and its potential to open up new avenues for progressive politics.

From the French Revolution to Mitterrand's turn to economic 'rigour': the French left and the national question

To say that the French left has relied on the apparatus of the nation-state to implement its policies would obviously be a truism, given that the political-administrative system of any state remains central to policy-making, despite the erosion of state power and the changes in how societies are governed (Smith 2009). However, it is argued here that parts of the French left have an attachment to the nation-state that goes beyond this instrumental dimension, an attachment that is intrinsically ideological and built on the firm belief that the French republic as a virtuous polity can and ought to be a progressive and emancipatory institution. The defining historical event that helped to develop such republican patriotism is, not surprisingly, the French Revolution of 1789. As it will not be possible in this article to explore this decisive moment in detail, I would like to restrict the argument to those points that are most relevant for situating the position of the current French radical left within the long-term trajectory of sovereigntist thinking.

It can hardly be denied that the history of modern France begins with the French Revolution (Hazan 2012; Lefebvre 2001; Mathiez 2012), and that this crucial juncture still shapes French politics today. Whereas the political right tends to regard the revolutionary period as either one milestone among many or a disruption of the long historical arc of the French nation and, hence, rather invokes pre-revolutionary figures such as Joan of Arc, who is a key reference for the far-right Front National, or Vercingétorix, a Gallic opponent of Caesar, to whom the conservative presidential candidate François Fillon likened himself in April 2017 (Auffray 2017), the political left widely considers the French Revolution as the founding moment of progressive politics – which is not surprising given that the distinction between left and right emerged in this period. Left-wing parties and movements see themselves as being tasked with completing the revolutionary work (Priester 2012) in order to close the gap between the Republican principles of liberty, equality and fraternity on the one hand and the socio-economic reality of contemporary France on the other.

This does not, however, mean that the French labour movement and socialist parties have shared a unanimously positive view of the French Revolution. As Judt (2011) and Sassoon (2010) show in detail, there have been diverse strands of the French left, some of which are distinctly critical of the legacy of the French Revolution and the centralising nature of the French state, arguing that it is rather economic conditions that determine the life of workers and citizens, regardless of the prevailing political system. The political struggles of Jean Jaurès in unifying the French left at the turn of the nineteenth and twentieth centuries illustrated well the difficulty of reconciling and then associating socialist movements with the republican model (Candar and Duclert 2014). But, despite this diversity of positions, the legacy of the French Revolution has solidified over the course of time and led to a revised understanding of the state – from a source of oppression and control during the absolutist period, to a potential guarantor of ever fragile individual rights (Sée 1973). We can see here a direct lineage to the political philosophy of Maximilien de Robespierre, for whom the protection of universal human rights, the democratic integration of all citizens regardless of income and wealth, and the provision of social protection ought to be the key objectives of all state action (Jessene 2013).

This benign view of the state as an agent for social progress has often been linked to a particularly homogeneous understanding of 'the people'. As Judt (2011: 108) notes with respect to the radical left, 'the imagined unity of a hypostacized "people" has repeatedly provided the incantatory justification for restrictive authority and undemocratic practices', creating an opposition between individual and common interest. Harking back to the time of the French Revolution, when national and popular sovereignty became intertwined (Pertué 2006), and when 'the people' emerged as a political actor and were identified as the sole source of legitimate authority within a democratic system that requires virtuous representatives and effective control by the people (Labica 2013), this mindset helps to explain why popular demands for social protection and prosperity continue to be primarily directed at the state, with intermediary institutions being seen as secondary (Judt 2011).

This consensus around the central role of the state has endured within the French parliamentarian left throughout the diverse episodes of twentieth-century socialism and was epitomised in the coalition government of socialists and communists that came to power after the election of François Mitterrand to the French presidency in May 1981. Traditionally Keynesian, as well as focused on the nationalisation of key industries and the expansion of social rights and protection systems to facilitate a substantive transformation of the social and economic order (Hall 1985), the government relied on 'one substantial instrument' (Sassoon 2010: 548) to implement these policies: the state. This experiment of introducing socialism incrementally within one nation-state was, however, abandoned quite swiftly in light of repeated currency devaluations and a deepening economic crisis, and the turn to economic 'rigour' in March 1983 began to align France with the dominating paradigm of European social and economic policies, with its focus on increasing international competitiveness while providing support to the increasing number of long-term unemployed (Lallement 2007). It is in this moment that the question of sovereignty returned centre stage, as it became apparent that the competitive pressures of a globalised economy, with its free circulation of capital, and the interdependencies within the European Community severely limited the ability of national governments to follow the policy orientation for which they had received an electoral mandate.

To ease this tension between popular demands and systemic constraints, the idea of a 'Social Europe' gained more and more traction over the course of the following years, despite a remaining core of EU-scepticism on the French left (Sassoon 2010). In particular, the prospect of political union, which was to follow the increased economic integration of the 1980s, was seen as an opportunity to use the weight of the unified Europe to serve as a bulwark against the pressures of the globalised economy and to uphold, if not expand, standards of social protection – a view that did, however, underestimate the extent to which European integration has always been an ambivalent project, combining social advances with moments of regression in the name of economic imperatives (Brunkhorst 2014). It was, hence, not surprising that support for this 'European approach' did not last long, and that European integration has been increasingly questioned (Cautrès 2017), including among more radical forces of the left that have perceived the EU more and more as an institutionalisation of neo-liberal economic policies (Dardot and Laval 2016), pitting national economies and employees against each other in what is interpreted as a race to the bottom of social protection and living standards. The referendum of 2005 on the European Constitutional Treaty crystallised this criticism of the EU, when a plethora of left-wing parties, movements and organisations, including the French Communist

Party and a minority of the Socialist Party, collaborated to campaign against the treaty and managed to remobilise otherwise disaffected voters (Mauger 2007) around an embryonic, not yet fully formulated, form of popular sovereigntism.

Nuit debout and La France insoumise: redefining and reviving popular sovereignty

After decades of policy and strategic shifts within the French left, shifts that weakened neither programmatic differences nor the ability of parliamentarian forces of the left to collaborate tactically whenever possible and necessary to gain power (Reuter 2014), we can identify today three distinct groupings: a centrist, economically liberal orientation, itself divided between its centralist, securitarian, and its decentralised, libertarian, wings; a critical left arguing against the neo-liberal mainstream and seeking broader popular appeal beyond party lines; and a reformist left attempting to bridge the increasing gulf between the first two orientations. These three groups remain unable to overcome their irreconcilable differences, while none of them is currently able to gain hegemonic power over the left (Rey 2017). It is for the second orientation that the loss of control over (economic) policymaking at the national level represents a serious challenge, and it is, hence, this orientation that formulates a critique of the existing economic, social and political order that can be described as radical, as it seeks not only an alleviation of social problems, but a far-reaching reorganisation of democratic governance and economic conditions. The social movement Nuit debout and the political movement La France insoumise, under leadership of the former member of the Socialist Party Jean-Luc Mélenchon, have represented in the last few years the two most visible and influential exponents of this radical left, even though both avoided the label. They shall now be discussed further, with a focus on their conception of sovereigntism.

Nuit Debout emerged as an urban social movement in March 2016, following on from mass protests against the French government's rewriting of employment law that prioritised sectoral agreements and deals within companies over collective bargaining and state regulation and that aimed at a further flexibilisation of labour markets. After repeated protests of trade unions, left-wing opposition parties and civil society organisations in all major cities that led to violent clashes between protesters and increasingly aggressively operating police forces, opponents of the labour law reform began to occupy the Place de la République in Paris (and later central areas in other French cities), inspired by similar occupations of urban places such as Occupy Wall Street, Tahrir Square in Cairo or the Spanish 'Los Indignados' (Birch 2016; Kokoreff 2016). Although the movement can, hence, be situated in the broader context of mass urban protests in the aftermath of the 2008 global financial crisis, it also emerged out of specific conditions in France, notably the combination, by a centre-left government, of openly neo-liberal supply-side economic reforms with a substantive erosion of civil liberties during the state of emergency declared after the terrorist attacks of 2015 (Cukier and Gallo Lassere 2016; Cusset 2016).

Built on the principles of direct democracy and open deliberation in popular assemblies, the movement has aimed at a convergence of different protest movements and civil society campaigns, while resisting attempts to be captured and instrumentalised by more established political organisations (Assennato 2016). It has remained without leaders or more permanent structures, in a fluid state, and failed to transmit its objectives through institutional or established political channels, but has arguably contributed to an opening of public debate and a re-politicisation especially of younger citizens (Guichoux 2016). Despite its transnational outlook and its criticism of the oppressive forces of the state, Nuit debout has, in my view, invigorated the debate around popular sovereignty in at least two ways.

First, the movement was initially driven by a concern for the consequences of a post-democratic politics (Crouch 2004) under global capitalist pressures, and the restrictions on national policymaking that these structural constraints entail. By combining a critique of contemporary capitalism with a questioning of how states exercise their power in practice (Cukier and Gallo Lassere 2016), Nuit debout formulated, despite all its diversity, the desire to defend the provision of social security and public services by the state, epitomised in the demand to 'have the right to have rights' (Guichoux 2016). Although the modus for making such claims was different from traditional left-wing politics of the past, the addressee for these demands remains the state – a state that is supposed to regain leeway and a willingness to enact policies that ensure the common good and individual well-being. In other words, Nuit debout sought to mobilise citizens to participate directly in politics, to overcome the perceived capture of state institutions by oligarchic elites (Maniglier 2016), while recognising, at least implicitly, that any nation-state whose institutions were reformed along such direct democratic lines would still be subject to external constraints arising out of the treaty obligations of the EU or the competitive pressures of global capitalism. It seems fair to say, however, that the focus of the movement was more on the reengagement with politics within the national polity than on the question as to whether and how a state such as France could regain its ability to decide independently on its policies.

Second, according to Maniglier (2016), Nuit debout has contributed to the construction of counter-hegemonic narratives to challenge the doxa of contemporary politics, in line with the political theory of Antonio Gramsci and following the prescriptions of Ernesto Laclau (2007) regarding the need for the radical left to break with the dominating 'way of thinking' and to move beyond the mobilisation of the working class to construct a national-popular alliance against the domination by powerful elites. It becomes apparent that Nuit debout (and also, as will be shown later, La France insoumise) are influenced intellectually by the concept of agonistic politics as defined by Mouffe (2005, 2013), within which there is 'a struggle between conflicting hegemonic projects aiming at presenting their views of the common good as the "true" incarnation of the universal', a struggle for which there is no rational solution (Mouffe 2013: 79). As highlighted in detail by

Priester (2014), this model of radical democracy and agonistic politics proposed by Mouffe and Laclau is inherently ambiguous and borders on political mysticism – for example, regarding the possibility of reconciling popular heterogeneity with an agreement on the common populist project, the ambivalent role of leaders, or the potential threat to liberal principles if these stand at odds with the will of the majority. It therefore remains a project that tends to understate the complexities of contemporary politics and that, hence, struggles to clarify how precisely 'the people' can constitute themselves as a coherent political subject, how existing lines of dissent can be overcome, and how fundamental principles of liberal democracy can be protected. Despite these reservations, it can be argued that this ability of the radical left to regain a voice in the public debate represents, notwithstanding all its limitations, progress for the quality of political discussions in comparison with past experiences, when the radical left had been inaudible while forces of the governmental left were absorbed within the dominant neo-liberal discourse of the last decades (Cusset 2016). This relative success of Nuit debout has, however, been short-lived, with the movement running out of steam in summer 2016 and being restricted in scope owing to the difficulty of reaching out to those parts of the population that were not actively engaged. It therefore seems that Nuit debout, as visible as it was for a short period of time, failed to reach escape velocity to gain a truly hegemonic position in the public sphere and effectively challenge the political status quo.

It remains to be seen whether La France insoumise will be able to avoid this fate by establishing itself as a key player in French politics. Founded in 2016 by the former presidential candidate of the now defunct left-wing party cartel 'Front de Gauche', Jean-Luc Mélenchon, this political movement combines direct and horizontal forms of democracy (such as web-based consultations on its programme and independently operating local support groups) with a vertical institutionalisation of a tight team of organisers around the movement's leading figure, a gifted public speaker and media communicator, as well as an experienced politician who left the Socialist Party in 2008 in protest against its continued drift to the right (Alemagna and Alliès 2012; Mélenchon and Endeweld 2016). Launched as an open movement above the fray of party politics, similar to the French President Emmanuel Macron's campaign movement En Marche, it attracted over time the support of more than 500,000 people (La France Insoumise n.d.), even if the degree of participation within the movement varies considerably, of course. After an innovative presidential campaign, Mélenchon obtained 19.58 per cent of the votes during the first round of the election on 23 April 2017, missing the qualification for the second round by fewer than 700,000 votes, but achieving a level of support for a radical left-wing programme not seen since 1969, when the candidate of the French Communist Party united more than 21 per cent of voters behind his candidacy (France-Politique n.d.). During the first round of the following parliamentary elections in June, support for La France insoumise fell, however, to 11.03 per cent in a context of overall weak voter mobilisation (Ministère de l'Intérieur

2017), which translated into only 17 representatives in the National Assembly, highlighting the challenge of sustaining the political fortunes of a movement that remains strongly dependent on its leader to galvanise support within the confines of the presidential system of the Fifth Republic. However, the parliamentary group of La France insoumise has managed, in the first period of Emmanuel Macron's presidency, to occupy a central opposition role, arguably punching above its weight.

Notwithstanding this relative weakness, the stance of La France insoumise with respect to the question of popular sovereignty warrants closer attention, as it arguably represents the foundation of its programme 'L'Avenir en commun' (L'avenir en Commun n.d.; Mélenchon 2016) on which all other proposed measures rest – underlining the centrality of this question for the radical left at the beginning of the twenty-first century. It is, for that reason, hardly surprising that the issue of sovereignty was at the core of Mélenchon's speech at the last mass gathering of the presidential election campaign, on the Place de la République, on 18 March 2017 (Mélenchon 2017a). The programme's first section encapsulates the idea of constitutional reform by calling for a constitutional assembly of citizens, half elected, half randomly chosen, to overcome the Fifth Republic with its 'presidential monarchism' (Mélenchon 2016: 26–27) by agreeing on a new set of institutional rules. This reform ought to aim, furthermore, at blocking the influence of wealthy private interests, in order to redevelop a sense of republican virtue for the benefit of the common good – a rhetoric and mindset that draws explicitly on the political legacy of Robespierre and is situated in the broader tradition of enlightened republicanism (and is conceptualised fully in Mélenchon and Amar 2017). Moreover, the new constitution should facilitate and encourage popular engagement with politics between elections, notably by giving voters the right to recall an elected official via referendum. The underpinning conception of 'the people' and their role in the political process is outlined by Mélenchon (2014) in his book *L'Ère du peuple*, in which he argues that, in becoming aware of its interdependencies and in identifying its needs – for example, for key public services or environmental protection – the multitude of individuals with their respective personal interests, beliefs and priorities becomes 'the people'. In other words, 'the multitude becomes the people when it enacts its sovereignty' (Mélenchon 2014: 115, own translation), when it turns into a conscious political subject that demands control over the conditions within which it exists. From this perspective, the task of political activism is to foster this rise in awareness and to facilitate the construction of political networks. The ultimate aim of this political project is counter-cultural, as it seeks to define a 'new humanism' that combines individual emancipation from all forms of illegitimate domination with a harmonious relationship between humanity and the environment (Mélenchon 2017b).

Similar to Nuit debout, an understanding of politics as agonistic, as defined and conceptualised by Mouffe (2005, 2013), underpins the strategic orientation of La France insoumise. For Mélenchon (2010, 2014), this agonistic opposition resides in the political conflict between 'the people' as a conscious, interconnected mass of interdependent and politicised individuals on the one hand, and the dominating oligarchic elite or 'caste' with its supporters in mass media and traditional parties on the other. Although it is undeniable that this view of contemporary politics allows the restraints of traditionally class-based political mobilisation to be overcome and also avoids the pitfalls of essentialist definitions of 'the people' as an ethnic or cultural entity, as they are espoused by movements and parties of the far right, it remains unclear how exactly this transformation 'from multitude to people' works and to what extent the inevitable differences in ideology and opinion among individuals can be respected without undermining the viability of the common political project. The proposal to call a constitutional assembly to deliberate on a new constitution illustrates this challenge well, as it is built on two quite demanding premises: first, that the task will politicise even those voters who have withdrawn or who have never engaged with politics; second, that the outcome of these deliberations will be in line with the eco-socialist and progressive project that La France insoumise seeks to incarnate.

Therefore, this approach represents a wager that is both interesting and banal. It is interesting because it assumes that a majority of the population can be convinced by a radical programme for change, to the extent that any substantive disagreements regarding the common good can be overcome in a process of deliberative and enlightened reasoning. Moreover, it is assumed that the process of deliberation and debate itself will enhance levels of politicisation and engagement to constitute 'the people' as an active political subject. What seems to resemble, at first sight, the Habermasian ideal of 'deliberative democracy' distinguishes itself by two features: first, a firm ambition to defend a definition of the common good that is comprehensive and goes far beyond an agreement on the basic tenets of liberal democratic decision-making and individual rights to also encapsulate substantive programmatic aspects; second, a willingness to see political conflicts and antagonisms as main drivers of history and as inevitable in any complex society, in line with the principles of historical materialism. The wager seems at the same time banal, as the question as to how individual interests and a concern for the common good can be reconciled in a democratic as well as emancipatory manner is at the core of any democratic order (Habermas 1990), even if this issue has been relegated and neglected in an era of neo-liberalism aiming at 'replace[ing] political judgment with economic evaluation' (Davies 2017: 5). In any case, the political philosophy of Mélenchon and La France insoumise, with its focus on popular sovereigntism, attempts to bridge the gap between usually antithetical positions: it is conflict-driven and agonistic, but also aims for the establishment of a majority consensus; it is openly unafraid of being seen as populist (Schneckenburger 2012), while upholding the principles of informed and reasoned public discourse.

There is a second dimension to the sovereigntist project of the movement, in addition to the described ambition of remaking 'the people' and putting them in charge of national politics: the necessity to address those regional and global constraints that may weaken the capacity of the French nation-state to conduct its policies as it sees fit. In other words, popular sovereigntism rests on two intertwined pillars: popular sovereignty within the national polity, and national sovereignty on the global stage. To achieve the latter, the programme of La France insoumise formulates the intention of making France a key actor within alter-globalist alliances and of reforming the EU profoundly, in order to harmonise social standards, end competition between member states and install a system of 'solidaristic protectionism' at the European borders (L'Avenir en commun n.d.; Mélenchon 2016). This ambitious agenda would represent nothing less than a realignment of European integration, and it would require the consent and support of all other member states. Although France, undoubtedly, is a key player in European politics and would, therefore, probably achieve more concessions than the British government when it tried to renegotiate membership conditions, it is, in light of the current political climate within the EU, impossible to achieve the kind of radical reform that La France insoumise demands – which is why the option of leaving the EU, despite its lack of popularity and inherent difficulties, would need to be more seriously examined to guarantee the coherence of the movement's programme.

Overall, La France insoumise and, to a lesser extent, Nuit debout have put the question of popular and national sovereignty firmly back on the agenda, reaffirming, in the process, the long-standing tradition in French politics of being preoccupied with this matter. Both movements share an understanding that the democratisation of national politics, to overcome the 'oligarchic tendencies' of the current order, necessitates more direct and more active participation of citizens. They also share an understanding of the limits imposed on national policy-making by external constraints, even if there is no clear assessment of how these constraints could be overcome. It seems, hence, appropriate to unpack these constraints in a bit more detail within the final section of this chapter.

The fiction of sovereignty in a world order without alternatives?

The notion of sovereignty has always been a fictitious construct, necessary for international relations to enshrine the principle of equal nominal rights of nation-states and of non-interference, and necessary domestically to underpin democracy and its core idea that citizens of a given state can decide independently how they organise their national community. At the start of the twenty-first century, the gap between fiction and reality seems to be so large that an unconscious awareness of the erosion of state power appears to have spread far beyond those who would usually concern themselves with this question. There are at least three reasons for making this observation.

First, there are a number of policy problems that are truly global in nature, most notably, of course, the fall-out of climate change and other environmental problems. Although nation-states theoretically could decide sovereignly on how they deal with these challenges, there are inevitable externalities that make decisions in one state spill over into other national entities, hence undermining de facto the ability of a state to protect its citizens in the context of 'a complex system of structural global vulnerability' (Held 2010: 216). Second, accelerated globalisation in recent decades has led to polycentric forms of governance, in which states remain crucial but have to interact with and accept interferences from local as well as international and supranational actors, rendering the notions of statism and sovereignty obsolete both materially and ideationally (Scholte 2005). Finally, economic globalisation, with its extensive international division of labour and the liberalisation of capital movements, has led to the development of competition states in which the economic imperative of upholding competiveness overrides social imperatives such as providing comprehensive social protection to residents (Jessop 2002). The volatility that arises out of the focus on flexibility within contemporary capitalism filters, therefore, more and more through to individuals, who are no longer shielded from the vagaries of the economy (Holst 2012), leading to a competition society in which not only do corporations and states have to compete continuously to attract investors and customers, but also the demands of adaptability, competitiveness and flexibility are imposed upon each individual (Dardot and Laval 2014), culminating in the ideal of the permanently mobile, active and adaptable 'entrepreneurial self' (Bröckling 2016).

The impact of European integration can be observed across all three of these dimensions, which highlights how globalisation and regionalisation go hand in hand to alter the conditions of national policy-making: First, the geographical density of Europe, with relatively small state territories in close proximity, in combination with high levels of interaction between populations – for example, due to the free movement of labour and the migrations it has facilitated – leads to a heightened level of interdependence, as well as awareness of these interdependencies. Second, the EU as supranational entity represents the complexity of multilevel governance par excellence, as it forms a dense network of treaty obligations, provides fora for binding intergovernmental decision-making, and intervenes directly in the domestic affairs of its member states in those policy areas that belong to the realm of community matters. This decision-making process can not only be seen as suffering from a democratic deficit owing to, at best, indirect lines of accountability between decision-makers and European citizens, but also arguably leads, in the words of Anderson (2009: 61), to an 'attenuation of politics of any kind', as national parliaments are 'short-circuit[ed]' and 'confronted with a mass of decisions over which they lack any oversight, without affording any supranational accountability in compensation'. Finally, as highlighted repeatedly by critics of European integration in its current form (Dardot and Laval 2016), the centrepiece of the EU is the single market, with the freedom of movement of goods, services, capital and labour, and the regulations that enshrine its functioning, creating a vast space for direct economic competition, not only between companies and member states, but also between workers. Whether the social consequences of this competition, such as the outsourcing of economic activity to parts of the EU with lower wages and the unemployment or precarious employment that follows logically in wealthier member states, or the trend to reduce corporation tax to attract companies, with its problematic impact on public finances, are outweighed by the benefits of the single market for aggregate economic prosperity is, at this stage, an almost moot point, given that the perception of injustice partly fuels the scepticism and rejection of the EU among a substantive share of the population (Cautrès 2017). Moreover, it confirms again the loss of state sovereignty within the EU, a loss that may have been chosen voluntarily by member states, but cannot easily be reversed, as the Brexit negotiations illustrate.

It is, in this context, not surprising that the debate around national sovereignty focuses on two interconnected questions (Keucheyan 2014): whether nationalism remains a relevant ideology today, and on the role of the state and its relations to civil society and global capitalism. What may appear as an academic debate gains in salience if we consider that, despite all criticisms of the state, the limited erosion of its power, as well as well-warranted and historically justified scepticism towards nationalism, no convincing alternative to the nation-state as organising principle for the regulation of public affairs in a peaceful manner and for the provision of welfare and public goods has yet been found, with supra- or international institutions lacking in democratic legitimacy and organisational effectiveness, and with smaller-scale, local forms of government suffering from potential communitarian tendencies and insufficient power and resources to provide the level of services and regulation that nation-states deliver. The discussion of post-national ideologies and approaches remains, therefore, ambiguous, as it remains somehow detached from the material and ideational realities in which people live and according to which they develop their political views (Delannoi 2017). Furthermore, the concern with the erosion of state power risks underestimating the extent to which especially more powerful states remain capable of exercising control and authority over national policy-making, and can overshadow the equally crucial question as to whether a given state apparatus actually chooses to use the power of which it disposes (Thompson 2010).

Thus, the preoccupations of the two exponents of the French radical left discussed in this chapter capture well the tension that faces progressive radical forces across the world, and in particular in Europe. On the one hand, there is the relative decrease in the ability of states to decide autonomously on public policies, as well as the increase in complex interdependencies between states and actors within multilevel governance networks, and the structural constraints of global capitalism in its neo-liberal form. On the other hand, there are the long-standing legacy of democratic practices bound to the nation-state, the remaining ability of states to impose their priorities, and the paucity of viable alternatives to the nation-state. The popular sovereigntism espoused by Nuit debout and, in particular, La France insoumise attempts to tackle this conundrum by staying attached to the nation-state as a framework for common decision-making, but reinvigorating its democratic credentials, while at the same time seeking to use the power of the French state to project the radical programme these movements incarnate beyond French borders, in the vague hope that this would suffice to create conditions that make it easier to resist the economic imperatives of global capitalism. In light of this uncertainty and the mentioned ambiguities regarding the ways in which 'the people' can actually constitute themselves and the simplistic opposition between 'the people' as a coherent entity and 'the caste', one can hardly avoid the conclusion that this reinvention of popular sovereigntism is neither the best nor the ultimate answer to these challenges. However, as John Gray wrote recently with respect to the United Kingdom:

> [b]y identifying liberal values with institutions and policies that cannot command democratic consent – European federalism, continuing large-scale immigration and unfettered globalisation, among others – the self-appointed guardians of liberal centrism in Labour and other parties have shirked the question of what liberalism means in the irrevocably changed conditions of our time.
>
> *(John Gray 2017: 31)*

This is a critique that does not apply to Nuit debout and La France insoumise, movements that arguably may not provide the answer, but at least have the merit of asking the right question.

Conclusion

The election of Emmanuel Macron as French president in May 2017 and the strong showing of his movement La République en Marche during the following parliamentary elections were interpreted by some commentators as a triumph of openness and liberalism, as a reassuring counterpoint to the rise of right-wing populist parties, in particular in Eastern Europe, the election of Donald Trump and the Brexit vote. His success was facilitated by the mentioned division of the left between centrist, reformist and critical traditions (Rey 2017), with the reformist strand represented by the Socialist Party and its candidate Benoît Hamon (6.36 per cent of the first-round vote), in a weakened state but not weakened to the point of full disintegration. From a more critical perspective, the election of Macron represents a continuation of the status quo, with critics such as Lordon (2017) highlighting the backing for Macron from political figures from the centre-left and the centre-right, as well as from key players in the mass media and business associations. Rather than a departure from the well-trodden path of European politics, Macron's parliamentary majority resembles the grand coalitions between parties of the centre that have dominated many European member states in recent years.

Regardless of how this political orientation is assessed, and irrespective of how long Macron and his movement can maintain momentum, cohesion and a sufficient modicum of popular support (and the signs at the point of writing are not too positive), it seems fair to say that the fundamental question of sovereignty that has been discussed in this chapter will not be addressed, given that it is a blind spot of the current presidency. This issue is thus likely to partially structure political debates in the years to come. Taking an overview of the landscape, three entrenched positions can be identified: a denial of the salience of this question by those political movements and parties that aim to defend the existing 'order of things'; an essentialist and ethnicised defence of national sovereignty with more or less xenophobic tendencies by the (far) right; and the notion of popular sovereigntism defended by parts of the French radical left. As has been shown here, the last position has gained in visibility in recent years in France, largely owing to Nuit debout and La France insoumise, but remains in its adolescence, despite its historical antecedents. It remains to be seen how well and how swiftly it can iron out its ambivalences and surmount obstacles to become a potent political force. But, whatever the outcome, those espousing the ideal of popular sovereigntism contribute to a renewal of radical politics, while strengthening notions such as 'the people' or 'the common good' in the political discourse – notions that, for a time, seemed at risk of disappearing (Deneault 2015) and that have the potential to be decisive in this phase marked by 'unstable configurations and chains of *surprising events* [that] take the place of *predictable structures*' (Streeck 2017: 166, emphasis in the original) into which our contemporary politics has entered.

References

Alemagna, L. and Alliès, S. (2012) *Mélenchon, le plébéien*, Paris: Robert Laffont.

Anderson, P. (2009) *The New Old World*, London: Verso.

Assenato, M. (2016) 'Voyage à travers la machine-temps du 37 Mars', *Les Temps Modernes* 691: 79–92.

Auffray, A. F. (2017) Sur les pas de Vercingétorix et de Sarkozy, *Libération*, at: www.liberation.fr/france/2017/04/08/fillon-sur-les-pas-de-vercingetorix-et-de-sarkozy_1561411 (accessed 3 June 2017).

Birch, J. A. (2016) French Spring, *Jacobin*, at: www.jacobinmag.com/2016/04/france-labor-code-hollande-nuit-debout (accessed 3 June 2017).

Bröckling, U. (2016) *The Entrepreneurial Self*, London: Sage.

Brunkhorst, H. (2014) *Das doppelte Gesicht Europas*, Berlin: Suhrkamp.

Candar, G. and Duclert, V. (2014) *Jean Jaurès*, Paris: Fayard.

Cautrès, B. (2017) 'La Remise en cause de l'Europe', in P. Perrineau and L. Rouban (eds), *La démocratie de l'entre soi*, Paris: Presses de Sciences Po.

Crouch, C. (2004) *Post-democracy*, Cambridge: Polity Press.

Cukier, A. and Gallo Lassere, D. (2016) '"Contre la loi travail et son monde": Autonomie et organisation dans le long mars français', *Les Temps Modernes* 691: 118–137.

Cusset, F. (2016) *La droitisation du monde*, Paris: Textuel.

Dardot, P. and Laval, C. (2014) *The New Way of the World*, London: Verso.

Dardot, P. and Laval, C. (2016) *Ce cauchemar qui n'en finit pas*, Paris: La Découverte.

Davies, W. (2017) *The Limits of Neoliberalism*, London: Sage.

Delannoi, G. (2017) 'Nation-solution ou nation-problème? Nation, nationalisme et anti-nationalisme en France', in P. Perrineau and L. Rouban (eds), *La démocratie de l'entre soi*, Paris: Presses de Sciences Po.

Deneault, A. (2015) *La médiocratie*, Montréal: Lux Editeur.

France-Politique (n.d.) *Élections présidentielles*, at: www.france-politique.fr/elections-pre sidentielles.htm (accessed 3 June 2017).

Geiselberger, H. (ed.) (2017) *The Great Regression*, Cambridge: Polity Press.

Gray, J. (2017) 'Liberal Britain Has Nothing to Say', *The New Statesman* (31 March–6 April): 30–31.

Guichoux, A. (2016) 'Nuit debout et les "mouvements des places": Désenchantement et ensauvagement de la démocratie', *Les Temps Modernes* 691: 30–60.

Habermas, J. (1990) *Strukturwandel der Öffentlichkeit*, Frankfurt am Main: Suhrkamp.

Hall, P. A. (1985) 'Socialism in One Country: Mitterrand and the Struggle to Define a New Economic Policy for France', in P. Cerny and M. Schain (eds), *Socialism, the State and Public Policy in France*, New York: Methuen.

Hazan, E. (2012) *Une histoire de la Révolution Française*, Paris: La Fabrique.

Held, D. (2010) 'Global Challenges: Accountability and Effectiveness', in C. Hay (ed.), *New Directions in Political Science*, Basingstoke: Palgrave.

Holst, H. (2012) 'Die Konjunktur der Flexibilität', in K. Dörre, D. Sauer and V. Wittke (eds), *Kapitalismustheorie und Arbeit*, Frankfurt am Main: Campus Verlag.

Jessene, J.-P. (2013) 'Robespierre, au défi de l'égalité et des politiques sociales', in M. Biard and P. Bourdin (eds), *Robespierre: Portraits croisés*, Paris: Armand Colin.

Jessop, B. (2002) *The Future of the Capitalist State*, Cambridge: Polity Press.

Judt, T. (2011) *Marxism and the French Left*, New York: New York University Press.

Keucheyan, R. (2014) *The Left Hemisphere*, London: Verso.

Kokoreff, M. (2016) 'Nuit debout sur place: Petite ethnographie micropolitique', *Les Temps Modernes* 691: 157–176.

Labica, G. (2013) *Robespierre: Une politique de la philosophie*, Paris: La Fabrique.

Laclau, E. (2007) *On Populist Reason*, London: Verso.

La France Insoumise (n.d.), at: https://lafranceinsoumise.fr/ (accessed 3 June 2017).

Lallement, M. (2007) *Le travail: Une sociologie contemporaine*, Paris: Gallimard.

L'avenir en Commun (n.d.) at: https://laec.fr/ (accessed 3 June 2017).

Lefebvre, G. (2001) *The French Revolution: From Its Origins to 1793*, Abingdon: Routledge.

Lordon, F. (2017). 'Macron, le spasme du système', 12 April, *Les blogs du 'Diplo': La pompe à phynance*, at: https://blog.mondediplo.net/2017-04-12-Macron-le-spasme-du-systeme (accessed 30 August 2017).

Maniglier, P. (2016) 'Nuit debout: Une expérience de pensée', *Les Temps Modernes* 691: 199–259.

Mathiez, A. (2012) *La Révolution Française*, Paris: Bartillat.

Mauger, G. (2007) 'Sur la participation des classes populaires aux nouveaux "jeux électoraux"', *Savoir/Agir* 1: 49–58.

Mélenchon, J.-L. (2010) *Qu'ils s'en aillent tous! Vite, la révolution citoyenne*, Paris: Flammarion. Also available online in an English translation, at: www.jean-luc-melenchon.fr/librairie/they-must-all-go.pdf (accessed 30 August 2017).

Mélenchon, J.-L. (2014) *L'Ère du peuple*, Paris: Pluriel.

Mélenchon, J.-L. (2016) *L'Avenir en commun*, Paris: Seuil.

Mélenchon, J.-L. (2017a) Défilé pour la 6e République, at: www.youtube.com/watch?v=b5atq_VZd2M (accessed 30 August 2017).

Mélenchon, J.-L. (2017b) L'insoumission est un nouvel humanisme, *Le blog de Jean-Luc Mélenchon, L'Ere du peuple*, at: http://melenchon.fr/2017/08/26/linsoumission-nouvel-humanisme/ (accessed 30 August 2017).

Mélenchon, J.-L. and Amar, C. (2017) *De la vertu*, Paris: Editions de l'Observatoire.

Mélenchon, J.-L. and Endeweld, M. (2016) *Le choix de l'insoumission*, Paris: Seuil.

Ministère de l'Intérieur. (2017). *Résultats des élections législatives 2017*, at: www.inter ieur.gouv.fr/Elections/Les-resultats/Legislatives/elecresult__legislatives-2017/(path)/legislatives-2017/FE.html (accessed 30 August 2017).

Mouffe, C. (2005) *On the Political*, London: Routledge.

Mouffe, C. (2013) *Agonistics*, London: Verso.

Pertué, M. (2006) 'Souverain', in A. Soboul (ed.), *Dictionnaire historique de la Révolution Française*, Paris: Presses Universitaire de France.

Priester, K. (2014) *Mystik und Politik*, Würzburg: Königshausen & Neumann.

Priester, K. (2012) *Rechter und Linker Populismus*, Frankfurt am Main: Campus.

Rendueles, C. (2017) 'From Global Regression to Post-Capitalist Counter-Movements', in H. Geiselberger (ed.), *The Great Regression*, Cambridge: Polity Press.

Reuter, E. (2014) 'In or Out: Political Strategies of the Radical Left in France and Europe', *Political Studies Association Conference Paper*, at: www.psa.ac.uk/sites/default/files/conference/papers/2014/Radical%20left%20in%20France_E%20Reuter_PSA%20con ference%202014_0.pdf (accessed 3 June 2017).

Rey, H. (2017) 'L'Identité (perdue?) de la gauche', in P. Perrineau and L. Rouban (eds), *La démocratie de l'entre soi*, Paris: Presses de Sciences Po.

Sassoon, D. (2010) *One Hundred Years of Socialism*, New York: I.B.Tauris.

Schneckenburger, B. (2012) *Populisme*, Paris: Bruno Leprince.

Scholte, J. (2005) *Globalization*, London: Palgrave.

Sée, H. (1973) 'The Economic and Social Origins of the French Revolution', in E. Schmitt (ed.), *Die Französische Revolution*, Darmstadt: Wissenschaftliche Buchgesellschaft.

Smith, M. J. (2009) *Power and the State*, London: Palgrave.

Streeck, W. (2017) 'The Return of the Repressed as the Beginning of the End of Neoliberal Capitalism', in H. Geiselberger (ed.), *The Great Regression*, Cambridge: Polity Press.

Thompson, H. (2010) 'The Character of the State', in C. Hay (ed.), *New Directions in Political Science*, Basingstoke: Palgrave.

11

THE EUROPEAN RADICAL LEFT

Transformation and political change

Marco Damiani

Introduction

The European radical left can be described as a heterogeneous political field in a state of profound transformation and adaptation. The European radical left takes the form of a political family similar to a mosaic, made up of many different tiles of various shapes and colours. The composition of all the tiles together, in this case made up of numerous political parties, gives the observer the outline of the whole final picture. The reasons behind the high degree of fragmentation observed within this political category are essentially ascribable to two orders of factor. The first was the fall of the Berlin Wall, which, according to Hobsbawm (1994), caused the premature conclusion of the 'Short Twentieth Century', characterized by the implosion of real socialist regimes and the disaggregation of the Soviet Union. The second was the causes of the large heterogeneity within the radical left, which is to be attributed to the advent of so-called globalization, which, at the turn of the twentieth and twenty-first centuries, determined the crisis of ideologies and their respective political models of reference, the overcoming of modern forms of capitalistic production and a different organization of industrial relations, the implosion of the Fordist model, the failure of mass bureaucratic schemes of Weberian tradition, the broadening of the international economy and financial markets, and, accordingly, the search for a renewed global political balance (Revelli 2013). Starting from these premises, in Europe, the conditions led to the transformation of national political systems and to the progressive weakening of the social-communist left. The transformed conditions of political behaviour provided the possibility of establishing a new space, within which it is possible to imagine a new European left, heir to the past tradition, but at the same time capable of an interpretation of the post-twentieth-century historical phase and the transformed forms of aggregation of contemporary interests and conflicts.

Given the frame of reference and the boundaries within which such changes are developed, in this chapter we intend to present and discuss the main characteristics of the post-1989 European radical left. In the following, we will provide, hence, the definition of this political category, describing its peculiarities, its character and the characteristics that differentiate it from all the other political organizations. In particular, regarding the radical left parties, we will discuss the structure of their values and fundamental political beliefs, their identity and the different models of political structure. In this chapter, in an attempt to conjugate theoretical reflection with the empirical level, we will refer to the numerous political organizations that, in the main European countries, in different contexts and times, prove able to interpret the traits attributed to the same family of political parties. On the methodological side, besides the contributions published in the literature, this work uses different primary sources (sometimes explicit in the text, otherwise not explicitly reported, but always useful for our research process). Among these, particularly important is the information drawn from the statutes and internal documents provided by the main political parties included in the same political category.

The post-communist radical left

After the crisis of communist ideology and the fall of real socialist regimes, in Western European countries the left-wing parties acquired three different political forms. The major family of post-1989 progressive parties remains that of the so-called reformist left. With this expression, we intend to indicate all the political organizations interested in strengthening the democratic institutions inside which they habitually operate through gradual political and institutional reforms. At the opposite end of the same continuum are positioned the extreme left parties. Such political organizations are identifiable as being capable of harsh criticism of the dominant political system, thence mobilizing strong opposition to the liberal democratic governments, in their turn considered to be bourgeois power systems to be overcome by revolutionary transformation of the existing balance of power. Compared with such considerations, the radical left parties are identifiable as parties set right in the middle of the space occupied, on one side, by the reformists and, on the other, by the extremists (March 2011). Ultimately, the radical left parties are those parties that, although criticizing 'radically' (i.e., at the 'root') the choices of the capitalist regimes' political classes, pursue the objectives they declare to bring about profound changes within the institutional framework in which they operate, accepting ipso facto the rules of the democratic game. If the reformists pursue the objective of gradually transforming the existing system, and if the ultimate aim of the extreme left parties is to establish a real socialist regime, to be pursued (even after 1989) without first excluding the use of physical and military force, the objective of the radical left parties is to bring about the change with a plan of 'root and branch' reforms that attempts to redesign the relationships of forces within the liberal democratic field.[1] For the main figures in the European radical left, the aim is to transform the existing system without overhauling the democratic institution. According to March and Mudde (2005), the political forces of the European radical left, for this reason, would be closer to the reformist option than to the revolutionary one.

With this definition of the outline within which the reformist and extreme left parties operate, the radical left parties certainly belong to the class of anti-liberalist parties and not to the class of the *tout court* anti-democratic parties (Mudde 2006). Substantially, if the reformist left parties accept operating in the liberal democratic field, definitively accepting the forms and relationships of production in a capitalist economy, and if the extreme left parties still have the objective of revolutionary destruction of the bourgeois state, the radical left parties constitute an intermediate route. They accept the rules of the democratic game, while nurturing expectations of 'radical' change in the dominant relationships of forces. In particular, these show two fundamental characteristics. First, the parties of the European radical left are not 'anti-establishment' parties according to the definition given by Giovanni Sartori (1976). Second, the same family of parties, made up of the heirs of the social-communist tradition – although not anti-system anymore – can be considered as real 'anti-political establishment parties', according to Andreas Schedler (1996) and Amir Abedi (2004). We will try to explain what we mean by such political categories more accurately in the following pages.

First consideration: the European radical left parties are not anti-system parties according to the traditional definition given by Sartori (1976). In this regard, the Florentine political scientist is very clear in his explanation. Anti-system parties include all the political organizations (from left to right) whose ideology categorically refuses the present system, and whose practice hinders its operation. More specifically, according to Sartori, the anti-system parties are those parties that, if called to govern the country, would not change – if possible – the governing team, because of their interest in surpassing the democratic state. The anti-system parties are those that express their hostility not only towards the leading elite of a certain country, but more generally towards the institutional architecture within which the same political organizations are found to be acting. At the time of the events, Sartori adds to this political category, besides the neo-fascist and neo-Nazi subversive political organizations, all the European communist parties, including those that, in certain circumstances (e.g. the Italian Communist Party), contributed to setting the democratic rules. Although, before 1989, the category of anti-system parties was without doubt attributable also to the far left of parliament, we believe that, in Western post-bipolar democratic regimes, the typology of anti-system parties includes (possibly) political groups ascribable to the far left, excluding the radical left parties, which are internal and, hence, on the side of the liberal-democrat system.

Second consideration: although not anti-system, the post-twentieth-century European radical parties are defined as true 'anti-establishment' parties, or better: 'anti-political establishment parties'. This type of party is qualified for the organization of strong opposition to all the forces that, in a certain political system, have the possibility of accessing government responsibilities (Schedler 1996). Normally, an anti-political establishment party presents three essential features: (1) it formulates a radical criticism of the liberal political system without wanting to destroy it; (2) it shows a perception of itself as the subject capable of challenging the institutions managed by the establishment; and (3) it interprets and represents the presumable strict division between the people's interest and that of the political class, be it the government or the opposition (Abedi 2004). The anti-political establishment parties are not to be considered as authentically anti-politics parties; they can be considered as subjects capable of institutionalizing a feeling diffused among the citizens of hostility towards the ruling classes (Poguntke 1987, 1996; Poguntke and Scarrow 1996). In this sense, this political category has a particular meaning, placing itself in contrast to the leading elite (Barr 2009). In this reference context, we believe that the parties of the European radical left are exactly definable as specific instances of anti-political establishment parties that are far from discrediting the democratic government systems in which they operate, claiming the leading role played by a new ruling class and substituting the political elite of the past, both that of liberal conservative and reformist origin. In a 'reopened society' after the facts that led to the implosion of real socialist regimes, at the end of the twentieth century and the beginning of the twenty-first, the conditions of politics changed in Europe (Dahrendorf 2005), thence opening a possible space for the radical left parties.

Besides what we have discussed so far, an assessment of the European radical left parties cannot leave out analysis of their internal political pluralism, which determines their fundamental character. From this point of view, the convergence of different political traditions is clear – in particular: (1) social-communist parties founded in the twentieth century; (2) political groups of social and social-democratic inspiration that either left or were never included in reformist parties because they were critical of them, or of some of the policies approved by centre-left governments; and (3) groups emerging from the *deuxième gauche* of the ecologist, environmentalist, pacifist, feminist and gender cultures. These and multiple political cultures give the European New Left parties an autonomous political approach, totally original compared with that which determined the political history of the twentieth century. In fact, starting from objectives linked to the construction of a utopian state and to the achievement of the socialist objective, the aim of such political groups is oriented towards the pursuit of root-and-branch reforms that do not set as a goal the overcoming of the capitalistic bourgeois state, aiming instead at the achievement of a democratic state simply shifted to the left on the axis of European political systems. Within this renewed political organization, the communist parties that survived the twentieth century chose to be part of it (often also with the role of fundamental actor), although they interpreted a search on the level of political practice that was truly pro-system and not revolutionary. All this gives, or should give, a contribution, according to the expectations of the stakeholders, to broaden the boundaries of such political groups, in order to enlarge the size of their electoral appeal.

Clearly, the foundation of such political actors requires a completely different political representation compared with the past. For this reason, the period after 1989 represents a completely new historical phase for the European left that (among other things) saw the constitution of renewed forms of political organization in the Western democracies. At the beginning of the 1990s, the European left was described as a 'retreating army', and, after the Soviet Union's implosion, a reshaping of the parties of the left seemed inevitable, in particular of those placed to the left of socialist and social-democrat parties. On the other hand, at the beginning of the third millennium, new possible options emerged that foresaw unedited experiences, capable of reaching even the government of single states. Starting from these thoughts, in the following pages we will try to go into more depth regarding two fundamental issues, the identity and the political structure of the European radical left forces, which, according to our argument, would show both their pro-system and anti-establishment character at the same time.

Establishing political identity

From the point of view of identity, the post-twentieth-century radical left parties steered clear of previous tradition. Instead of being distinguished for their homogeneity in ideology, they are recognizable for a plurality of ideas that make them unique. In fact, these parties show a complex internal structure that allows diverse values to be present in the same political organization. Whereas, in the past, ideology in the social-communist parties had been unitary and non-negotiable, in the post-twentieth-century parties of the radical left the plurality in the structure of their identity and values is an element of absolute novelty.

Given these premises, let us now analyse the values behind the political structure of the parties in the European New Left. Both the plurality and the proliferation of ideas during the years bridging the twentieth and twenty-first centuries can be explained by the relationship of forces between politics and society being overturned. If, in the past, ideology seeped down from above into people's individual experience and governed their main modes of action, in the following era, the relationship between politics and society was substantially turned upside down, and values and ideas are consequently produced mainly by the social sphere. The concept of 'social imaginary' thus appears in the literature and, in the European political system, tends to take the place of traditional monolithic ideology. By social imaginary we mean a great warehouse of ideas made up of contributions from diverse social groups, each of which bears specific content, even though often provided in limited and involuntary form (Santambrogio 2015). Whereas ideology, being the fruit of systemic reflection produced by a given group of intellectuals and political thinkers, is called upon to show a logical connection capable of proposing a coherent interpretation of reality, these concerns disappear with the social imaginary. The social imaginary is based upon everyday experience and builds upon a thought system that is not necessarily structured. With these conditions, within a specific community of people, the values, principles, ideas and symbols that make up the social imaginary can be pursued and promoted by a single political organization.

We therefore consider it useful to apply George Lakoff's concept (1987) of 'radial categories' to this reasoning. Lakoff makes a distinction between 'primary category' (or 'central subcategory') and 'secondary categories' (or 'no-central subcategories'). In the case at hand, our idea is that the central subcategory of the European New Left is defined by the principle of equality, whereas the no-central subcategories can be seen in the plurality of values that distinguishes the same family of parties (see Figure 11.1). In particular, in reference to what we are examining in this context, the primary category pinpoints the central nucleus that characterizes the New Left parties, and the secondary categories share a part in common with the primary nucleus and can be graphically represented by a series of concentric circles around the central subcategory. The definition of the values of the post-twentieth-century radical left proposed in this chapter is based on the analysis of statutes presently in force and political programmes adopted during elections following the cold war years. It refers to the speeches and writings (in specialist essays and publications, newspapers, conventions and political congresses) of the main leaders of parties in the European New Left.

In the first place, what we are trying to point out is that, after 1989, the values of the European radical left are such when they are conceived in relation to the formal principle of equality of conditions. In the European parties of the

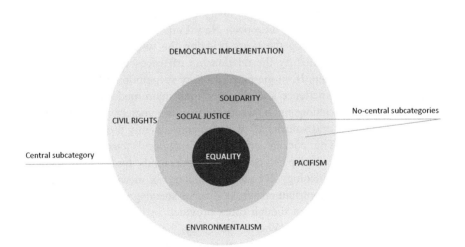

FIGURE 11.1   The values of the European radical left

New Left, any value of reference – far from being an end in itself – must be seen, or should be seen, as aiming to reduce inequality between people, as an idea of changing relationships in forces and providing all individuals with the possibility of imagining a progressive process of economic, political and cultural emancipation. In this regard, whereas the utopian approach of the social-communist parties tended towards theoretically reaching a society of 'equals', once freed from the logic of private profit and social conflict, the European New Left claims new motions of change. Having abandoned the anti-system role of the revolutionary parties (Damiani 2016), in the radical left's social imaginary there is no place for totalitarian egalitarianism. The need to ensure a better distribution of wealth takes its place to ameliorate people's lives and, in particular, the conditions of poorer people.

In this context, going back to our reasoning on radial categories, if the principle values of the New Left can be traced back to the idea of social justice and solidarity among individuals, these values can be integrated with a long list of other values that do not necessarily belong merely to the left. These values could altogether contribute to defining the meaning of equality in starting conditions, which in turn points to the operating principle of the new political parties in the radical left. Together with values of a materialist nature, concerned more with closing the gaps between the different categories of people in economic terms, the radical left also took on post-materialist values (Ingleart 1977). All values, materialist and post-materialist, together define the field of the radical 'ideas' of the post-twentieth-century left. The underlying principle remains that of pursuing conditions of equality, which represents the inspiration and determines the aim of each single reference value. The post-materialist values that complete the identity of the New Left essentially embrace pacifism, respect for the environment, the civil rights of citizens and the will to widen the democratic process towards a maximum degree of political participation. The outstanding question in this reasoning is that these are values that are not inherently just those of the radical left and refer also to other political cultures: liberal, Christian, Catholic, pacifist, and so on. However, these values also share some of the characteristics of the New Left's value system in so much as they aim to pursue the principle of equality of initial conditions.

Let us now give an example by taking 'pacifism' as a reference of value. Pacifism is not only an attribute of the European radical left, but is rather a universal value of mankind. Many very different people share this value, ranging from believers in the Christian sphere, inspired by ideals of brotherhood and the New Testament, to representatives of anarchical and revolutionary groups whose followers are of anti-American and anti-imperialistic conviction (and, therefore, opposed to post-modern warfare conducted under NATO's control), without being ideologically against violence and the use of military intervention. In this case, these two realities, Christian believers and anarchists, both belong, together with other players, to the same movement – pacifism – sharing a common point of view, although totally divergent in their long-term aims. On the other hand, these same subjects, although united in their struggle for pacifism, will find themselves divided in other political controversies. The same dynamics can be found in the entire field of values that characterizes political pluralism in the European radical left. The peculiarity of these parties is that their political ideologies are a strange mixture that assumes the value of being 'leftist' merely by the measure of being conceived with the aim of pursuing conditions of equality among the members of that same political community. Ipso facto, the pluralism of ideas, typical of the European radical left parties, converges on the formal principle of equality, determining a total packet of values that more precisely defines their social imaginary.

Apropos of this, by continuing to apply Lakoff's concept of radial categories, what we can state is that the no-central subcategories do not possess the same characteristics of value – that is, they do not posses the same value structure, even though they share a portion of values with the primary (or central) subcategory. This means that value attributes – for example, pacifism and respect for the environment (and/or any other no-central categories) – are not equal to each other, but rather each one shares a part of the significant attributes of the central subcategory, which in this case corresponds to the principle of equality in initial conditions. Only the sum of all no-central categories returns the total content of the central subcategory (Collier and Mahon 1993).

Once the values of the New Left have been defined, it becomes important to take their functional relationship into consideration. Not all the formations of the radical left present an identical priority. Apart from the centrality of equality in initial conditions, which constitutes a matrix of identity within which all the other values that make up the field of the radical left must necessarily be contained, it will be the prerogative of each singular political organization to define its priorities. In fact, according to each specific case, some parties will be able to conserve – for example – the value of class solidarity as a fundamental reference of identity; others may see their main reference point as international peace, or the environment and ecology, reaching out to civil rights, or (depending upon each case and that particular historical moment) the necessity to start a further process of democratic growth. It is through these diverse choices that the scale of values of the European New Left defines and redefines itself regarding real power relations. Unlike the socialist-communist parties, with strong ideological stability, with the radical left we are facing a political category that is forever changing and adapting to new values, according to the situation.

The political structure

Of course, what we have discussed so far about values cannot influence the process of construction of the real forms of political organization that these parties choose to give themselves. After 1989, in fact, the transformations recorded in the European radical left parties, besides having an impact on the values, are also identifiable on the basis of their organizational structure. Having abandoned the role of the twentieth-century revolutionary party of Marxist-Leninist origin, with a strong ideology and over-centralized functioning model, the parties of the New Left show very different features. In comparison with the past, the first element that characterizes the organizational model of such political groups is the complete abandonment of 'democratic centralism' as a principle, in favour of a decision-making model founded on the transparency of internal debate and the effective participation of all the political components in the endogenous decision process. Democratic centralism, in fact, developed with the aim of pursuing the criteria of stability in the decisions it adopted and assumed sovereignty of the party over the individual autonomy of each single party member. In a centralist democratic regime, the choices made collectively in respect of the criteria of majority could not be argued over by any of its members. This mechanism collapsed with the communist parties' crisis. After the fall of the Berlin Wall and the disaggregation of real socialist regimes, the European New Left parties, far from adopting such criteria, founded their political identity on an open debate between the different political groups, being organized openly and sometimes conceived in competition between each other for the formation of their management and the occupation of the main roles of power.

Once the era of communist parties founded on strong ideological sharing was over, the political groups that were heirs to that experience started to work on the construction of an alternative organization, capable of integrating different political cultures with reference values and social imaginary in common. This kick-started the process of political convergence, capable of joining together communists (of different identities: libertarian, Troskyists, Leninists and even neo-Stalinists), socialists critical of the reformists, environmentalists, feminists, pacifists and exponents of the no-global world. In this new framework, regarding political pragmatism and realism, it is certain that, with these conditions of internal pluralism, the different political parts that form the parties of the radical left would have had difficulty living together and respecting democratic centralism. Thence, respect for the criterion of pluralism in ideas, as a constituent element of the post-ideological European New Left parties, becomes an essential condition for the construction of a unitarian political subject, placed to the left of the socialist and social-democratic parties.

However, despite abandoning democratic centralism, not all the radical left parties adopt the same model of internal operation. Considering respect for political pluralism, intended as the foundation of the new form of party, it is possible to identify organizational models, even very different from each other, that characterize the structuration process of the same political category. From this point of view, we put forward a classification of the organizational models adopted by the radical left parties (Damiani 2016). We are dealing with five ideal types that will be described at the empirical level as follows:

The *late-ideological party*: this is a party model that, at the turn of the twentieth and twenty-first centuries, continues to take its inspiration from the typical organization scheme of the mass party. The political formations still influenced by this scheme continue to emulate the more traditional form of twentieth-century party (not always with encouraging electoral results), also facing the on-going historical change. In the configuration adopted by the European radical left parties, the late-ideological party model is still the benchmark for the Spanish Communist Party, the French Communist Party, the Italian Communist Refoundation Party and the German Party of Democratic Socialism (just to mention the most important cases). This form of party, however, is possible only as long as the parties constituted around a sole political identity survive, which, in the cases mentioned, converges around the social-communist ideology. The gradual failure of a homogeneous ideological content and the growing internal pluralism recorded within the political groups of the post-twentieth-century New Left imposed upon these parties the need to structure themselves in a very different manner. All this determined the rise of new organizational models.

The *plural party*: This represents a political organization model that shows different features from those of the *late-ideological* party, from which it normally originated. The plural party maintains the traits of the unitary political organization, operating inside the fusion of different components that, instead of being structured around a federate model, prefer to fuse together in one single political organization. In this case, all the parts merged into the plural party decide together (at the risk of their project failing) to elect their management, converging into a single and shared political line and proposing the same public policies. Among the best-known ones, typical examples of plural parties are represented by the Greek and German radical left. In both cases *Die Linke* and *Syriza* contain different internal political factions and/or currents that, instead of claiming their own statutory autonomy, manage to reach an agreement that allows them to operate a real organizational synthesis. This typology of radical left parties was born in Germany and Greece exclusively, or nearly, owing to the pressure exerted in that direction by the institutional rules and material subsidies laid down in electoral regulation.

In the German case, with the aim of achieving strong government stability, electoral law obliges the parties to present themselves at the elections for the renewal of the Bundestag as a unity. It is on these premises that, in 2005, the *Linkspartei* was born. The *Linkspartei* emerged from the union between the PDS (the German Party of Democratic Socialism), heir to the SED, the historic leading party in the former East Germany, and WASG (Labour and Social Justice – The Electoral Alternative), which comprises a group of heterogeneous political components. Among these, it is worth mentioning the officers of IG Metal, the union that was historically close to the Social Democratic Party of Germany (SPD), critical exponents of the same political group and a non-negligible part of the Greens (Jesse and Lang 2008). From this experience, in 2007, *Die Linke* (the Left) was born.

The Greek case is practically identical, where the system of institutional rules favours the unity of the forces in the field, awarding a majority premium of fifty seats to the party with the most votes (no coalitions or electoral cartels are allowed). In this context, *Syriza* (in English: Coalition of the Radical Left) tried to take a step forward. It was founded in 2004 as a coalition of parties, capable of adding together sixteen political components, all placed to the left of Pasok (Panhellenic Socialist Movement), in consequence of an explosion of the traditional Hellenic party system (produced by the negative impact of the 'great recession' that exploded in Europe at the beginning of the twentieth century). In 2014, with national elections in the coming year, the Greek Coalition of the Radical Left shed the clothes of political coalition to become a real plural party in order to run for the majority premium provided by the electoral law previously mentioned. After the transformation from political coalition to plural party in 2015, *Syriza* managed to win the majority premium twice in one year (January and September) to establish the government of the country. In both circumstances, Alexis Tsipras was elected prime minister (Mudde 2017).

The *party–front*: This consists of an organizational model that adds together different political components that, while preserving their identity and their statutory autonomy, decide to merge into a party–front, delegating to it some of the strategic tasks (among others, the electoral one) while still retaining the party's symbols, management bodies, local clubs and national headquarters, together with those of the party–front. This political organization model describes exactly the functioning scheme of Izquierda Unida (IU), the Spanish party of the radical left (Ramiro Fernández 2004). Several different elements are merged inside IU, in fact, the most important of which is represented by the Spanish Communist Party, which, while keeping its organizational structure intact, decided not to run directly for the elections, contributing to the foundation of a single political organization together with other minor parties of the left. In this circumstance, the Spanish Communist Party represents a traditional political formation as promoter of a broader political project, applying its forces to found a single actor of the post-ideological radical left. In the Spanish case, double membership is also possible, offering the possibility of being a member of both IU and one of the individual affiliated political formations. What we have described is the 'soft' version of the party–front. Besides IU, there is a 'hard' version of the same organizational scheme, which, as a matter of fact, corresponds to the Portuguese case Bloco de Esquerda and the Danish case of the Red–Green Alliance. In both cases, the sum of the parts merged into the party-front organization, giving birth to a strongly structured subject with great political autonomy, which leaves a secondary role to the constituent political formations, making the external representation of a single political subject possible.

The *front*: This is a kind of political organization that is surely 'lighter' than the models presented so far. The front represents little more than an electoral cartel, with almost exclusively electoral tasks and with an external image not yet attributable to the sum of the single parts. In the European New Left experience, all the components that make up the fronts continue to represent the coalition's identity autonomously, conferring the image of a container whose survival is at risk owing to the low political structuration and the strong authority represented by the single parts compared with the whole coalition. The front model, with a clear linguistic reference, is that interpreted in France by the Front de gauche (Left Front), established in 2008 in order to try to avoid the risk of the French Communist Party disappearing – in the previous decade, it had suffered a series of heavy electoral defeats. The Left Front also originated in numerous political parts. It is major elements are represented by the French Communist Party and the Parti de gauche (Left Party), born out of separation from the socialist party (Damiani and De Luca 2016). In its specific configuration, the French *Front* does not enjoy true territorial political penetration within the country, it does not have its own real-estate assets and it does not organize an autonomous membership campaign. In order to enrol in the *Front* in France, it is sufficient to enrol in one of its single constituent parts. Considering its low political structure and the internal conflicts between its different constituent forces, it was not difficult to foresee the difficulties of survival that this form of political organization would have had within the French borders. The end of the Left Front experience was declared in 2016. After the Front de gauche, the French radical left relied on a new political formation, which in 2016 led to the formation of France insoumise (Unsubmissive France). France insoumise launched the candidacy of Jean-Luc Mélenchon for the presidential elections of the following year as its first political act. Already candidate of the *Front* in 2012, with about 11 per cent of the votes, in the 2017 presidential elections Mélenchon obtained a good result, obtaining a surprising 19.6 per cent in the first electoral round. From the point of view of organization, Unsubmissive France is hardly classifiable. What is sure is that it is not a post-ideological party, nor is it a pluralist party, but, considering everything said so far, it is neither a front nor an electoral cartel, because it does not represent a group in which diverse political forces merge close to the electoral deadline. Such a *rassemblement* can more easily be considered as a movement–party.

The *movement–party* is the last of the organizational models that we will use to describe the different internal operational models that characterize the European New Left parties. This specific political form shows its truest representation in the Spanish case of Podemos (Torreblanca 2015). The movement–party is a very particular organizational model that gives birth to political formations considered something between a party and a movement (Gunther and Diamond 2001). The movement–party, although presenting itself to regular electoral turns and taking on the role of a real political party in such circumstances, still maintains the distinctive traits of a social movement. Its success is due to the surpassing of the traditional *cleavages* identified by Lipset and Rokkan (1967) and is marked by the discontinuity found in our contemporary age with the classic structure of social conflicts. In particular, during the formation process of movement–parties, an essential role is played by the growth of 'postmaterialistic' values (Inglehart 1977) generated within the youth and anti-authoritarian movements outside the political divisions founded on economic factors. Such renewed forms of political organization are generated from the dissatisfaction expressed by citizens towards the classic institutions of representative democracy and the mechanisms that regulate the life of traditional parties. From this point of view, movement–parties are characterized by non-conventional policies, and their success depends not only on the results obtained in the electoral rounds, but also on their ability to push their demands and arguments forward within organized society. As specific kinds of movement–party, Podemos and France insoumise propose a highly fragmented political organization model where some fundamental features emerge. Among these, the most important are the substantial centrality of the leader, the extensive use of media and the use of the Internet and 2.0 web platforms. In addition, such political groups, organized in movement–parties, often use internal referendums and elections, in which both members of local headquarters and members registered online participate. These consultations are normally convened to vote for the leadership or to decide on actions regarding certain programmatic issues.

Obviously, the difference found in the party models just discussed cannot be considered a factor of electoral success or failure on its own. It is not the choice of a model that grants a certain outcome. However, what it is possible to state is that the most reliable models in the long term are those that respond to a larger political unity, either in the plural parties, the front–parties or the movement–parties, suggesting that the front model is at risk of undergoing a negative conditioning owing to the internal conflict dynamics that can arise between the individual constituent parts.

Conclusions

Compared with the framework set out in this chapter, in the concluding considerations, we would like to take the discussion back to what we have already mentioned regarding the pro-system nature of the post-1989 radical left parties. In fact, both the values and the structure of the working model within these political organizations confirm the indications given in the initial pages of this chapter.

In regards to the values, none of those indicated has an anti-system nature. The principle of equality, one of the fundamental historical functions attributed to Western democratic regimes, is not against the system. According to Norberto Bobbio (1995), a society is democratic when the individuals that make it up are freer and more equal than those who live in any other form of coexistence experimented with by mankind. Again, with reference to the European radical left, the desire for better social justice or ample solidarity among people is certainly not anti-systemic. On the other hand, they are coherent and perfectly in line with the values of liberal Western democracy and with the objectives of mankind's full development. The same thing can be said of feminism – a value that directly aims at equality between the sexes and overcoming gender unbalance that is still perceived in many aspects of social, economic and political life in the main Western countries. Continuing to look at the values assigned to the

European New Left, in pacifism we cannot find a possible element of an anti-systemic nature. On the contrary, pacifism is the value that more than any other seems to break away from the twentieth-century social-communist tradition, which saw physical (even military) force as a useful instrument to achieve a real socialist regime. Finally, the values to be recognized in environmentalism and ecology can certainly not be considered to be against the system. The pursuit of improving the care of the environment and the world's ecosystem is intimately linked to the counsel of a democratic political regime, where all citizens should be able to respect the environment with the aim of pursuing and reaching so-called 'sustainable development', with reference to which the satisfaction of the present generation's needs must not compromise the possibility of future generations achieving their goals.[2]

Regarding the model of political organization, we can state the very same. Although the Western Marxist-Leninist party of twentieth-century origin was founded with the (theoretical) aim of realizing real socialism, it was organized around the concept of democratic centralism, whereby command was given to a directive structure that coordinated political action; the parties of the New Left are very far removed from this. Far from pursuing a single utopian aim of constructing a political regime with strong ideological content, the organizations belonging to the radical left are necessarily obliged to find a way of operating internally that allows them to sustain the coexistence of a plurality of political values of reference. As they consist of numerous political elements with distinctive histories, cultures and ideals, the New Left parties have to organize themselves around a light party model to be able to ensure the conditions for the coexistence of an elevated internal diversification. Nevertheless, apart from the form of political organization they decide upon, the parties on the radical left normally find themselves within a political organization that induces them to coexist within a flexible set of rules that are devised to guarantee the survival of the very same organization. From this point of view, it is obvious that the fragile model of organization in such a set of political parties cannot constitute a danger to the system, as it is incapable of operating in common agreement when faced with the first occasion of political divide.

Notes

1 The expression 'root and branch' meaning the pursuit of objectives of radical reform within that particular political system without questioning the democratic set-up.
2 Definition provided in 1987 by the World Environment Committee (Bruntland Committee) of the UN programme.

References

Abedi, A. (2004) *Anti-Political Establishment Parties*, London: Routledge.
Barr, R. R. (2009) 'Populists, Outsiders and Anti-Establishment Politics', *Party Politics* 15(1): 29–48.

Bobbio, N. (1995) *Eguaglianza e Libertà*, Torino: Einaudi.
Collier, D. and Mahon, J. E. (1993) 'Conceptual "Stretching" Revisited: Adapting Categories in Comparative Analysis', *American Political Science Review* 87(4): 845–855.
Dahrendorf, R. (2005) *La Società Riaperta. Dal Crollo del Muro Alla Guerra in Iraq*, Rome-Bari: Laterza.
Damiani, M. (2016) *La Sinistra Radicale in Europa*, Rome: Donzelli.
Damiani, M. and De Luca, M. (2016) 'From the Communist Party to the Front de Gauche: The French Radical Left from 1989 to 2014', *Communist & Post-Communist Studies* 49(4): 313–321.
Gunter, R. and Diamond, L. (2001) 'Types and Functions of Parties', in L. Diamond and R. Gunter (eds), *Political Parties and Democracy*, Baltimore and London: Johns Hopkins University Press.
Hobsbawm, E. J. (1994) *Age of Extremes*, London: Abacus.
Inglehart, R. (1977) *The Silent Revolution*, Princeton: Princeton University Press.
Jesse, E. and Lang, J. P. (2008) *Die Linke*, Munich: Olzog.
Lakoff, G. (1987) *Women, Fire and Dangerous Things*, Chicago: University of Chicago Press.
Lipset, S. M. and Rokkan, S. (1967) 'Cleavage Structures, Party System, and Voter Alignments: An Introduction', in S. M. Lipset and S. Rokkan (eds), *Party System and Voter Alignment: Cross-National Perspective*, New York: Free Press.
March, L. (2011) *Radical Left Parties in Europe*, London: Routledge.
March, L. and Mudde, C. (2005) 'What's Left of the Radical Left? The European Radical Left after 1989: Decline and Mutation', *Comparative European Politics* 3(1): 23–49.
Mudde, C. (2006) 'Anti-system Politics', in P. Heywook, E. Jones and M. Rhodes (eds), *Developments in European Politics*, London: Palgrave.
Mudde, C. (2017) *Syriza. The Failure of the Populist Promise*, London: Palgrave.
Poguntke, T. (1987) 'New Politics and Party Systems: The Emergence of a New Type of Party?', *West European Politics* 1(1): 76–88.
Poguntke, T. (1996) 'Anti-party sentiment – Conceptual Thoughts and Empirical Evidence: Explorations into a Minefield', *European Journal of Political Research* 29(3): 319–344.
Poguntke, T. and Scarrow, S. E. (1996) 'The Politics of Anti-party Sentiment: Introduction', *European Journal of Political Research* 29(3): 257–262.
Ramiro Fernández, L. J. (2004) *Cambio y Adaptación en la Izquierda. La Evolución del Partido Comunista de España y de Izquierda Unida (1986–2000)*, Madrid: Centro de Investigaciones Sociológicas.
Revelli, M. (2013) *Finale di Partito*, Torino: Einaudi.
Santambrogio, A. (2015) 'Essere di Sinistra Oggi: Dall'ideologia Politica All'immaginario Sociale', *Quaderni di Teoria sociale* 9(2): 33–58.
Sartori, G. (1976) *Parties and Party Systems*, Cambridge: Cambridge University Press.
Schedler, A. (1996) 'Anti-Political-Establishment Parties', *Party Politics* 3(1): 291–312.
Torreblanca, J. I. (2015) *Asaltar los Cielos: Podemos o la Política Después de la Crisis*, Barcelona: Debate.

INDEX